INFRASTRUCTURE OF INJUSTICE

This book examines the dynamics of infrastructure development in Northeast India, especially Manipur, from a socio-anthropological perspective. It looks at the pattern and distribution of infrastructure in the region to analyse the impact of education, roads and health care on the livelihoods, ecosystems, governance and social futures of communities.

The volume examines the infrastructure deficit in the conflict-ridden state of Manipur, focusing especially on electricity and roads. The author shows how problems arising from poor infrastructure are further complicated on account of corruption, insurgency, ethnic unrest and the politics of marginalisation. Looking at the discourse around development in the northeast, the volume also highlights the structural inequality in Manipur and other states. It further shows how infrastructure development can become a means for enabling trade, creating markets, diluting boundaries between varied ethnic groups and connecting people.

This book will be useful for researchers and scholars of development studies, economics, social anthropology, sociology and public policy – particularly those interested in India's northeast.

Raile Rocky Ziipao teaches in Tata Institute of Social Sciences, Guwahati Off Campus, Nagaland Regional Centre. He was the former Raghunathan Family Fellow, Harvard University. His research interests include critical infrastructure, political economy of development, northeast studies and tribal and indigenous epistemologies.

INFRASTRUCTURE OF INJUSTICE

State and Politics in Manipur and Northeast India

Raile Rocky Ziipao

Routledge
Taylor & Francis Group
LONDON AND NEW YORK

First published 2020
by Routledge
2 Park Square, Milton Park, Abingdon, Oxon OX14 4RN

and by Routledge
52 Vanderbilt Avenue, New York, NY 10017

Routledge is an imprint of the Taylor & Francis Group, an informa business

First issued in paperback 2021

British Library Cataloguing-in-Publication Data
A catalogue record for this book is available from the British Library

Library of Congress Cataloging-in-Publication Data
Names: Ziipao, Raile Rocky, author.
Title: Infrastructure of injustice : state and politics in Manipur and Northeast India / Raile Rocky Ziipao.
Description: Abingdon, Oxon ; New York, NY : Routledge, 2020. | Includes bibliographical references and index.
Identifiers: LCCN 2020001549
Subjects: LCSH: Infrastructure (Economics)—Political aspects—India—Manipur. | Equality—India—Manipur. | Manipur (India)—Economic conditions. | Manipur (India)—Social conditions. | Manipur (India)—Politics and government.
Classification: LCC HC437.M33 Z55 2020 | DDC 338.954/17—dc23
LC record available at https://lccn.loc.gov/2020001549

ISBN: 978-1-138-38459-0 (hbk)
ISBN: 978-1-138-38459-0 (pbk)
ISBN: 978-1-003-04589-2 (ebk)

Typeset in Sabon
by Apex CoVantage, LLC

TO OUR PARENTS, YAONAI AND RAILE,
WHO RAISED US AGAINST ALL ODDS

CONTENTS

ILLUSTRATIONS

Tables

Figure

PREFACE

My interest in the study of infrastructure began in my home village of Hiimai (Purul). During monsoons, the roads are not drivable, and electricity is so irregular that in some places, there are electric poles with no wires. People have to climb to the top of the mountain for cell service. To get to school, students have to walk for miles. When I go to other parts of the country, the infrastructure is much better. I began to wonder why infrastructure is so bad in tribal-dominated areas. Hence, I began my research project to understand the politics and social dynamics of building infrastructure. In the sensitive social and political context of India's border and frontier regions, it is crucial to research the impact of infrastructure development on ecosystems, communities and livelihood.

Infrastructure entails connectivity, circulation of goods and movements of people. It establishes ideas, crosses socio-cultural boundaries, maintains and expands social intersections and deepens community relations. However, in a state like Manipur, characterised by persistent social conflict, infrastructure is an extremely political issue. From an academic point of view, infrastructure provides deep insight into issues of access, inclusion and exclusion, equity, social justice and state policy and practice. Drawing from my ethnographic study of these processes, my analysis gives primacy to infrastructure within the development discourse and argues that infrastructure development has always been an act of power, which at different times has been leveraged for and against communities. While it smooths relationships, connects people, enables trade and dilutes boundaries between varied ethnic groups, infrastructure also rigidifies boundaries, ruptures relationships, hinders trade and commerce and disconnects peoples.

Broadly, one can map out three perspectives on knowledge production: (1) the perspective from above stemming from the long venerable tradition of the western and brahminical world views, 2) the perspective from below echoed from the subaltern studies and 3) the emerging perspective from the Tribal Intellectual Collective India (TICI), what came to be called perspective from within. This book is premised within the framework of infrastructure of injustice wherein I echoed the perspective from within. The focus of the book is on roads and electricity. Although there are other areas of critical infrastructure, such as airways, waterways, railways and telecommunication which are equally important, these are either at the nascent stage or yet to be developed in Manipur. And, therefore, they have had minimal impact on the political and economic power play in the state. The infrastructure of roads and electricity has been the most politicised in the border state and most visible upon breakdown, thus presenting a rich subject of study. The responsibility for the development imbroglio in the conflict-ridden border state of Manipur lies with multiple agencies. Yet each of the stakeholders finds an excuse for the lack of development, and the general tendency amongst them is to blame the others. In a nutshell, Manipur's development resonates with a scapegoat syndrome.

The book is a majorly revised version of my doctoral work at Tata Institute of Social Sciences, Mumbai. I am indebted to many precious supports in the process of preparing my manuscript. I am afraid I will not be able to mention them all. Needless to say, I owe an intellectual debt to Professor Virginius Xaxa. I was one of the fortunate budding researchers to be supervised by Professor Xaxa for my M.Phil and Ph.D. His instructive insights helped me to formulate my study into a researchable one and to create a space to learn, unlearn, relearn and think beyond the obvious. Though I feel immense gratitude for him, I fell short of words, and I can only say, thank you sir. I am particularly grateful to Dr. Bodhi S.R. He always gave me intellectual direction with his insightful and thought-provoking ideas to think beyond common sense and shaped me to engage in the realms of meaning making. I have learnt so much from him, especially on deepening the perspective from within. I am equally thankful to Dr. Alex Akhup for his invaluable insight on issues in Manipur. My sincere appreciation and gratitude to TICI for giving me a space to share my ideas and deepen my understanding of the lived and shared reality of non-caste societies (tribes) in India. Interacting and engaging with them has been a great learning experience and a source of much intellectual enrichment.

I am thankful to Professor Ajantha Subramanian, Harvard University, for her keen interest in my work and agreeing to be my advisor during my post-doctoral fellowship at Harvard. Professor Sai Balakrishnan, Harvard University, shared with me her rich and invaluable ideas and insights in many conversations about my manuscript. I am particularly grateful to the Lakshmi Mittal and Family South Asia Institute, Harvard University, for offering me the Raghunathan Family Fellow (2017–18). My appreciation to Professor Stephen Kingsley Scott for allowing me to audit his course Infrastructures and Their Imaginaries, where I was introduced to a range of literature on infrastructure.

This manuscript would have just remained a proposal without the community's encouragement and commitment. I would like to acknowledge the insights I gained during my fieldwork interacting with different communities.

I am thankful to those who have given me their valuable time to share their ideas, perspectives, opinions and lived and shared realities. All my major arguments in this volume are built from their voices. Thank you all for helping me translate my proposal into a book. I shall continue to write for the cause of the struggling communities, through which we can grow together collectively.

I would like to acknowledge and express my gratitude to all my peers who have contributed in different ways in shaping my manuscript. Needless to say, I am indebted to Dr. Joseph Riamei, Dr. Dominic Leo, Dr. Roluahpuia, Dr. Moses Thangal, (late) Andrew Lathuipou Kamei, Hitoho Sumi, Richard Kamei, Zach Yanthan, Hinatoli, Pavei, Lallian, Chongnei Moi, Aashish Khakha, Danii Victor, and Philemon Shangne, amongst others, for they did not only contribute to my research but also created a space where research became a joyful experience. Thank you all. Alomi S. Yepthomi was generous in helping me read the proof.

Getting the manuscript to completion would not have been possible without the enthusiasm and support from the Routledge team and especially Antara Chaudhary Ray and Shloka Chauhan. I am also thankful to anonymous reviewers for their invaluable suggestions.

And last, but not least, I am deeply indebted to my parents and my siblings (Rosemary, Rebecca, Regina, Rolenson, Roccos, Reapson and Rustum) for their continuous support of my unbridled flight to pursue knowledge. My indebtedness to my parents could not be expressed in words. I dedicate this book to them.

Raile Rocky Ziipao

ABBREVIATIONS

AA	Alternative Arrangement
ADB	Asian Development Bank
ADC	Autonomous District Council
AH	Asian Highway
AMUCO	All Manipur United Clubs' Organisation
BADP	Border Area Development Programme
BRO	Border Road Organisation
BRTF	Border Road Task Force
CDA	Contractor Dealing Assistance
CM	Chief Minister
CMC	Constitutional Making Committee
CSO	Central Statistics Office
GoI	Government of India
GoM	Government of Manipur
HAC	Hill Area Committee
ICC	Indian Chamber of Commerce
ILP	Inner Line Permit
JONGL	Jubilant Oil and Natural Gas Limited
KCP	Kangle Communist Party
KNA	Kuki National Army
KNF	Kuki National Front
KNO	Kuki National Organisation
KRA	Kuki Revolutionary Army
MANIREDA	Manipur Renewable Energy Development Agency
MGNREGS	Mahatma Gandhi National Rural Employment Guarantee Scheme
MIMSTEC	Multi-sectoral Technical and Economic Cooperation
MLA	Member of Legislative Assembly
MLR&LR	Manipur Land Revenue and Land Reform Act
MNPF	Manipur Naga Peoples' Front
MoDONER	Ministry of Development of North Eastern Region
MSPCL	Manipur State Power Company Limited

MSPDCL	Manipur State Power Distribution Company Limited
MSRRDA	Manipur State Rural Road Development Agency
NEC	North Eastern Council
NER	North Eastern Region
NH	National Highway
NHAI	National Highway Authority of India
NHPC	National Hydroelectric Power Corporation
NNC	Naga National Council
NNL	Naga National League
NPCPR	Non-lapsable Central Pool of Resources
NPMHR	Naga Peoples' Movement for Human Rights
NRRDA	National Rural Road Development Agency
NSCN (I-M)	National Socialist Council of Nagalim (Isaac-Muivah)
NSCN (K)	National Socialist Council of Nagalim (Khaplan)
NSS	National Sample Survey
PLA	Peoples' Liberation Army
PMGSY	Pradhan Mantri Gram Sadak Yojana
PPP	Public-Private Partnership
PREPAK	Peoples' Revolutionary Party of Kangleipak
PWD	Public Works Department
R-APDRP	Restructured Accelerated Power Development and Reform Programme
RGGV	Rajiv Gandhi Grameen Vidyutikaran
RMSA	Rashtriya Madhyamik Shiksha Abhiyan
SDSA	Senapati District Students' Association
SEZ	Special Economic Zone
SOC	Social Overhead Capital
SPA	Special Plan Assistance
STDCM	Scheduled Tribe Demand Committee of Manipur
UCM	United Committee Manipur
UNLF	United National Liberation Front
UPF	United People's Front
ZRA	Zomi Revolutionary Army
ZRO	Zomi Re-unification Organisation
ZUF	Zeliangrong United Front

INTRODUCTION

Infrastructure of injustice

This book disentangles the pattern and distribution of infrastructure in Manipur, a chronically conflict-ridden state, with a specific focus on roads and electricity. Although there are other areas of infrastructure, such as airways, waterways, railways and telecommunication, which are equally important, these are in their nascent stage and, therefore, have had a minimal impact on the political and economic power play in the state. Disparately, the infrastructure of roads and electricity has been most politicised in the border state. My analysis gives primacy to infrastructure within the development discourse and argues that infrastructure development has always been an act of power, which at different times has been leveraged to smooth relationships, (dis)connect people, enable trade, create spaces of contestation and dilute boundaries between varied ethnic groups.

Infrastructure entails (dis)connectivity, goods, people and ideas, as well as the maintenance and expansion of social relations. However, in a chronic conflict state like Manipur, infrastructure also provides a basis to understand the issues of access, inclusion and exclusion, equity, social justice and other contemporary practices and processes of the state. Over the years, studies of infrastructure from a socio-anthropological perspective in the form of an ethnography of infrastructure have offered a new theoretical lens to understand the materiality and forms of infrastructure and its relationship with society, power dynamics, authority, everyday politics, governance, emblem of exclusion and social future, amongst others. However, the fundamental question remains, what is infrastructure? To address this, it may be worthwhile to begin with the argument from Start and Rudleder's (1996) seminal paper, 'Steps towards an Ecology of Infrastructure'. They hold that 'infrastructure is a fundamentally relational concept. It becomes infrastructure in relation to organised practices'. Hence, they suggest we ask 'when' not what is an infrastructure. Drawing from this perspective, road becomes road infrastructure only when it is constructed and maintained regularly and fit for traffic. They also presented a list of infrastructure's constitutive dimensions, including embeddedness, transparency and reach/scope, being learnt as part of a membership, conventions of practice/standards possessing an installed base and becoming visible upon breakdown (Start and Rudleder, 1996).

Socio-anthropological work on infrastructures began to draw together a set of diverse interests in technology, in material relationships and in material agency, fostering close relationships between science and technology studies and ethnographic approaches to the analysis of technological system, social change and development (Harvey and Knox, 2015). Larkin (2013: 329) posits, 'Infrastructure also exist as forms separate from their purely technical functioning, and they need to be analysed as concrete semiotic and aesthetic vehicles oriented to addressees'. For him, infrastructure occupied a peculiar ontology that 'they are things and also the relation between things' (ibid.). Thus enabling the movement of other matter. Hannah et al. (2015) makes a similar argument by theorising that contemporary infrastructures are critical sites through which social and political systems are given form and performed. While they promised circulation and distribution, at the same time, these precarious assemblies also threatened to break down and fail. The material and political lives of infrastructure reveal fragile relations between people, things and the institutions (both public and private) that seek to govern them.

The materiality of infrastructure on the one hand and the dimension of aesthetics on the other hand offer an enriching theoretical lens. Echoing from the Aristotelian concept of *aisthesis*, Buck-Morss (1992) noted that it does not refer to the mental appreciation of a work of art but to a bodily reaction to lived reality. 'Aesthetics in this sense is not a representation but an embodied experience governed by the ways infrastructures produce the ambient conditions of everyday life: our sense of temperature, speed, florescence, and the ideas we have associated with these conditions' (as cited in Larkin, 2013: 336). Infrastructure creates a sensing of modernity (Mrazek, 2002), a process by which the body, as much as the mind, apprehends what it is to be modern, mutable and progressive (Larkin, 2013). Building large infrastructure projects, such as mega dams, railways, airports, highways, economic corridors and waterways, amongst others, is seen as developing for modernity. The post-independence Nehruvian state embarked upon industrialisation for a prosperous and modern India with Nehru terming such projects as, 'temples of modern India'. The primacy of this vision was building massive infrastructure projects that focused on select industries, such as irrigation, power generation and heavy industries. While on one hand such large infrastructural projects are seen as heralding the arrival of modernity and economic development, on the other hand, these 'temples of modern India' are more often than not a reflection of the exclusion, displacement and marginalisation of certain communities.[1] This brings us back to infrastructure as a relational concept, as posited by Star and Rudleder (1996).

Edwards (2003: 186) argued that 'infrastructures simultaneously shape and are shaped by – in other words- co-construct, the condition of modernity' and serve the interest of the state and dominant communities'. For Anand (2011), infrastructure is the material articulation of imagination, ideology and social life, while de Boeck (2012) referred to infrastructure as a system of built forms around which the public thickens. Stewart (2011: 452) saw the materiality of infrastructure as an affective experience of 'worldling' and 'attunements' where 'incommensurate elements hang together in a scene that bodies labour to be in or to get through'. In all cases,

> infrastructures are built networks that facilitate the flow of goods, people, or ideas and allow for their exchange over space. As physical forms, they shape the nature of a network, the speed and direction of its movement, its temporalities, and its vulnerability to breakdown.
>
> (Larkin, 2013: 327)

Scott (2009) makes the case for infrastructure, such as construction of bridges and all-weather roads, forest felling, accurate surveying and mapping and the telegraph, which provided a means of quick communication as 'distance-demolishing technologies', making it possible to project their power and technological prowess to the highland communities resisting colonial expansion.

This book takes a critical position in order to unravel multiple ways of seeing infrastructure. Theoretically, it is located within the framework and concept called *infrastructure of injustice*. It analyses the materiality of infrastructure, but in conceptualising this phenomenon, I am positioning it within this concept called infrastructure of injustice. It, nevertheless, dovetails well with the socio-anthropology of infrastructure and political economy of development literature. In addition to this domain, I elaborated on and added the dimension of conflict, injustice and lived experience into the studies of infrastructure. The book presents the intersection of development studies, socio-anthropology of infrastructure and science, technology and society.

Infrastructure of injustice

It is beyond the scope of this book to discuss the theory of justice in detail. Hence, I shall limit my discussion to what is relevant in the context of justice and injustice of infrastructure. The liberal-utilitarian principle of social justice espouses that the 'greatest happiness of the greatest number' in the context of infrastructure in Northeast India would amount to injustice to those communities that are at the margin of the state and the dominant communities. Hence it is problematic to conceptualise justice from the perspective of utilitarianism in this study and more so in the domain of infrastructural distribution. John Rawls critiqued and bemoaned the utilitarian conception of justice. For Rawls (1971), 'justice is the first virtue of social institution' wherein he theorised 'justice as fairness'. Echoing from Rawls's theory of justice in the context of infrastructural accessibility and distribution, infrastructure in Manipur and Northeast should ensure a fair or just manner amongst different social categories (here tribals and non-tribals). If one community appropriates all the resources and avails all primary goods, including basic infrastructure, for itself, then this would amount to injustice. Rawls's conception of justice as fairness provides the basic structure of the argument. This basic structure becomes unfair when one community appropriates the benefits of all goods and services. Hence, the benefits of infrastructure should be fair and just for all communities, irrespective of their social location and geographical terrain within a nation-state framework.

It is also interesting to note the conception of social justice as propounded by Dr. B. R. Amkedkar in the context of Indian society, which is marked by a pervasive caste system. His concept is based on the principles of equality, liberty and fraternity in all social categories. For him, social justice would mean to annihilate the caste system based on graded inequality and removal of all inequalities existing in the society. Echoing Ambedkar's perspective, infrastructural justice would mean equal access to all infrastructure facilities irrespective of caste, tribes, creed, religion, gender, etc. When certain social groups support a dominant caste-appropriate infrastructure and deny access to other social groups, this is injustice. Fair and just distribution of materiality amongst varied social categories in India and the northeast in particular is one way forward to address the question of infrastructural injustice. Differential access to material resources or physical infrastructure (roads, electricity, telecommunication, hospitals, schools, colleges and universities, amongst others) based on social location and power dynamics is the hallmark of Indian society and germinates social exclusion. Xaxa (2008) posited that differences have been the hallmark of Indian society. These differences emerged as the result of various long and complex historical processes. Hence, it is imperative to address the historical injustice meted out to certain social groups, such as tribes/Adivasi and Dalits in India.

Amartya Sen, in his seminal work titled *Idea of Justice*, dealt with the concepts of justice in early Indian jurisprudence between *niti* and *nyaya*.

> Among the principal uses of the term *niti* are organizational propriety and behavioural correctness. In contrast with *niti*, the term *nyaya* stands for a comprehensive concept of realized justice. In that line of vision, the roles of institutions, rules and organization, important as they are, have to be assessed in the broader and more inclusive perspective of *nyaya*, which is inescapably linked with the

> world that actually emerges, not just the institutions or rules we happen to have.
>
> (Sen, 2009: 20)

He further augments his ideas about justice by deepening the capabilities approach. This approach of Amartya Sen is seen primarily as attributes of people, not of collectivities, such as communities. However, he also posits that the capabilities approach has a 'concern with people's ability to live the kind of lives they have reason to value brings in social influences both in terms of what they value and what influences operate on their values' (Sen, 2009: 244). The central idea of justice is indeed the removal of all injustice in the society. The prevalence of injustice in India can be found at all levels, ranging from poverty to structural inequality. In this domain, tribes/Adivasis face injustice at a much greater degree than other social groups in India. Tribes in Manipur and other northeastern states echo similar experiences where they bear the brunt of infrastructural injustice. In the words of Amartya Sen at an event hosted by the Asia Society Northern California (2010),

> Neglect of tribals is a huge spot on India's pursuit of justice. I very much rebel against the view saying we ought to do something about it otherwise they would join the Naxalites (*insurgent in the case of Northeast India*). The reason we should do something about them is precisely because it's matter of justice.[2]
>
> (Emphasis added)

Justice thus refracts the ideology of development. Hence addressing the historical injustice meted out against certain social groups in India would echo the development of justice.

Social scientists pay scant attention to the materiality and form of infrastructure that manifests injustice. How is injustice embedded in infrastructure? One way forward to unearth this phenomenon in relation to tribes is through the lens of the decolonial perspective[3] or what came to be called the 'perspective from within' by the TICI. The socio-politico-economic issues plaguing tribes in India are too complex for the existing dominant social theories to adequately address the issues of situating, as well as explaining, the reality. Hence, it is imperative to approach from different perspectives, drawing on the experience from indigenous studies across the globe. Indigenous people in South America assert concepts such as perspectivism[4] and decolonial thinking. In North America, the focus is on decolonial method, while indigenous scholars from South Africa engage with decolonisation and indigenisation processes. The Maori's of New Zealand, especially the writings of Linda Tuhiwai Smith, posit decolonising methodology as the way forward. Indigenous people from Australia assert truth telling, healing and decolonisation of the stolen generation by the colonisers. The seminal work of Boaventura De Sousa Santos (2014) titled *Epistemologies of the South: Justice Against Epistimicide* gives an emancipatory approach to knowledge production and departs from the Eurocentric critical tradition.

In the context of tribal/Adivasi/indigenous studies in India, Bodhi and Jojo (2019: 6) succinctly summed up that until about early 2000,

> it was going through an interregnum crisis: as in the old was dying and the new not yet born. However, in the midst of this theoretically saturated state, a minor historical rupture took place and the contour of the new is beginning to unravel, framed around the perspective from within.

The connotation, concept, category and usage of the term *tribes* in this study is markedly different from what is commonly understood in Europe/western or caste-centric anthropological writings, which categorise tribes as savage, barbarian, backwards people without histories, amongst others. Tribes in this book refer to non-caste societies in India and people with a distinct history, culture, tradition, identity, autonomy, sense of territory/boundary, intrinsic relationship with nature, varied mode of production, political entity and victims of several waves of colonialism. The book analyses the social and political processes of infrastructure building which breed injustice at the same time, and it builds on my research work in Manipur from 2013–17.

Tribes in Manipur, as elsewhere in the country, were (are) experiencing waves of colonialism or, in other words, layers of colonial power imposing themselves. The first layer fundamentally took place with the British. In the pre-British period, what is today commonly known as Northeast India consisted of various kingdoms and independent village republics (or what Yonuo called village-states) ruled by various kings and chiefs. Geographically and politically, the region falls into two broad categories – namely, hills and valleys. The hilly regions predominately inhabited by tribes were neither ruled by kings nor followed the monarchical system. They had their own system of autonomy and were self-governed.[5] The hills were outside the control of valley administration, and they flourished more or less as an independent region (Roy-Burman, 1961).

Invasions and expansion of kingdoms were part of the history of the region, as elsewhere in the country. Burma (Myanmar) was a rising power in the early 19th century,[6] making repeated invasions into the Ahom and Manipuri kingdoms. This led the Ahom and Manipuri kings to seek assistance from the British East India Company, which was then based in Calcutta and had already established the Bengal Presidency in 1765. British India responded, and in preparation for the first Anglo-Burmese War (1824–26), roads were constructed for the military campaigns in the region. The Burmese army was defeated in the war, which eventually led to the signing of the Treaty of Yandabo in 1826. This treaty between the East India Company and the king of

Ava brought to an end the Burmese invasions and occupations of the Assam, Manipur, Cachar and Jaintia kingdoms. Thus, the treaty officially paved the way for colonial rule in the region.[7] Mention may be made that the king of Manipur entered into a formal relationship with the British by signing the first treaty for defence alliance on 14 September 1762.[8] Henceforth, various Manipuri kings colluded and worked in close alliance with the British throughout the colonial period. Theoretically, Manipur was an independent kingdom until 1891, but for all defence purposes, it depended on the British government[9] through the political agents stationed in the kingdom.

The colonialisation and territorialisation of the northeastern states and their resources were streamlined with the construction of roads. Roads for territorial expansion and resource extraction were the core agenda of the British East India Company. With the discovery of fertile land for commercial exploitation of tea and later coal and oil resources in Assam there came the need to improve the transport and communication systems. The expansion and prosperity of tea plantations was directly dependent upon such infrastructural facilities (Xaxa, 1985). Construction of roads was within the domain of the British military department, which controlled the public works; thus, road building was undertaken with a view towards strategic military expeditions, expansion of the colonial administration and control over the region. The region, therefore, became strategic in two ways: first, to protect British commercial interests and second, to safeguard the empire from external aggression. Hence, they introduced and enforced various acts, regulations, laws and policies.

One amongst many such regulations was the Bengal Eastern Frontier Regulation Act of 1873. This regulation introduced an inner line concept that demarcated a line between the plains and foothills of Assam. The entry of both tribals and non-tribals beyond that line required permission from a competent British authority. This was the beginning of division between hills and valley. Until today, an inner line permit (ILP) was required by non-tribals to enter the states of Mizoram, Arunachal Pradesh and Nagaland. The colonial policy of non-interference in dealing with the hill communities was replaced by regular expeditions to quell their opposition to the colonial extension of commercial activities in and through their land. Eventually, the hill communities were brought under a different territorial administrative authority and thus the concept of territorial politics was introduced, hitherto unknown to these communities (Shimray, 2001). The colonial rulers further introduced concepts such as 'backwards tracts,' 'excluded areas,'[10] 'partially excluded areas',[11] etc., by passing the Government of India (Excluded and Partially Excluded Areas) Order, 1936. It was the British who redefined space, landscape, forests and infrastructure, and they created many categories, such as hills, valleys, frontiers, partially excluded areas, administered areas and political agents, amongst others.

The second wave of colonialism which the tribes experienced in Manipur and elsewhere in the country stemmed from dominant communities.[12]

During the same period of British colonisation, there was an emerging power and narratives – i.e. the Meitei monarch. What the king of Ava did to the Meitei state in the early 19th century was replicated by the Meitei maharaja towards the tribes – i.e. subjugation and invasions into tribal territories with the help of the British military might. Gambhir Singh,[13] who was recognised as the king of Meitei state by the king of Ava and the British in the aftermath of the Treaty of Yandabo in 1826, carried out multiple military expeditions in tribal territories. The Manipur Levy, during the reign of Gambhir Singh, was increased to 3,000 men, equipped, trained and commanded by the British officers.[14] Kamei (2015: 33) pointed out that 'the Levy was used for subjugation of the hill tribes of Manipur: 1826–29, the defeat of Khasi rebels, the conquest of the Naga villages including Thibomei in 1832'. Manipur valley/state was connected to British territories by roads: on the west, it is connected via Cachar district and on the north via Kohima road to Assam. This provided easy access to Manipuri raja to British power. These two roads continue to be the lifelines today, forming with the name national highway (NH) No. 37 and NH-2.[15]

The Manipur state was geographically located in the valley encircled by hills, predominately inhabited by tribes. Tribes, or in other words used to describe the hill people, were outside the state, and they were an independent village republic with their own political structure and governance. However, as Gambhir Singh gained popularity and military power with the help of the British government, he was determined to consolidate the surrounding hill territories to his rule and expand his kingdom. Hence, he launched various punitive military expeditions[16] into tribal countries to subdue tribes and captured men as prisoners, as well as livestock and paddy as booty. Hill men were also used as corvée labour for road construction, rest houses, carrying loads and other infrastructure development for the state. Tribal labourers were thus invested for building the valley state. Tribes continue to live in a colonised state, even in post-independent India. In fact, they are experiencing what Xaxa (2016: 227) called two forms of colonialism: one at the hands of the British and the other at the hands of the non-tribal Indian population.

Fundamental to the life of physical infrastructure is its intrinsic connection to land. Infrastructure is built on land. Land and identity amongst tribes are intrinsically related to each other. Mega-infrastructures invariably fragment land, village community and identity. The fragmentation of the holistic construction of identity in the processes of infrastructure build on the injustice and create varied kinds of conflict within the community vis-à-vis community and state. Infrastructure, as much as it connects and builds network, also destroys community structure and identity. When land is turned into a commodity and the state and dominant community appropriate such land for infrastructure development, then the original inhabitants lose control over their land, leading to injustice. More so, when the benefits from such infrastructure development does not accrue for tribes, which is often the case, this perpetuates injustice or what may be called infrastructure of injustice. With such development, new governance systems are put into place, and tribes are forever dispossessed of their land.

Colonising by discourse

A more pervasive form of colonisation is what I identify as 'colonising by discourse'. This practice is common to both the British and the dominant community that colonises tribes. Tribes, unlike the valley state and the British, do not have a written history. This does not mean that they do not have a history. In fact, they have a rich oral history in the form of folktales, folksongs, legends, oral narratives and folklores, amongst others. And yet it was the British, particularly the colonial administrators – commissioners, political agents and army officers – who wrote memoirs, monographs, reports and tour diaries, giving birth to an alternate history. Their texts became the basis on which the notion of geography, landscape, tribal culture, customs, religions, people, villages, occupations, languages, ethnicities, histories, boundary lines and so on were constructed and taken to be the truth from their own perspectives.[17] It was the British who first created discourse for themselves, embedded tribes in their discourse and legalised it. This process continued throughout the colonisation period.

Concurrently, the Meitei state was also asserting its narrative in a written form, with the Cheitharol Kumbaba (the Royal Chronicle) being a notable instance. In this 'history claiming and writing' process, the dominant Meitei community was able to adapt in a varied way to the overarching discourse of the British. Tribes, or the hill people, were sandwiched between these discourses. Hence their narrative, lived experience and shared history became distorted and entangled by the written text of the dominant communities. Not frequently, Meiteis from the plains invaded the formidable Naga village-states. It was common for the Meitei kings to frequently invade Naga villages across mountains, conquer them, demand tribute from them and attach whatever name appeared convenient to the hills, mountains, villages and people, whom they considered 'savages' (Yonuo, 1974: xi). This has a ramification until the current day, with many of the tribal villages, districts and other places named in Manipuri and legalised by notifying the official gazette. The present-day names of villages such as Purul Atongba (Hiimai Dunamai),[18] Oinam (Onaeme), Koide Mathak (Naa Reimai), etc., are all names provided by the Meiteis. This was nothing but an attempt to deny the very existence of the local language by the dominant community. 'These dominant epistemological frameworks emerging from such locations have bounded "tribes" under rigid "waves of colonial" frames' (Bodhi and Jojo, 2019: 3). Thus tribes experienced two forms of domination under colonial rule: physical and narrative control. Bodhi and Jojo (2019) succinctly summed this up:

> Most Tribes were self-reliant communities before the British began entering their habitats. Later, many non-tribal traders, merchants, and moneylenders also entered. It is important to note that it is under the British that the numerous tribal communities were subjected to British India's laws, rules, and regulations. Later, they were also subsumed under an overarching economic system through land, labour, credit, and commodity markets giving rise to a new politico-administrative system that steadfastly eroded their control over, and access to natural resources such as land, forest, and water.
> (Ibid. 3)

This has a bearing on infrastructure development in tribal territories. Under British rule, roads were explicitly built for the quick transportation of men and military supplies and to advance colonial control over resources, trade, people and territories. Where it suited their commercial and military interests, they extended roads to outlying tribal territories, but they hardly did anything to develop the economy of the tribes (Ziipao, 2018). It is important to note that colonialism and the colonial mindset did not have any genuine interest in developing infrastructure, except in cases where infrastructure extended their power and territories.

To understand the poverty of infrastructure in tribal areas, we need to understand the different aspects of its history, which set it on its particular development path followed by the colonial rule and subsequently by the dominant community's narratives. Hence one could locate the poverty or crumbling of infrastructure in tribal-dominated districts of Manipur as the by-product of colonial rule and the Meitei state hegemony. This brings us to the argument of infrastructure of injustice: Why is there so much poverty of infrastructure in the hills? Is there a poverty of infrastructure in the valley? What are the constraints of the state on infrastructure development in the hills? What are the perspectives of the communities on infrastructure? Above all, the book attempts to analysis the socio-politico-economic processes that breed injustice in infrastructure development in the conflict-ridden state of Manipur.

Imperial infrastructure policy

What we call Northeast India today, or in the touristic lexicon 'seven sisters' before India's independence, consisted of (1) Assam Province (2) Assam tribal areas (3) Manipur state (4) Tripura state and (5) Khasi states (Shullai, 1981, as cited in Bodhi and Jojo, 2019). Within the province of Assam, the British created various administrative categories – namely, the normal areas, partially excluded areas and excluded areas. The *normal areas* were Goalpara, Kamrup, Darrang, Nowgong, Sibsagar, Lakhimpur and Cachar district. The *partially excluded areas* includes Garo Hills, Khasi and Jaintia

Hills.[19] The *excluded areas* include the Naga Hills and the Lushai Hills. Further, within the Cachar District, the Cachar Hills subdivision was regarded as an excluded area and within two districts of Nowgong and Sibsagar, the Mikir Hills portion was regarded as a partially excluded area. The Assam tribal areas were the North East Frontier Tracts, including Balipara Frontier Tract, Abor and Mishmi Hills District and the Naga Tribal Area (Bodhi and Jojo, 2019).

All the hill territories, with the exception of a small area in Shillong, were demarcated as either partially excluded or excluded areas by the British India. Hence it was the British who created the binary between the hills and valley on the basis of geospatial differences, civilisation, culture and tradition. The geographical location of varied communities in Northeast India invariably fits into Scott's argument about Southeast Asia; the tribes (Nagas, Mizos, Garos, Khasis, Kukis, etc.) in his terms, would form a non-state space – an 'illegible space' from the perspective of the states in the lowlands (Scott, 2009). Today, the region is experiencing the ramification of the colonial geopolitics. This has a bearing on infrastructure, sense of belonging, territories, boundaries, culture and so on for those communities that later came to be known as scheduled tribes (ST) in India or, more specifically, hill people in Northeast India. One could historically locate the infrastructure of injustice within the region from the framework of colonial administration and the panoply of laws, policies and regulations.

Infrastructural facilities such as roads, bridges, irrigations, waterways, dispensaries, postal services and guest houses, amongst others, in the normal areas of the then Assam Province were much more well equipped than those partially excluded and excluded areas. The first notable form of commercial transportation the East India Company initiated was the waterway. The company started a steamer service from the Brahmaputra River, connecting Calcutta to Guwahati, in 1847. Guwahati, located in the district of Kamrup, was the official residence of the viceroy. Connectivity (to ensure easier access to the frontier) constituted an important element in colonial policy, and the British expansion into the frontier was actualised by its persistent focus on the development of efficient lines of communication (Dzuvichu, 2013). In 1866, the government initiated the project of making a connected trunk road through the province (Hunter, 1879a). The Assam Truck Road (24-feet wide) connects Guwahati to Agia (81 miles) and Guwahati to Kalang river (15 miles). The Guwahati-Shillong Road via Byrnihat and Nongpoh covers a total distance of 65 miles. These roads were constructed under the superintendent of the Public Works Department (PWD) from the imperial funds. The Kamrup District was well connected with local roads, repaired and maintained by the local administration within the district. The Assam Trunk Road extended and covered the whole length of the District of Darrang – i.e. from Kurughat to the eastern boundary of Darrang (158 miles). Tezpur, the British administrative headquarters of the district and the largest town, was well connected both overland and waterway to Guwahati. The road from Bengbari to Kaigaon to Mangaldai and Rangamati (25 miles) on the bank of the Brahmaputra River was constructed and extensively used by the planters for the transportation of tea. The Nowgong District of the Assam Province is connected to Guwahati via a road. The roads from Nowgong to Dihing River (54 miles) and Kaliabar to Silghat (4 miles) were constructed through the imperial funds. Similarly, Goalpara, Sibsagar, Lakhimpur and Cachar Districts were well connected via roads. In addition to road infrastructure, all these districts have schools, dispensaries, jails and postal service facilities.

The Garo Hills District comes under the partially excluded areas. Hunter (1879b), in his *Statistical Account of Garo Hills District*, stated that the district contains nothing worthy of the name of a town, but the civil station is at Tura. 'The people often travel immense distances with loads of from eighty to a hundred twenty pounds on their back, to the market villages situated within the Goalpara district'. The poverty of infrastructure prevails across Garo Hills District. The main line of connectivity was through a 'tolerably road runs from Harigaon, on the western borders of the Garo hills, to Tura (about 29 miles in length)' (Hunter, 1879b: 167). The government proposed to construct a road to Shillong through Garo hills and another from Durgapur to Jira. By and large, infrastructural facilities in the said district were left untouched by the British. The Naga Hills District was formed by the British in 1867, and it was categorised as an excluded area, similar to that of the Lushai Hills District. Nagas, particularly the Angamis, were most often cited in colonial discourses, tour dairies, expedition reports and surveys reports, amongst others, as the most difficult tribes to rule over due to strong retaliations from the Angami side. As Hunter noted, owing to the want of roads, the only means of transport for goods across the Naga Hills District is by coolies (Hunter). The construction of the Golaghat-Samaguting Road (67 miles) linking the British headquarters at Samaguting with Assam in 1873 and the road linking Samaguting to the Kohima road (40 miles) (Dzuvichu, 2013) drastically changed the transportation and communication routes to the advantage of the British military logistics and political control. Other roads were more footpaths prior to 1876. There was no provision for road construction under imperial funds nor fairs or religious festivals; permanent markets were held in the district, unlike other districts, which were under normal areas of Assam Province.

In the Khasi and Jaintia Hills Districts, with the exception to Shillong proper, infrastructural facilities remain underdeveloped. Shillong, the administrative headquarters of the then chief commissioner of Assam was well equipped infrastructurally. British India took an interest in developing infrastructure, even though Shillong is located in a hilly terrain mainly due to favourable weather conditions for the Europeans. In the words of Hunter (1879a: 172), 'The climate of Shillong is pleasant and congenial to Europeans'. Hence, Shillong was made the headquarters for the British Assam

Province. The Shillong-Guwahati Cart Road (67 miles) was constructed with imperial funds and opened for wheeled traffic in 1877. Besides road construction, the British also constructed rest houses and hotels along the route for the convenience of the British officers. Large amounts of money went into the erection of the public building and bungalows for the offices and residences of the administration (ibid.). A printing press was already in place at Shillong, from which all the official documents and reports for the province were printed. There were in total three police stations and police outposts, along with two jails. By 1874–75, there were already 64 primary schools wherein 45 were of English medium. The enrolment of pupils totalled 1,226 pupils (Hunter, 1879a). Sanitation facilities, such as public toilets and drainage systems, were in place in addition to proper water supply systems and markets within the town. However, the moment one crossed out of Shillong, poverty of infrastructure was the common phenomenon, which continues to this day. The poverty of infrastructure is much more visible in what was called as the North-East Frontier Agency (NEFA) or the Assam Tribal Areas, which today form the state of Arunachal Pradesh.

There was (and continues to be) a sharp difference in the level of infrastructural development between those districts which were in Assam Province proper and those which were included in the category of partially excluded and excluded areas.[20] Tribes in the *northeast, as elsewhere in the country*, were incorporated into the colonial state structure through war, conquest and annexation(Xaxa, 1985 emphasis added), not so much for the development of the tribes but for the extension of the imperial power and to protect their interests on the plains of Assam, Manipur and Burma. The Samugating-Golaghat and Dimapur-Imphal are pointers in this direction. These roads were constructed to ease the mobility of the British military forces and to connect with Manipur and Assam rather than improving the connectivity of the hills tribes. Thus infrastructure for spatial control, territorialisation, political supremacy, military surveillance and taxation in the hill territories was paramount to the British infrastructural policy towards the hill peoples of the region. Social and anthropological surveys were carried out alongside geographical mapping surveys.

The politics of othering the tribes[21] and categorising them as 'savages' and 'uncivilised' created the binary between the coloniser and colonised. Within the framework of civilisational evolutionism, the whites (British in India) saw themselves as the civilised core and the tribes as the uncivilised periphery. This perception was perpetuated and replicated by the Ahoms and Meiteis who converted themselves to Hinduism. Thus, psychologically, tribes experienced two layers of power imposed upon them and the inferiorising tribes from the caste category. Tribes were ensnared on the one hand by racial inferiorisation and on the other by material/physical domination by the British, as well as the dominant communities in the region. Besides poverty of infrastructure in tribal areas, their culture, traditions and intrinsic relationship with nature were destroyed by the imperial rule as they did not co-opt with the colonial administration unlike the likes of Meitei and Ahom monarchies. Physically, the tribal areas were made more accessible to the rest of the country; while psychologically, an image of their being different was gradually built up; and administratively they were kept in isolation (Roy-Burman, 1961). The post-colonial Indian state further extended the misery of tribes with militarisation and military-led road development. Tribes have been subjected to extreme forms of state brutality and subjugation in the name of nation-building. This trend began under colonial rule and has been reinforced by the independent Indian state.

Post-independent infrastructure development

The colonial construction of the northeast as a 'frontier space' has been transformed to its position as a 'border region' in post-independence India. However, to this day, the legacy of colonial practices is seen in policies implemented by the Indian state towards the region. Infrastructure development is a case in point. 'An important challenge that India faced after independence vis-à-vis the northeast was the restoration of severed communication links' (Das, 2008: 102). With the formation of East Pakistan and Burma, all major links to the rest of India were cut off, except for the 20-km-wide 'Siliguri Corridor', popularly known as the 'Chicken's Neck', that connects the northeast with other parts of India. This resulted in a serious threat to nation-building projects coupled with insurgency, border disputes and secessionist movement from the region. Hence the top priority for the Government of India (GoI) was to build physical infrastructure that connects the region with other parts of India, which legitimises the political integration as a sovereign nation. Thus, in 1950, a rail link from Takiragram to Siliguri through the foothills of the Himalayas was constructed, bypassing the East Bengal (Rao, 1972). Similarly, a NH was rerouted through Siliguri which would connect with northeastern states.

It is interesting to note how the GoI's strategy towards, or rather its engagement with, Northeast India shifted from cultural, security and political paradigms to development paradigms in the 1990s. Hence, there is also a shift in infrastructure projects. During the 1940s and 1950s, the various ethnic communities in the region were taken as contributing richly to India's mosaic of cultures, and it was thought best to leave them alone and untouched – in other words, the government adopted an isolationist policy towards them.

> Northeast cultures were seen as exotic, endangered, which needed to be kept in museums and protected from the big bad wolf called economic development. And, if one looks at writings and the dominant

> discourse in government during those years, it was these that really animated much of our policies towards the Northeast.
>
> (Jairam, 2011: 1)

This was reflected in policy advocacy by the likes of Elwin, who recommended an isolationist framework, and was endorsed by Nehru.[22]

However, India's defeat by China during the 1962 war, the mushrooming of insurgent movements and the realisation of the geo-strategic importance of the region led to what Ramesh calls the security paradigm in this period – i.e. the 1960s. The questions about the infrastructural disparity within the region largely remain unaddressed, with the government prioritising punitive militarisation to suppress the insurgent operations, secessionists and other nationalist movements stemming from various ethnic communities. It was evident that the region required political representation of the diverse communities. Hence, in the 1970s and early 1980s, various states were formed, and union territories were granted full-fledged statehood. This period witnessed the emergence of what is called a political paradigm in the region. The Indian state, on the one hand, fails to comprehend the intricate social reality of Northeast India stemming from various ethnic communities. On the other hand, to quell the ethnic demands for separate states and sovereignty movements, the states of Nagaland (1963), Meghalaya (1972) and Mizoram (1987) were carved out of Assam. The union territories of Manipur and Tripura were declared full-fledged states in 1972. Arunachal Pradesh, which was until then the NEFA was granted full-fledged statehood in 1982. Today, what is known as Northeast India encompasses the states of Assam, Arunachal Pradesh, Meghalaya, Manipur, Mizoram, Nagaland, Tripura and Sikkim.

India remained relatively isolated from the global economic system until the economic reforms were introduced in the 1990s. Following the reforms, there was a fundamental shift in economic policy – i.e. economic reform was in tune with the neo-liberal policy and so too was development policy. This framework was applied across the states in the country. This approach and its application to tribal-dominated northeastern states[23] has its limitations due to the existing legal framework.[24] In order to resolve these constraints, the GoI formulated the Look East Policy (LEP) (now rechristened the Act East Policy (AEP)). This system altered the way the Indian state perceived Northeast India, with its focus shifting from the earlier cultural, security and political approaches in the decades since independence to the development paradigm of the present era. Development became the core thrust of state policy given the region's underdevelopment, the threat of external interfaces and insurgency and the prospects of linking India's economy with Southeast Asia, amongst other considerations. Development is perceived as a panacea to all problems in the region. And yet this notion of development is concentrated in urban areas (Guwahati, Imphal, Shillong, etc.) covering only a small proportion to the total geographical areas. Infrastructure development is a case in point.

Thus, building infrastructure became the premise for nation-building, political integration and channelling state power in post-independent India. If infrastructure for territorial expansion and resource extraction were the core agenda of the colonial project in the hill areas of Northeast India, then in post-independent India, infrastructure is a means for national integration, securing the region from external threat and a gateway to Southeast Asia. In the process, infrastructure also becomes emblematic of exclusion and injustice, as well as the site of protests. The interest of the Indian state in 'securing' the region has activated various infrastructural projects, amongst which road construction and tapping hydropower resources are the key elements. Thus it also meets the vested interest of the government's AEP.

AEP and its agendas

With the rise of LEP, Northeast India is projected as the gateway to Southeast Asia. As part of the policy, massive infrastructural projects are on the pipeline, promoted by the GoI through its institutions, such as North Eastern Council (NEC), Ministry of Development of North Eastern Region (MDoNOR) and the likes of the World Bank and Asian Development Bank (ADB). The major infrastructural projects include, 127 dams in Arunachal Pradesh, Special Accelerated Road Development Programme for North East (SARDP-NE), Asian Highway (AH) No. 1, frontier highways and trilateral highways, amongst others. In the road sector,

> the Government is planning to invest about Rs. 1.45 lakh crore (24.5 billion) in the North East for development of NH: It plans to invest about Rs. 48,000 crore in Assam, Rs. 22,000 crore in Manipur, Rs. 20,000 crore in Nagaland, projects worth Rs. 17, 000 in Sikkim, Rs. 12,000 crore in Mizoram, Rs. 10,000 crore in Arunachal Pradesh, and Rs. 8,000 crore each in Meghalaya and Tripura.[25]

The World Bank and ADB, on the other hand, stepped in by giving loans for infrastructure development in the region for grand Asian connectivity and for greater mobility across the nation-states. This raises some interesting questions: who would benefit from such infrastructure development when it bypasses the local economy and people? Does this contribute to the state imaginary of regional integration and assimilation and to its counter-insurgency operations or to the neo-liberal agenda of capitalist expansion in the region? How are subversion of funds and projects taking place at the same time? What are the vested interests embedded in this policy?

Infrastructure is being projected as a tool for economic growth, development and greater mobility of goods and services from one part of the country to another country. Is the northeast the new gateway to facilitate this process, which bypasses the local communities? Highway development is a pointer in this direction. While the GoI prioritised mega-road development projects, such as SADRP and AH-1, the rural and feeder roads are either poorly developed or non-motorable – i.e. unfit for wheeled traffic. There is a lack of feeder roads connecting NHs in rural/tribal areas of Northeast India. Infrastructure such as highways, as much as they facilitate greater mobility/connectivity of goods and services, also effectively disconnect the rural/tribal communities.

> The roads are built not so much to connect villages, towns, and cities, but to facilitate speedy movement of goods and services within and across the countries by conceiving the shortest road and train routes possible, linking cities with industrial corridors, sea port and airports. (Srikanth, 2016: 46)

This approach of bypassing the local economy and communities is an act of injustice.

The massive government push for highway development in the region coincided with the proposed construction of more than 127 hydropower projects, which would generate 56,000 MV of electricity. The largest dam in India with a capacity to generate 12,000 MV is been constructed at Siang River basin in Arunachal Pradesh. Northeast India not only projected as the gateway to Southeast Asia but also became a hot-belt/energy frontier of hydropower generation through building small to large dams. It is interesting to note that most of the large hydropower plants (dams) are located in tribal territories: Ranganadi Dam in Arunachal Pradesh, Doyang Dam in Nagaland, Khuga Dam in Manipur, Tuirial Dam in Mizoram, Subansiri Dam on the Assam and Arunachal Pradesh border, Tipaimukh Dam in Manipur and so on. Yet it is in these areas that the power supply is most irregular with inadequate infrastructure in place, leaving aside large displacement of natives due to the submersion of villages. To cite the volume of displacement due to hydropower projects, 'Five hundred villages have been submerged by the flash flood generated by release of stored water from the Ranganadi-Dikrong project alone which has a capacity to 283 MW' (Gohain, 2008: 20). There are numerous other examples stemming from hydropower projects in the region where thousands of tribes were displaced (including forceful eviction), lost their livelihoods, traditions and cultures permanently and suffered the destruction of the eco-system, amongst others. The benefits of national development projects, which Nehru described as the temples of modern India, did not accrue to the tribal people: the employment created by these projects did not go to tribes; power projects did not electrify tribal villages and irrigation projects did not irrigate tribal land (Guha, 2007 as cited in Xaxa, 2016). Injustice is thus embedded in infrastructural projects.

The political economy of megaprojects in the region is in tune with the neo-liberal agenda streamlined and vouched for by the AEP. Rather than promoting basic infrastructure development of the local communities, Northeast India, as elsewhere in other parts of the country, is witnessing an increasing trend of private participation in the form of public-private partnership (PPP) in infrastructure development. The building of dams for hydropower generation is a classic example which promotes the PPP model of development. Bamang, citing the empirical evidence stemming from hydropower projects in Arunachal Pradesh, stated, 'The government is auctioning off Arunachal Pradesh without the consent of its people. Our land and water rights are being transferred to large companies to generate hydro-dollar for the elite' (as cited in Gohain, 2008: 20). The hydro-energy frontier under the AEP is fast transforming into facilitating the distribution of power energy not only to other parts of the country but also to export to neighbouring countries. Echoing from this perspective, Northeast India truly emerges as a new gateway and a power hub for corporate states and other parts of the country. However, what is often being overlooked is the contradiction of perspectives and conflict emanating from infrastructure projects between the tribal people vis-à-vis the state, dominant communities and the likes of World Bank, ADB and multinational companies in the region. This contradiction is not merely a conflict of interest or materiality but also about the conflict of values. Essentially, the philosophical foundation of tribal society is embedded in the principles of egalitarian society, interconnected and interdependent ecology and culture, environmental conservation and creation of sustainable livelihood (Bodhi, 2014). The waves of the neo-liberal state agenda penetrating into tribal society in the forms of megaprojects and layers of power/colonialism imposed upon tribes pose a threat to their values, thus escalating the contradiction of perspectives. One might question why tribes still feel that the state does not serve their interests, even when they have their own government, the state belongs to them and funds are in their hand. The simplest answer is because there is some form of colonisation still taking place. Thus, tribes are ensnared in the realm of the neo-liberal state agenda of development on the one hand, and on the other, they are under the dominant community's hegemon. Manipur, the site for this book, is an interesting case to disentangle these complex, dynamic and intricate processes. Characterised by a great degree of diversity while soaked in a history that speaks of waves of colonialism, tribes in the area have been excluded and denied agency from the infrastructural development.[26]

Often, there is a misconception, making Look/AEP synonymous with Northeast India development. But as Srikanth succinctly summed up that the Look/AEP is conceived more as a national policy for promoting trade, technology and investment opportunities: development of northeastern states was not its primary concern. He reiterates that it was only after the initiation of subregional forums like Bay of Bengal Initiative for Multi-sectoral

Technical and Economic Cooperation (BIMSTEC), Bangladesh-China-India-Myanmar (BCIM), Mekong-Ganga Cooperation (MGC), etc., that Northeast India is being projected as a gateway to East and Southeast Asia (Srikanth, 2016). Hence, this justified why there are massive investments by the government in megaprojects in the region and why the Indian state bypassed the interests of tribal people.

Tribes and infrastructural injustice

The use of the term 'tribe' is fraught with certain difficulties in Northeast India as elsewhere in India, as it tends to generalise communities that are quite different from each other in respect to language, culture, tradition, customs and so on. Amidst these differences, Xaxa drew out one commonality of tribes in India: i.e. exclusion from many social groupings that have historically, socially and culturally been associated with India (Xaxa, 2016). And yet for the purpose of this study, as many as 139 societies that constitute the ST in the region have been subsumed under one distinct social category – i.e. tribe. According to the 2011 census, amongst the northeastern states, Mizoram has the highest proportion of ST population (within the state) of 94.43 per cent, followed by Nagaland (86.47 per cent), Meghalaya (86.14 per cent), Arunachal Pradesh (68.78 per cent), Manipur (35.12 per cent), Sikkim (33.79 per cent), Tripura (31.75 per cent) and Assam (12.44 per cent). So how did the tribes, which otherwise were self-governed, each with its clear boundary/territory, sense of identity, culture, language and intrinsic relationship with nature, continue to experience poverty and crumbling infrastructure? What are the structural constraints that disallowed easy infrastructure development in tribal areas?

Tribes are experiencing a superimposed notion of development. Resistance to infrastructural creation is a common phenomenon and more so for mega-infrastructure projects, such as dams. Tribal communities resist because they the experience fear that with this kind of process, their lifestyles will change, including their culture, tradition, livelihood, eco-system and social relation, amongst others. Their existing social structures, landownership patterns and customary laws also disallow easy infrastructural development. Whatever little public infrastructure has been built by the state, tribes have not taken ownership of the same. Hence, there is no sense of accountability for the maintenance of the infrastructure, even when it reaches the point of wear and tear. We have not reached a point where the people have begun to take ownership and build public infrastructure. The nonchalant nature and attitude that there is someone (government) to do it for them still prevails amongst tribal communities. The pace of infrastructure creation is very slow amongst tribal societies. However, say if A wants to colonise B and if that colonisation process requires A to appropriate from B, then A will not mind building it. On the other hand, for building intra-village assets, such as village roads, water tanks, morungs and others, a collective labour force constitutes centre stage. However, this phenomenon has not translated beyond a village. Hence, one could witness the crumbling of inter-village roads, community halls, government offices, schools and veterinary centres, amongst others.

It is true that the tribal social reality and social structure does not allow easy infrastructure development. But on top of this, there is a pervasive structure – i.e. the politics of dominant communities that disallowed the growth and rise of an alternative centre. Manipur, the focus of this book offers an interesting case of suffocation and subversion of funds for infrastructure development. There is a sharp difference in terms of infrastructure facilities between the valley and hill districts, with the former being the power centre where the dominant community dwells and the latter predominantly inhabited by tribes that undergo multiple marginalities, layers of power and manipulation by the dominant community and the state. It is imperative that social transformation and growth involves infrastructure development.

The salient feature of infrastructure is that the moment it arises – i.e. when schools, colleges, universities, hospitals, government offices, roads, electricity, telecommunication, airports and multi-stadia, amongst others, are built – then that particular place begins to grow and deepen itself. If my interest is in positioning my place as the centre then there is conscious effort[27] to deny the growth of an alternative centre. The social reality of the dominant community stemming from Manipur points towards this direction. So the question of justice and injustice is also embedded in the mindset of the people who want to create and dominate the centre while at the same time denying the rise and growth of alternative centres. Echoing from this perspective, Imphal (the power centre) and other valley districts constitute the centres' hill districts, such as Senapati, Ukhrul, Tamenglong, Churuchandpur and Chadel, which are the alternative centres whose growth is denied.

For instance, if hill districts start developing as an alternative centre – for example, the Ukhrul District started highway construction linking to the state of Nagaland – then the dominant community would make a conscious effort to destroy that project in the form of delaying, suspension, non-release of funds, delay in issuing utilisation certificates, etc., since the state is controlled by the dominant community. On the other hand, if developing a highway (NH-37) from Imphal to Jiribam,[28] which is an extension of its power, the dominant community would bypass all the existing legal hurdles and build it. This book details how the dominant community creates, dominates and protects the centres and, in the process, denies the rise and growth of an alternative centre. Essentially, the concept of infrastructure of injustice is embedded within the mindset and how the very act of building infrastructure manifests injustice. It is imperative for an inclusive development to take place that the historical infrastructural injustice meted out to tribal societies be taken into serious consideration by the state and that it equally promotes the growth of alternative centres. Theoretically, it is meaningless to talk about tribal development and welfare, political rights, autonomy, cultural preservation and sustainable development, amongst others, without addressing the issue of historical injustice meted out against tribes in this subcontinent called India.

Plan of the book

Chapter 1 focuses on the imperatives of infrastructure development in a landlocked state. In the sensitive social and political context of India's border and frontier regions, infrastructure resonates with a unique material agency, fostering a close correlation with ethnicity. The chapter unfolds how infrastructure build-out in the region is ensnared in a binary space of military vs. civil, hills vs. valley, tribes vs. non-tribes and centre vs. alternative centre infrastructure. It posits that the state approach to building infrastructure in the hills is more of a future investment rather than a response to the needs emerging from the communities. This chapter argues that the concept of modernity framed within the perspective of the state at the behest of the dominant communities amounts to the denial of justice to tribal societies.

Chapter 2 details the political economy of development in Manipur. This chapter locates how the hill-valley divide continues to be a defining political space and the laying of infrastructure in the state. The chapter concludes by arguing that Manipur's development experience illuminates how the unequal power relations of various ethnic communities led to social unrest, development disparity, deep hostility and structural inequality. It unearths an emerging perspective of development from the lived experiences of tribal societies and illustrates how tribes are subjugated in the ambit of the dominant hegemon.

Chapter 3 looks at various communities, relationships and issues of contradiction and contestation. It traces the historical location of communities known as STs in Manipur. The political economy of the state is vividly brought out and so too is the deprivation of the STs in the state. This chapter also provides a historical outline of the state's power structure and argues that the state of Manipur has always put the interests of the dominant community at the forefront, while the tribes remain marginalised.

The political highway and its tributaries are mirrored in Chapter 4. It examines the ontology of roads and how the very act of building a road breeds injustice. It traces the budgetary allocation of funds for road development from 1947 to 2014 and its outcome. Combining empirical evidence and secondary data, it vividly captures road disparities in the state and examines the concept of roads from Poumai Naga tribal narratives and lived experiences. The chapter describes how roads have become political highways that are frequently the targets of blockades used to intensify protest movements that draw attention to local issues.

Chapter 5 looks at the political economy of electricity and budgetary discrimination. This chapter raises the following questions: how are rural villages electrified yet without electricity? Is the new policy change in electricity a reform in itself or mere prepaid metering? The chapter captures the hill-valley electricity divide and the dynamics of bill generation. The chapter argues that electricity, as much as a circulatory regime and network of connectivity, effectively transmits injustice.

Chapter 6 studies the intricate nexus of various stakeholders in building infrastructure and subsequently sheds light on the social and political processes of creating and maintaining infrastructure. This chapter discusses in detail the inter-linkages between various stakeholders such as tribal elites, bureaucrats, ministers, contractors and insurgents. This chapter points out how the parallel forms of civil administration, one by the Government of Manipur (GoM) and the other by insurgent groups, have paraded the common citizens in a perpetual state of insecurity and anxiety.

Chapter 7 argues that the nexus in building infrastructure is not only limited to politicians, and bureaucrats contractors; rather, it also includes insurgents, valley-centric elites and even civil society in the web of corruption of varied kinds. This chapter posits that the political life of infrastructure, the non-human agency enveloped in a shadow of ethnic contestation and insurgency, steeped in corruption and nexus, reveals contemporaneous development practices. Chapter 7 shows how infrastructure opens up new avenues to unfold the spaces of injustice, as well as sites for protest and negotiation. In a nutshell, Manipur's development resonates with a scapegoat syndrome.

Notes

1 The GoI data estimated that from 1951 to 1990, mega-development projects, such as dams, mining, wildlife sanctuaries and factories, have displaced over 21 million people in India. Out of this 21 million, 8.54 million have been enumerated as tribal. Thus, tribes constitute more than 40 per cent of the total displaced population, even as they comprise less than 9 per cent of the total population.

2 Retrieved from https://asiasociety.org/amartya-sen-and-idea-justice (accessed on 24 September 2018).

3 Broadly, there are two dominant perspectives concerning tribal studies in academia in South Asia: (1) colonial anthropologists/western/nationalist caste centric perspective, which can be located as 'perspective from above', and (2) the subaltern studies approach that takes the form of 'perspective from below'. The emerging perspective as theorised by the TICI came to be known as 'perspective from within', which coalesced with the decolonisation theory. Bodhi (2016) posited that perspective from within gives a space for a respectful engagement across fluid community boundaries yet propeled researchers to search, locate and position themselves around the ability to occupy a point of view firmly grounded from within rather than from without. Grosfoguel (2011) reiterated that 'decolonial perspective cannot be based on an abstract universal (one particular that raise itself as universal global design), but would have to be the result

of the critical dialogue between diverse critical epistemic/ethical/political projects towards a pluriversal as oppose to a universal world'.

4 For details, see Castro de Viveiros. 1998. 'Cosmological Deixis and Amerindian Perspectivism,' *Journal of the Royal Anthropological Institute*, 4 (3): 469–488.

5 For detailed discussion of hill peoples in Southeast Asia, see Scott, C. J. 2009. *The Art of Not Being Governed: An Anarchist History of Upland Southeast Asia*. New Haven: Yale University Press.

6 For detailed, see Kamei, G. 2015. *A History of Modern Manipur (1826–2000)*. New Delhi: Akansha Publishing House.

7 This paragraph was paraphrase from Ziipao, R. R. 2018. 'Roads, Tribes, and Identity in Northeast India.' *Asian Ethnicity*, 20 (1): 1–22. https://doi.org/10.1080/14631369.2018.1495058.

8 This treaty was signed by Haridas Gossain on behalf of Bhagyachandra, Raja of Manipur and Harry Verelst, Chief of Chittagong factory. For details, see Lal Dena. 2008. *British Policy Towards Manipur, 1762–1947*. Imphal: Nongeen Publication.

9 Had Manipur being truly an independent kingdom, its kings would not have been required to be recognised by the British government. Maharaja Gambhir Singh was recognised by the king of Ava after the Treaty of Yandabo, and, subsequently, all the kings of Manipur were subjected to being recognised by the British government.

10 The excluded areas were under the direct jurisdiction of the British through the executive control of the Assam governor, and no act of the federal legislature or the Assam legislature was to apply to these areas.

11 In a partially excluded area, the administration was primarily the responsibility of the cabinet, but the governor of Assam was charged with special responsibility for provinces' peace and good government. Assam had elected representatives in the legislature (Reid, 1944).

12 Meitei is the dominant community in Manipur.

13 Gambhir Singh was given the title of Maharaja by the British government.

14 The officers who commanded the Manipur Levy includes, Major F.J Grant, Lt. R.B. Pemberton, Lt. Francis Jenkins, Lt. George Gordon, amongst others.

15 For details, see *political highway* in Chapter 4.

16 Military expedition of Gambhir Singh includes the conquest of Khoupum, 1828; the Kuki expedition in the Southern hills, 1828; invasion of Tangkhul villages, 1826; and expeditions to Naga country, 1832–33; amongst others. For details, see Kamei, *Modern History of Manipur*; Laldena, *British Policy Towards Manipur*; *The Royal Chronicle* (Cheitharol Kumbaba).

17 Writing of such texts is in fact a political activity and often associated with power, which the British has.

18 The name in parenthesis denotes the name in local language.

19 Within Khasi states, there are small areas – namely the cantonment areas, European ward and police bazar in Shillong – which were under British rule. Outside these British areas are the Khasi states that constitute 25 mostly semi-independent states.

20 The polarisation of infrastructure between the plains and hills of Northeast India continues to be visible in post-independent India.

21 Most of the hill tribes during the British rule in the region were either in the category of excluded or partially excluded areas.

22 Jawaharlal Nehru, then prime minister of India, put forward the famous Panchsheel principles in his foreword to Verrier Elwin's book *A Philosophy for NEFA* (1957).

23 It includes the states of Meghalaya, Mizoram, Nagaland, Arunachal Pradesh and part of the Manipur hill districts.
24 These limitations or constraints include Article 371 (A), (B), (C), Sixth Schedule of the Constitution of India and other persistent issues, such as insurgency, law and order problems, ethnic strife, lack of infrastructure development and various secessionist movements in the region.
25 As stated by Shri Nitin Gadkari (union minister of road transport and highway). Retrieved from https://economictimes.indiatimes.com/news/economy/infrastructure/states-told-overcome-land-hurdles-in-ne-road-projects/articleshow/62661613.cms (accessed on 10 September 2018).
26 Paraphrased from Bodhi, S. R. and Jojo, B. *Problematics of Tribal Integration: Voices from India's Alternative Centers*. Hyderabad: The Shared Mirror, 2019, p. 2.
27 These efforts include budgetary cuts, planning, diversion and subversion of funds, policy twists, denial of agency, etc.
28 Jiribam was part of the Imphal East District until 2016, and Meiteis constitutes the major population. It lies at the tri-junction of Nagaland, Assam and Manipur hill district of Tamenglong.

References

Anand, N. 2011. 'Pressure: The PoliTechnics of Water Supply in Mumbai'. *Cultural Anthropology*, 26 (4): 542–564. https://doi.org/10.1111/j.1548-1360.2011.01111.x

Asia Society Northern California. 2010. Amartya Sen and the Idea of Justice. Retrieved from https://asiasociety.org/amartya-sen-and-idea-justice

Boaventura de Sousa Santos. 2014. *Epistemologies of the South: Justice Against Epistemicide*. New York: Routledge.

Bodhi, S. R. 2014. 'Tribal Social Work: Reflection on Its Philosophical Foundation'. *Indian Journal of Dalit and Tribal Social Work*, 2 (6): 64–74.

Bodhi, S. R. (ed.). 2016. *Social Work in India*. Kolkata: Adivaani.

Bodhi, S. R. and Jojo, B. 2019. *The Problematics of Tribal Integration: Voices from India's Alternative Centers*. Hyderabad: The Shared Mirror.

Boeck, D. 2012. 'Infrastructure: Commentary from Filip De Boeck,' Curated Collections, *Cultural Anthropology*.

Buck-Morss, S. (1992). 'Aesthetics and Anaesthetics: Walter Benjamin's Artwork Essay Reconsidered'. *October*, 62: 3–41.

Castro de Viveiros. 1998. 'Cosmological Deixis and Amerindian Perspectivism'. *Journal of the Royal Anthropological Institute*, 4 (3): 469–488.

Das, P. 2008. 'Evolution of the Road Network in Northeast India: Drivers and Brakes'. *Strategic Analysis*, 33 (1): 101–116. https://doi.org/10.1080/09700160802518635.

Dzuvichu, L. 2013. 'Roads and the Raj: The Politics of Road Building in Colonial Naga Hills, 1860s–1910s'. *The Indian Economic and Social History Review*, 50 (4): 473–494. https://doi.org/10.1177/0019464613502416.

Edwards, N. P. 2003. 'Infrastructure and Modernity: Force, Time, and Social Organization in the History of Sociotechnical Systems'. In T. J. Misa and P. Brey (eds.), *Modernity and Technology*. Cambridge, MA: MIT Press.

Elwin, V. 1957. *A Philosophy for NEFA (North East Frontier Agency)*. Berkeley: University of California.

Gohain, H. 2008. 'Big Dams, Big Floods: On Predatory Development'. *Economics and Political Weekly*, 43 (30): 19–21.

Grosfoguel, R. 2011. 'Decolonizing Post-Colonial Studies and Paradigms of Political-Economy: Transmodernity, Decolonial Thinking, and Global Coloniality'. *Transmodernity*, 1 (1): 1–38.

Hannah, A., et al. 2015. 'Introduction: The Infrastructure Toolbox. Theorizing the Contemporary'. *Cultural Anthropology*. Retrieved from https://culanth.org/fieldsights/714-introduction-the-infrastructure-toolbox (accessed on 7 March 2018).

Harvey, P. and Knox, H. 2015. *Roads: An Anthropology of Infrastructure and Expertise*. Ithaca and London: Cornell University Press.

Hunter, W. W. 1879a. *A Statistical Account of Assam I*. London: Truner and Co.

Hunter, W. W. 1879b. *A Statistical Account of Assam II*. London: Truner and Co.

Jairam, R. 2011. 'North East India in a New Asia'. In A. K. Agarwal and B. Singh (eds.), *Understanding India's North East*. Guwahati: DVS Publishers.

Kamei, G. 2015. *A History of Modern Manipur (1826–2000)*. New Delhi: Akansha Publishing House.

Lal Dena. 2008. *British Policy Towards Manipur, 1762–1947*. Imphal: Nongeen Publication.

Larkin, B. 2013. 'The Politics and Poetics of Infrastructure'. *The Annual Review of Anthropology*, 42: 327–342. https://doi.org/10.1146/annurev-anthro-092412-155522.

Mrazek, R. 2002. *Engineers of Happy Land: Technology and Nationalism in a Colony*. Princeton, NJ: Princeton University Press.

Rao, V. 1972. 'Reorganization of North East India'. *The Indian Journal of Political Science*, 33 (2): 123–144.

Rawls, J. 1971 (1999). *A Theory of Justice* (Revised Edition). Cambridge, MA: Harvard University Press.

Reid, R. 1944. *History of the Frontier Areas Bordering on Assam From 1883–1941*. Shillong: Assam Government Press.

Roy-Burman, B. K. 1961. *Demographic and Socio-Economic Profile of the Hill Areas of North East India, in Census of India*. New Delhi: Ministry of Home Affairs.

Scott, C. J. 2009. *The Art of Not Being Governed: An Anarchist History of Upland Southeast Asia*. New Haven: Yale University Press.

Sen, A. 2009. *The Idea of Justice*. Cambridge, MA: Harvard University Press.

Shimray, U. A. 2001. 'Ethnicity and Socio-Political Assertion'. *Economic and Political Weekly*, 39 (28): 3674–3677.

Srikanth, H. 2016. 'Look East Policy, Subregional Connectivity Projects and North East India'. *Economic and Political Weekly*, LI (47): 45–51.

Star, S. and Rudleder, K. 1996. 'Steps Towards an Ecology of Infrastructure: Design and Access for Large Information Spaces'. *Information Technology and Organizational Transformation*, 7 (1): 111–134.

Stewart, K. 2011. 'Atmospheric Attunements: Environment and Planning D'. *Society and Space*, 29: 445–453. https://doi.org/10.1068/d9109.

Xaxa, V. 1985. 'Colonial Capitalism and Underdevelopment in North Bengal'. *Economic and Political Weekly*, 20 (39): 1659–1665.

Xaxa, V. 2008. *State, Society, and Tribes: Issues in Post-Colonial India*. New Delhi: Pearson Education Society.

Xaxa, V. 2016. 'Tribes and Indian National Identity: Location of Exclusion and Marginality'. *Brown Journal of World Affair*, XXIII (I): 223–237.
Yonuo, A. 1974. *The Rising Nagas: A Historical and Political Study*. Delhi: Vivek Publishing House.
Ziipao, R. R. 2018. 'Roads, Tribes, and Identity in Northeast India'. *Asian Ethnicity*, 20 (1): 1–22. https://doi.org/10.1080/14631369.2018.1495058.

1

THE PLACE OF INFRASTRUCTURE IN DEVELOPMENT

Introduction

For over 30 years, the state government has neglected the Tamenglong-Haflong Road. The construction of this road was included in the sixth five-year plan. During 1980–93, the PWD executed some initial work. However, the road remained impassable due to faulty alignment and non-completion. In 1997, the state entrusted the Border Road Organisation (BRO) with the construction of this road, but it declined, citing faulty alignment. Even after repeated assurances from the central government, including the former union tribal affairs minister Shri P. R. Kyndiah (2006) and Home Minister Shri P. Chidambaram (2011) during their visits to the district, the government did not build the road, and the people's dream of better facilities remained unfulfilled. The acts of non-implementation and delaying the project are themselves politics amounting to denial of justice to tribal societies. The temporalities and suspension nature of basic infrastructural projects is a common phenomenon across pan-tribal belt/territories in India. The GoI initiated a flagship programme known as Pradhan Mantri Gram Sadak Yojana (PMGSY) in 2000 to provide rural connectivity to all villages in the country with all-weather roads. Yet more than 17 years after the implementation of the programme, many tribal villages remain outside the radar of connectivity.

Inadequate basic infrastructure limits the movement of goods, people and ideas, especially in the hill areas predominantly inhabited by tribes. Even basic needs, such as all-weather roads connecting all villages, minimum electricity supply, health-care centres, primary schools and potable water, remain inaccessible for most tribal communities in the State of Manipur. This demonstrates how over India's seven decades of independence, the state has been negligent when it comes to addressing the problems of tribal people. Tribes are the ones that suffer the ramifications of the Indian state's indifferent attitude. Consequences of inadequate infrastructure include villagers carrying their sick in bamboo stretchers to the nearest health centre. Oranges and Naga chillies (commonly known as ghost peppers in international markets) grow abundantly in Tamenglong, a hill district in Manipur. However, surplus agricultural products are left to rot, as villagers are unable to transport them to the market due to a lack of road access.

A native-born, young and dynamic Indian Administrative Service (IAS) officer, Armstrong Pame, took up road connectivity as an immediate requirement in the area after witnessing the hardships faced by people in remote villages in and around the supposed route of the road. While posted as subdivisional officer (SDO) of Tousem subdivision, he and his elder brother mobilised resources and local communities. They created a Facebook page seeking donations to construct a 100-km rural road. Previously disconnected from social media, this rural village resorted to Facebook in order to establish infrastructure. A dedicated local resident, Haingiabuing Pame, mobilised the village with the following statement: 'I shall give all that I have to see the completion of this road. We have waited for too long. This has been my dream. Let us celebrate when it is finished'. The response from across the globe was overwhelming. The local communities took ownership of the road and contributed in a variety of ways, including labour, materials, bulldozers, fuel, food, accommodation and more. The People's Road, which connects the states of Manipur, Nagaland and Assam in India, was completed in seven months (August 2012–February 2013), after the state government neglected to complete it for over 30 years. Inaugurated on 17 February 2013 and opened for public use, the motto of this road stands as 'together we began, together we built and together we finished'. The monolith commemorating the inauguration of the road reads as follows:

> THE PEOPLE'S ROAD
> Dedicated unto the glory of God
> With the celebration of the people's endeavour
> by ARMSTRONG PAME, IAS
> SDO, Tousem
> In the August presence of all
> the donors, volunteers and well-wishers
> May the present and the future generations
> Remember every single drop of sweat, tears, and contribution
> Rendered for the construction of this road from all over the world
> Date: 17 February 2013
> KATANGNAM VILLAGE

Despite considerable odds, the tribal people from India's most remote district resisted marginalisation and surmounted structural obstacles by constructing 100 km of road. By doing so, they succeeded in carving their own path to mobility where the state failed miserably. The condition of the tribes' infrastructure development in Manipur stands as a testimony of the state's failure to discharge its duties and responsibilities. Rather than addressing the historical injustice and political aspirations of the tribes, the state suppressed and denied agency, thereby forcing the tribes to look after themselves. The Tamenglong's construction and maintenance of roads for livelihood, economic sustenance and maintenance of the ecological balance between people and nature have become the model in other parts of the state. If the state or development practitioners need a consultant on building roads, they should ask the true trailblazers – the tribal people. This is the extent to which rural habitats need connectivity and other basic infrastructure.

In landlocked states, the role of physical connectivity in overall development of a country or region assumes a place of critical importance. This is much more so in regions such as Northeast India and its states, as they are not only landlocked but also marked by hills and difficult terrain. Manipur is no exception. With this being the case, connectivity turns out to be critical given the landlocked nature and difficult geographical terrain. The overarching impact of infrastructure on the existing social relationship between a community and its environment, and on the socio-politico-economic development, are crucial in states like Manipur and Northeast India.

In the sensitive social and political context of India's border and frontier regions, infrastructure resonates with a unique material agency, fostering a close correlation with ethnicity. The current debates on infrastructure development by social scientists focus on budgetary allocations, inter- and intra-regional variations and deficits in infrastructural development. There is hardly any serious engagement with infrastructural development in a specific political context, which takes into account social composition and people at the micro-level. Northeast India is often projected as an *infrastructural deficit and backwards region*. However, this can be contested from the empirical evidence stemming from different states and geographical locations of varied ethnic communities. Mishra and Upadhyay (2017) noted,

> There is no doubt that significant gaps remain in the availability of physical, financial and social infrastructure across the region. However, it is wrong to reduce the development challenges of the region to the infrastructure deficit not only are there significant differences across the plain and hilly areas, but even within these regions, the challenges of development are multi-level, diverse and complex. Given this diversity and complexity, problems of the region cannot be neatly aggregated to fixed notions of 'backwardness'.
>
> (:9)

In fact, within the region, minorities have experienced infrastructural injustice since colonial times. The very act of not building and investing in infrastructure in the hill areas amounts to injustice. This is much more so in a chronic conflict-ridden state like Manipur where infrastructure in the valley is better developed as compared to those of the hill areas. The hilly areas where tribes predominantly reside could very well fit into the criterion of *infrastructural deficit* area. However, districts such as Imphal East, Imphal West, Kamrup Metro, Kamrup Rural, East Khasi Hills and Nagaon, Kokrajhar, amongst others, are on par with other developed districts in India in terms of infrastructure index. There is a spatial and social concentration of infrastructure within particular ethnic or economic groups – an aspect that is rarely presented through aggregate secondary data (ibid.). There is a need to critically examine the social dynamics of infrastructure development with the changing contours of development policies and programmes. This would pave the way for theorising structural inequality, which has been inadequately addressed in Manipur and Northeast India. Development policies and programmes of the GoI are crucial factors leading to infrastructure disparities within the region and states. Hence, it merits a revisit of infrastructure policy in India vis-à-vis its approach to northeastern states in the post-independent era. It is imperative to unearth what constitutes infrastructure in India.

Contextualising infrastructure in India

The term infrastructure gained currency with the emergence of development economics in the early 1950s, which is used interchangeably with social overhead capital (SOC). Amongst the early development economists, Lewis (1955) stressed the importance of public utilities, ports, water supplies and electricity, and Higgins (1959) focused on transport, public utilities, schools and hospitals in promoting economic development. The services referred by Levis and Higgins are today thought of as infrastructure. However, it was Hirschman (1958) who gave a very wide meaning to SOC or infrastructure. In his formulation, SOC includes education, public health, law and order, transportation, communication, power, water supply, irrigation and drainage. Infrastructure has thus meant different things to different people at different points in time and place depending on the changes in the technology, lifestyles of the people and the socio-economic and political environment under consideration (MoS&PI, 2010).

The Central Statistics Office (CSO), in its *Manual: Infrastructure Statistics*, operationalised infrastructure based on the *Rangarajan Commission Report* (2001). According to the Rangarajan Commission, infrastructure does not refer to the user and user-specific structure but to long-lasting engineering structures. They identified six characteristic features of infrastructure: (1) natural monopoly, (2) non-tradability of outputs, (3) bestowing externalities on society, (4) high-suck costs or asset specificity, (5) non-rivalness (up to congestion limits) in consumption and (6) possibility of price exclusion. The commission was of the view that the following infrastructures have all six characteristics identified in defining infrastructure:

- Railway tracks, signalling system, stations
- Road, bridges
- Transmission and distribution of electricity
- Telephone lines, telecommunications network
- Pipelines for water, crude oil, slurry, etc.
- Waterways, port facilities
- Canal networks for irrigation
- Sanitation or sewerage

(Rangarajan Commission, 2001)

It is interesting to note how economists and socio-anthropologists see infrastructure. The former perceive infrastructure from the material and value perspective, whereas the latter see infrastructure as a relational concept.[1] Star and Rudleder (1996) posited that infrastructure is fundamentally a relational concept. For them, infrastructure has the following dimensions/properties:

> (1) embeddedness: it is sunk into other structures; (2) transparency: it does not have to be reinvented each time; (3) reach or scope: it is not a one-off event or one-site practice; (4) being learned as part of membership: it is associated with a community of practice; (5) being linked with conventions of practice: it both shapes and is shaped by the conventions of a community of practice; (6) becomes visible upon breakdown.
>
> (:113)

Nevertheless, economists and urban planners distinguished two types of infrastructure: economic and social infrastructure. Economic infrastructure is defined as those infrastructures that promote economic activities, such as roads, railroads, airports, seaports, electricity, telecommunication, water supply and sanitation. Social infrastructures are those that promote the health, education and cultural standards of the people. They include schools, libraries, universities, clinics, hospitals, courts, museums, theatres, playground, parks, fountains and statues (Central Statistics Office, 2012).

The GoI felt the need to systematically capture infrastructural data based in India and to resolve the arbitrariness of the concept of infrastructure. Hence it constituted a Cabinet Committee on Infrastructure (henceforth CCI) on 6 July 2009 with the prime minister as its chairman. The CCI acknowledged and incorporated some features of infrastructure as defined by the Reserve Bank of India, income tax department, *Rakesh Mohan Committee Report* (1996), Insurance Regulated and Development Authority, Economic Survey and World Bank. However, it was the *Rangarajan Commission Report* (2001) which formed the basis for defining infrastructure in India.

Following this, the GoI came out with a list of infrastructure under six broad categories: (1) transport, (2) energy, (3) communication, (4) drinking water supply and sanitation, (5) irrigation and (6) storage.[2] These infrastructure activities are central to households and economic production. Thereafter, the Ministry of Statistics and Programme Implementation (MoS&PI) came out with an infrastructure indicator under two broad categories: outcome or performance and institutional reform indicator.

India's infrastructure development approach

India, with a population of 1.21 billion (2011 census), contributes over 17 per cent of the world's population. It is characterised as a multi-ethnic, multi-cultural, multi-lingual and multi-religious society. The country consists of 29 states and 7 union territories. It has 640 administrative districts. Thus, its citizens are spread far and wide. Over 72 per cent of the population lives in about 638,000 villages. The remaining 27.8 per cent reside in over 5,100 towns and over 380 urban agglomerations (Census of India, 2011). Since independence, the administrative division has been rearranged from time to time with a view to address development and social identity issues. In spite of such rearrangements, the development status of India has been far from uniform. There are differences along the lines of region, state, district and even villages. India's development experience points to a scenario of dichotomy that is of the best and the worst. This is well captured in the World Bank development policy review (2006)

> It is the best of the world, it is the worst of the world- and the gaps are growing. The top students from the Indian Institute of Technology are not just globally competitive; they have set the global standard. Yet, many, if not most, children in India finish government primary schools incapable of simple arithmetic. While there is increasing 'medical tourism' where people travel to India for high-quality, low-cost medical treatments- the typical Primary Health Centre doctors in Delhi are less competent than doctors in Tanzania. India's Supreme Court is justly world renowned, but local courts are backlogged and ineffective and local police are frequently a miasma of corruption and brutality. Similarly, in economic performance, while parts of urban India compete for business in software engineering and biomedical research, parts of rural India have poverty rates comparable to borderline 'failed states,' such as Haiti and Nigeria, and have child malnutrition rates higher than any country in the world.
>
> (:1)

To overcome the economic hurdles, the GoI followed a planned economy and set up the Planning Commission in 1950. The first five-year plan was introduced in 1951. The initial five-year plans in India focuses on the development of heavy industries and infrastructure besides agriculture sectors. The Table 1.1 provides the changing contour of India's development policy or rather political economy in post-independent India.

The trend in infrastructure policy and development in India followed the changing dynamics of leadership and its political orientation at the centre. Accordingly, India witnessed four waves of infrastructure build-out. Lall and Rastogi (2007) succinctly summed it up:

> The first wave of infrastructure build-out corresponding to the Nehru era covers the period of the first three five-year plans, the formulation of each of which was presided over by Nehru. The second wave corresponds to the period next three plans, formulated under the leadership of Indira Gandhi. And the third wave of build-out covers the period of the 7th Five-Year Plan which was guided by Rajiv Gandhi. The 8th, 9th and 10th Plans were formulated in the era of Decentralised Politics.
>
> (:5)

During the Nehruvian era, the focus was on increasing food production, developing basic and heavy industries and restoring the lost and damages from India-Pakistan partition. The first three five-year plans echoed Nehru's approach to development ingrained with his socialist ideology. Henceforth, his priority of development was on heavy industries, mega dams, multipurpose irrigation projects, hydro projects and roads, amongst others. In fact, his famous slogan 'temples of modern India' became the guiding principle of infrastructure development. The primacy of this vision was building

Table 1.1 Political economy in post-independent India

Era	*Political Orientation*	*Policy Focus*
Jawaharlal Nehru (1950–67)	Fabian socialist	Industrialisation, pro-public sector and central government bias
Indira Gandhi (1967–84)	Rhetorical socialist with anti-urban bias trending to populist	Food security, anti-private sector, import substitution
Rajiv Gandhi (1984–91)	Populist	Industrial de-licensing and deregulation, technological modernisation
Decentralised Politics (Post-1991)	Neo-populist (coalition based)	Structural economic reforms, globalisation

Source: Rajiv Lall and Anupam Rastogi (2007)

infrastructure for prosperous and modern India. Strangely, however, it was during this period that rural India experienced massive displacement due to megaprojects for building modern India. Tribes constitute the single-largest population enumerated from development-induced displacement. This was the beginning of the first wave of displacement in post-independent India. It is estimated that from 1951 to 1990, mega-development projects, such as dams, mining, wildlife sanctuaries and factories, have displaced over 21 million people in India. Out of this 21 million, 8.54 million have been enumerated as tribal. Thus tribes constitute above 40 per cent of the total displaced population, even as they comprise less than 9 per cent of the total population (as cited in Xaxa, 2018).

The Indira Gandhi regime, on the other hand, deepened the Nehruvian model of development but shifted its focus to building rural infrastructure, particularly roads and irrigations. The primacy of her vision was focused on reducing the long gestation projects with shorter initiatives and the focus on food security and poverty alleviation programmes. The total road length of India in 1971 was 9,14,970 km and went up to 14,85,421 km by 1981. Out of this total road length, rural road constitutes above 42 per cent (Basic Roads Statistics, 2013). India witnessed a growth of road infrastructure by more than 61 per cent from 1971 to 1981. The focus of infrastructure built on during the Rajiv Gandhi era was based on telecommunication and ground water irrigation. Lall and Rastogi (2007) observed that

> given Rajiv Gandhi's pre-occupation with modernisation and technology, significant investment was made in the country's telecommunications infrastructure. Telecommunications technology and services assumes high national priority in the seventh economic development plan (1985–90), during which expenditure on this sector grew very substantially.
>
> (:16)

The fourth wave – i.e. the decentralisation phase – is marked by the coalition government with a focus on structural economic reform and globalisation. The Indian government initiated economic reforms, citing twin crises of fiscal crunch and balance of payments deficits. This led the Indian economy to open up and the process of privatisation, deregulation and delicensing was initiated and pursued vigorously. Economic reform in India on the one hand promises a higher growth rate, generation of employment and poverty reduction, amongst others, but on the other hand, it widens economic inequality and massive displacement due to megaprojects, such as dams, special economic zones (SEZs), etc. The question of economic reform in India remains a point of contention and highly debated. Nevertheless, global economic integration became the order of the day in Indian economic policy, favouring privatisation with much larger participation from the private sector in the form of a PPP, hence reducing the role of the state in market regulation. Ahluwalia (former deputy-chairman, Planning Commission) pointed out that 'infrastructure problems were not the central focus of policy when the reform began in mid-1991. The agenda for reforms in the early years was understandably dominated by crisis management and the need for domestic and external stabilisation' (nd: 18). Yet infrastructure remains the bottleneck for economic growth in India; hence, there was a need to shift its infrastructural policy in tune with the neo-liberal agenda. Accordingly, during the eighth five-year plan, the GoI incorporated PPP in building strong infrastructures. The PPP became the preferred model of development, particularly in cultivating infrastructures in the lens of the policy makers. Subsequently, the government introduced the national PPP policy. The 11th five-year plan reiterated and deepened the PPP in building and delivering infrastructure. It stated,

> The approach to PPPs must remain firmly grounded in principles which ensure that PPPs are formulated and executed in public interest with a view to achieving additional capacity and delivery of public services at reasonable cost. These partnerships must ensure the supplementing of scare public resources for investment in infrastructure sectors, while improving efficiencies and reducing costs. PPPs must aim at bringing private resources into public projects, not public resources into private projects.
>
> (Government of India, 2007: 256)

International financial institutions, such as the International Monetary Fund and the World Bank, played a crucial role in India's approach to the PPP model in the form of policy prescription. The World Bank opined that India must invest around 3–4 per cent more of gross domestic product on infrastructure to sustain growth of around 8 per cent, address existing gaps and meet policy-driven coverage goals. The private sector can play an important role in providing such levels of resources through PPP, although improving implementation capacity and the quality of investment will be more important than increasing the quantum of funds available (World Bank, 2006: xv). Over the years, India's commitment on private investment has increase threefold. It initiated various large-scale infrastructure projects under its ambitious programme of building economic corridor with active participation from private sector. This includes the Golden Quadrilateral, international airports and ports, North-South and East-West Corridor, SEZs and hydropower projects, amongst others. These projects envisage the rationality of greater mobility and interconnected economic systems not only within the country but also across the globe.

Though the PPP approach to infrastructure development became the order of the day, empirical evidence suggests that access to infrastructure is limited to certain strata of society with the introduction of user fees under build, operate and transfer. The promise of PPP and economic reform for efficient service delivery, reduction of poverty, generation of employment or the trickle-down effect failed to translate into reality in rural India. Athreya (2008) elicited the weakening and relative stagnation of the rural economy under the economic reform dispensation, which also meant that the rate of growth of rural employment had been rather slow. Between 1993 and 1994 and 1999 and 2000, rural employment grew only by 0.66 per cent per annum as opposed to 2.07 per cent between 1987 and 1988 and 1993 and 1994. Data from the National Sample Survey (NSS) suggests that between 1999 and 2000 and 2004, the growth rate of employment for rural males was only 0.5 per cent per annum (females: 1.2 per cent). Urban employment growth rates also sharply declined during this period. Correspondingly, NSS data shows that the rate of unemployment amongst rural males by current daily status rose from 5.6 per cent in 1993–94 to 9.0 per cent in 2004 and that for rural females it rose from 5.6 per cent to 9.3 per cent. The economic reform and its infrastructure build-out are not as cosy as they were envisaged, particularly for rural inhabitants. The urban-rural divide becomes even more visible in the light of current development policies and programmes. The GoI has introduced smart cities, superhighways and bullet trains for urban populations. It is also equally important and more so for rural inhabitants to have smart villages, super-village roads and smart cultivation, amongst others. Hence the imperative for widening the role of the state in providing basic infrastructure to rural India. Besides stagnation in rural employment and economic inequality, there is also a phenomenon of regional disparity within the country. Northeast India echoes this disparity, coupled with inadequate infrastructure in the hills, identity politics, insurgencies, centre-state and centre-regional relationships, ethnic territoriality movement and unique landownership patterns, amongst others.

Locating Northeast India: frontier to region

The northeastern states were popularly known as the seven sisters until Sikkim was made part of the NEC in the year 2002. The present northeastern states consist of Arunachal Pradesh, Assam, Manipur, Meghalaya, Mizoram, Nagaland, Sikkim and Tripura. The region of Northeast India shares 98 per cent of its borders with the neighbouring countries of Bangladesh, Bhutan, Myanmar and China and only 2 per cent with other states of India. Scholarly engagement on Northeast India is an emerging line of research. Over the years, the northeast region has been theorised and variously described as India's frontier (Elwin, 1957), infrastructure-deficit (Shukla Commission, 1997), conflict-ridden (Shimray, 2004), India's periphery (Misra, 2000), region of durable disorder (Baruah, 2005), instability at the gate (Egreteau, 2006),

India's troubled periphery (Bhaumik, 2009), region of underdevelopment (Biswas and Sukhlabaidya, 2008), economically backward (Brunner, 2010; Sharma, 2011; Sharma, 2012), region of hostile geography and unfortunate history (Bhattacharya, 2011), new gateway (GoI, nd), hinterland (Patgiri and Hazarika, 2016) and the list goes on. Thus, the socio-politico-economic issues stemming from the region have created multiple discourses. And yet the question of Northeast India as an entity/region still remains largely contested both in academia and public discourse. To understand why Northeast India is the way it is today, we need to understand the aspects of its history that set it on this particular development path.

It is imperative to revisit the historical events that shaped India's northeast as an entity/region in the Deluesian language to examine how territorialisation took place. One could locate two dominant streams of discourse: colonial and post-colonial. The former refers to the northeast as a 'frontier' and the latter as a 'region'. The Bengal presidency was the basis upon which the concept of the frontier region was constructed and formulated. The present northeastern states and parts of Myanmar were categorised as the 'northeast frontier of Bengal'[3] following the first Anglo-Burmese War, which eventually led to the signing of the Treaty of Yandabo in 1826. This treaty was signed between the East India Company and the king of Ava and brought to an end the Burmese occupation of Assam, Manipur, Cachar and Jaintia. The Treaty of Yandabo officially paved way for colonial rule and the formation of a separate Assam state in 1904 (which comprised the present-day Assam state and adjoining regions that are today the separate states of Meghalaya, Nagaland, Mizoram and Arunachal Pradesh) under British administration. The treaty also demarcated the boundary line between present-day Myanmar and India. The ramifications of the Treaty of Yandabo are experienced in the northeast even today.

The inclusion of the northeast in the Bengal Province until 1874 turned the socio-politico-economic history of the region in a different direction, producing a new reality. The region was known as the North-East Frontier Non-regulated Province. The British policy of colonial expansion encountered stiff resistance from the hill tribes, and they made regular raids on the villages that were in the vicinity of roads. In the words of Mackenzie (1884),

> When in 1835 our hill villages in North Cachar were found to be constantly suffering from Naga exactions and raids, the Government conceived that the duty of controlling the hostile Nagas developed jointly upon Tukaram and the Manipuri State, as the two powers holding jurisdiction over at least some portions of the Naga Hills. It was proposed, therefore, that a line of posts to protect our subjects should be established along the neighbouring Naga frontier.
>
> (:103)

The colonial rulers introduced concepts such as 'backwards tracts,' 'excluded areas,' 'partially excluded areas', etc., by passing the Government of India (Excluded and Partially Excluded Areas) Order, 1936. With this order, the following territories were declared as excluded areas: the Naga Hills, the Lushai Hills, the North Cachar subdivision of the Cachar District and the frontier tracts – i.e. the present state of Arunachal Pradesh. The partially excluded areas from the region include the Mikir Hills, the Garo Hills and the British portion of the Khasi and Jaintia Hills. These excluded and partially excluded areas are predominantly inhabited by tribes. Many of the colonial acts were adopted by the post-colonial Indian state – for instance, the ILP requirement for non-tribals to visit three states as mentioned earlier and protective mechanisms under the Constitution of India – i.e. Article 371(A) for the state of Nagaland, Article 371(C) for the Manipur hills areas and Article 244(2) of the Sixth Schedule which applies to the states of Assam, Meghalaya, Mizoram and Tripura. The concept of Northeast India as an entity today referring to a geographical area stems from the historical events discussed earlier.

With India's independence, British territories and princely states were merged into the Union of India through the transfer of power, in direct contradiction to the political aspirations of various ethnic communities in the border regions. As a result, one can see even to this day the various political demands stemming both from insurgent groups and civil society in the northeastern states, prominent amongst them being the Naga movement, which was amongst the first to make itself felt post-independence (Hassan, 2006). In order to quell the Naga aspirations, Nagaland was carved out of Assam in 1963. The formation of the Nagaland state became a contentious issue as various ethnic groups inhabiting Assam started demanding separate states and autonomy for their respective areas. Following this, the Parliament of India enacted the Assam Reorganisation Act in 1969 to enable the formation of more states in the region and thereby to meet the demands of various hill areas within the state of Assam. As a result, the Meghalaya Autonomous State was created in 1970, elevated to full-fledged state in 1972. Following the recommendations from the State Reorganisation Commission, the GoI passed the North-Eastern Areas (Reorganisation) Act, 1971, which led to the formation of the states of Meghalaya, Manipur and Tripura. Arunachal Pradesh and Mizoram were given the status of Union Territories in 1972. In 1982, Arunachal Pradesh was elevated to a full-fledged state. The Mizo uprising and formation of the Mizo National Front (MNF) culminated in 1987 with the signing of the 'Mizo Accord' between the MNF and the GoI.

The northeast as a region was formalised as a political entity with the enactment of the NEC Act in 1971. NEC is the nodal agency for economic and social development and acts as a mini-planning body for the present eight states. This was taken further by the GoI with the establishment of a separate MDoNER in 2001. Apart from political formalisation of Northeast

India as a region, academic institutions of higher education joined the choir in establishing separate centres dedicated solely to studies of Northeast India, for example the Centre for North East Studies at Jawaharlal Nehru University (JNU) and the Centre for North East Studies and Policy Research at Jamia Millia Islamia in Delhi and regional bodies, such as the North East Student's Association, North East India History Association and Northeastern Political Science Association, amongst others. The terms 'Northeast India,' 'Northeastern Region,' 'India's northeast' and 'northeastern states' became popular in political, academic and public discourse. Thus, the transition from frontier to region can be seen from this perspective.

Misra (2000) points out that the use of the term 'northeast' is problematic as the region represents a varied cultural mosaic and has never considered itself to be a compact unit. He further argues that one has to recognise that there are many different communities in the region and the dynamics of each single movement have to be taken care of if any solution is to be achieved. Hussain (2004) also makes a similar observation and states that by bracketing the eight states, each with its diverse tribes, customs and cultures, into what is called the 'northeast' we tend to ignore the distinct identity and sub-national aspirations of the various ethnic groups. The nomenclature, as pointed out by Baruah (2005), is simply a reflection of bureaucratic or intellectual arrogance or carelessness in the attitudinal approach towards the region or mere ignorance about its history at the pan-Indian level. However, despite the diversity of issues such as levels of socio-economic development, the disparity between hill and valley dwellers, lived experiences of tribes and non-tribes, political aspirations, etc., there are common issues shared by the northeastern states. These include the issues of insurgency, ethnic unrest, lack of infrastructure and markets in most of the hill areas, amongst others.

Place of infrastructure in Northeast India

Northeast is a frontier space marked with difficult topography, and it shares 98 per cent of its boundary line with international countries; physical infrastructure thus occupies the vein of its circulatory network. The realisation of such infrastructure involves financial, regulatory and technical relations that often fold international, national, and local regimes into a single and specific location (Dalakoglou and Harvey, 2012). The interest of the Indian state in securing the region has activated various infrastructure projects, amongst which road construction is the key element. It pressed into service the Indian military for road construction and other development projects in the region (Ziipao, 2018).

The security-centric infrastructure development approach continues to dominate in the region. Over the decades, the People's Republic of China (PRC) has aggressively built overland transport facilities and airfields along and across the disputed border areas. It has doubled the length of its road transport network in Tibet to nearly 40,000 km. The Chinese Western Highway (3105 km) runs from Lhasa-Kashgar/Aksai Chin eastward, connecting Tibet to Xinjian. The highway with a capacity of 3,200 tonnes per day runs all along the Sino-Indian border. The PRC has also built the Qinghai-Tibet railway line of 1,142 km, 14 major air bases and numerous helipads on the Tibet Plateau (Bhatia, 2016). The extensive communication infrastructure that China has put in place on its side of the border in recent years enables it to deploy military strength quickly, further escalating an already tenuous situation (Das, 2008). Connectivity in terms of overland transport facilities on the Indian side of the border still remains underdeveloped, with the region being devoid of roads until recently. In the aftermath of the 1962 war,

> the government of India realised the need to establish better connectivity in Arunachal Pradesh and started building roads in the state. But the roads laid were mostly concentrated along foothills and were primarily aimed at providing lateral movement to the troops.
> (Ibid.:102)

Mohan warned that China's roadmap is India's wake-up call (Mohan, 2018)

As a countermeasure to the Chinese aggressive physical infrastructure development, in recent years, the GoI has begun focusing on strategic roads in the northeast in general and in Arunachal Pradesh in particular. Goswami is critical of the Indian strategic mindset, which viewed the lack of roads in the border areas of the state as a defence mechanism that would stop Chinese troop movement into India in case there was a repeat of 1962 (Goswami, 2012). She reiterates that this mindset continued to influence New Delhi's policy towards Arunachal Pradesh right up to mid-2000, with the result that Arunachalis were denied basic infrastructure and cut off from other parts of the country, and even movement within the state was difficult (ibid.). Infrastructural bottlenecks continue to be the main hurdle for local mobility and goods. New Delhi's excessive security-centric approach – i.e. its focus on national security and strategic considerations – remains the main hurdle for lack of connectivity in frontier states.

It was in May 2006 that the Cabinet Committee on Economic Affairs approved the construction of strategic roads in Arunachal Pradesh. This project was implemented under the Special Accelerated Road Development Programme in North East (SARDP-NE).[4] Yet there is no scope for local participation in any form since the project is under the Indian armed forces – i.e. the Indo-Tibetan Border Police (ITBP) and BRO.[5] Hence, there has been further militarisation and suppression of tribal rights over their lands, forests and other resources, apart from depriving them of connectivity and easy accessibility to markets. Thus state power and authority are mostly visible in the form of military presence (Goswami, 2012) rather than in the provision of basic infrastructure for connectivity and communication. The military-led infrastructure development has widened the relationship between the state and its citizens. Kikon and McDuie-Ra noted, 'This militarised frontier, the purported lack of infrastructure contrasts with the proliferation of modern infrastructure in the military-controlled parts of the state; infrastructure is bifurcated between civilian (underdeveloped, un-modern) and military (developed, modern)' (Kikon and McDuie-Ra, 2017: 775).

Infrastructure build-out in the region is ensnared in a binary space of military vs. civil infrastructure, valley vs. hill, tribal vs. non-tribal areas, centre vs. alternative centre and so on. The polarisation of this binary space is the key to the question of justice in terms of infrastructure distribution and investment. Hence the notion of infrastructure deficit cannot be generalised and applied across the region and states. The poverty or crumbling of infrastructure is mostly seen and experienced in tribal/hill areas, alternative centres and civilian spaces. Infrastructure facilities in valley districts and centres (Guwahati, Shillong, Imphal, etc.), and military spaces/zones[6] are well equipped within the region and state. On the other hand, the state's presence in tribal-dominated territories/districts has been in the form of militarisation to buttress the ethnonationalism stemming from various ethnic communities in the region. It was the British in India who first raised the paramilitary battalion specifically for the region known as the Cachar Levy in 1835. Their main task was to provide security for colonial expeditions, to guard the Assam plains from raids by the hill men from the surrounding hilly tracts and to aid the civil administration.[7] They also played a monumental role in road construction. What was known as the Cachar Levy was rechristened as the Assam Rifles in 1917. Since then, the Assam Rifles has continued to expand in Northeast India. It is the oldest paramilitary force in the country and the single-largest force present in the region, followed by the state police and the Indian Army. In the name of counter-insurgency, citizens face the brunt of the military operations, undergoing torture, numerous fake encounters, extrajudicial killings and routine frisking along the highways and at border areas. Militarisation is not a new phenomenon; the region has been experiencing it since colonial times, and today they experience it in a more stringent manner. Mention may be made that the Armed Forces Special Power Act (AFSPA) is in full force in the states of Arunachal Pradesh, Assam, Manipur, Mizoram, Nagaland and Tripura. Northeast India is thus perpetually experiencing the conditions of a 'military state', and this has ramifications for the development of the region. The military infrastructure has dominated much of the landscape; in contrast, civilian infrastructure is lacking and underdeveloped (Kikon and McDuie-Ra, 2017), particularly in tribal-dominated districts.

In the lights of India's LEP (rechristened as AEP under the Modi government), the GoI is shifting its approach to infrastructure development in the region. Dr. Manmohan Singh, the former Prime Minister of India, said, 'The Government views infrastructure development in the North East as a key element in the strategy for developing the region and increasing connectivity with the rest of the country'.[8] Accordingly, the northeast 'Vision 2020' document focuses heavily on infrastructure development. In fact, the main strategy to achieve its vision is stated as follows:

i Augmenting infrastructure particularly connectivity and transport infrastructure.
ii Ensuring adequate resources for public investment in infrastructure along with a framework for private participation in augmenting infrastructure and an enabling environment for the flow of investment.

The Indian Chamber of Commerce (ICC; 2011) in its report *Powering Infrastructure in North East India* has pointed out that

> while the significant initiatives taken by the Government to promote economic growth, tourism and development in the NER can be largely welcomed, it is important to identify the issues of absence of proper road connectivity and non- tapping of the immense hydro-power potential in the region, among other issues that need to be given special emphasis in order to help the region achieve high growth. The government needs to promote, focused, balanced, sustainable economic and infrastructure development that will enable NER to fulfill its role as the 'Gateway to South East Asia'.
>
> (:4)

As part of the LEP, several measures were undertaken by the GoI. First amongst these were the proposals to build the AH, the Asian Railway Link and a natural gas pipeline. The basis of the AH is the road that runs from Imphal (India) to Tamu (Myanmar), which connects with the Kalemyo railway via Mandalay (Goswami, 2009). In an endeavour to reinforce the LEP and link the northeastern region with the dynamic economies of Asia, India joined several subregional groupings.[9] The Bangladesh-Bhutan-India-Nepal initiative on subregional connectivity promises greater mobility for cargo and passenger traffic amongst the countries. While Bangladesh, India, and Nepal ratified the Motor Vehicles Agreement in 2015, Bhutan has yet to do so. Bangladesh and Myanmar are very crucial for India's AEP implementation, as they are the true gateways to the east (Ziipao, 2018).

The creation of physical infrastructure is imperative in order to implement the AEP. Primarily, road infrastructure becomes crucial for connectivity in the region if it is to act as a gateway to Southeast Asia. Roads are directly related to markets in the context of the so-called frontier region marked by its landlocked nature. The inadequacy of basic infrastructure limits the movement of both goods and people, especially in the hilly areas predominantly inhabited by tribes. With this being the case, connectivity turns out to be the main stumbling block in the way of the AEP. Echoing this, Barua (2005) opined that heavy investment in road and communication facilities is necessary in a landlocked region, such as the northeast, in view of its peculiar topographical features to enable expansion of markets within, as well as between, the states.

Historically, the British introduced the region to the world economy through tea plantations. Subsequently, various roads linking Bengal and the northeastern region, as well as roads connecting various towns within the region, were constructed (Haokip, 2015). However, 'most roads were built only up to the foothills, the higher reaches being left undisturbed, as communications to them were deemed economically unviable' (Das, 2008: 102). This colonial legacy still continues in the region as most of the rural roads are either poorly maintained or not constructed at all. The internal imperatives and external factors, such as China's aggressive infrastructure development along the border, have led the GoI to initiate various road development projects in the region. Yet these national road development projects have in many ways bypassed the local economy and people. Nevertheless, it is a welcome initiative in light of inadequate infrastructure in most of the northeastern states. In fact, infrastructure is considered the single-most important factor for promoting the region's economic growth to enable it to catch up with other parts of the country. Even though the northeastern states largely fare well in terms of the human development index compared to other states, as indicated in Table 1.2, their position on the infrastructure index is very low.

As shown in Table 1.2, all eight northeastern states fall into the category of the low infrastructure index. In contrast, however, none of these states figure in the low category of the human development index. In fact, Mizoram is ranked high in the human development index, whereas it is ranked low in the infrastructure index. One component of India's LEP is to bridge the infrastructural gap existing in the region and facilitate trades in relation with South East Asia. Goswami (2009) has argued that

Table 1.2 NER human development and infrastructure indexes

Category	*Human development Index*	*Infrastructure index*
High	Mizoram	
High middle	Manipur, Nagaland, Sikkim	
Middle	Arunachal Pradesh, Meghalaya, Tripura	
Lower middle	Assam	
Low		Arunachal Pradesh, Assam, Manipur, Meghalaya, Mizoram, Nagaland, Tripura, Sikkim

Source: Census of India, 2001 and Report of the Twelfth Finance Commission, GoI, 2005

India's conceptualisation of the LEP allows no room for the unique local ways of doing trade. The trade envisioned is of a high order, which these ethnic societies are ill equipped to handle. A huge flow of trade between the northeastern states and South East Asian markets will require sophisticated markets and infrastructure, at present available only in Guwahati, Assam's capital. Echoing a similar perspective, Haokip (2010) asserts that the AEP needs to be reoriented in keeping with the development interests of the northeastern region by focusing on the ground realities of the growth in border trade between the region and neighbouring countries, which has been rather slow. It is imperative that AEP also places emphasis on local-level infrastructure for inclusive growth and development of trade across the border.

Contextualising poverty of infrastructure in tribal districts of the northeast

In other parts of the country, industrialisation leads to urbanisation. With the rise of industries, there was a need for more labour. Hence, there is large migration from rural to industrial sites for jobs and residences. In 19th century Britain, the Industrial Revolution gave birth to rapid urbanisation and economic growth. Infrastructure such as roads, electricity, telecommunication, ports, airports, hospital, colleges and universities, amongst others, came as a response to these processes of change and needs created by industrialisation. However, in Northeast India, with the exception of Dispur/Guwahati (capital of Assam), infrastructure became the responsibility of the state. This was aimed at creating infrastructure rather than as part of the organic process. Hence the disparities of infrastructure within the region and state are alarming.

The MDoNER in 2009 came up with a database on the composite NER district infrastructure index. They took into account seven broad categories of infrastructure: (1) transport facilities (road density and road qualities), (2) energy, (3) water supply, (4) education, (5) health facilities, (6) communication infrastructure and (7) banking facilities. The data revealed a wide variation of infrastructure distribution and availability. The Imphal West District, located in the state of Manipur, ranked at the top in the overall district infrastructure index amongst all the districts in Northeast India with an average score of 328.96. The Chandel District, Manipur was ranked at the bottom with an average score of merely 70.49. Both Imphal West and Chandel Districts are located in the State of Manipur. Yet the difference in their ranking and composite score is of the extreme. Similarly, the Kamrup District in Assam is ranked at 7th with a composite score of 241.82, whereas the Dhemaji District in the same state is ranked at 79th with a composite score of only 69.14. Coming to the state of Nagaland, a similar trend follows – i.e. the Kohima District is ranked at 10th with a score of 213.52, whereas the Kiphire District is ranked at 80th with a composite score of 65.17.[10] This echoes to what I discussed in the introduction about the centre and denial of rise and growth of alternative centres. The polarisation of centres and alternative centres as revealed by this district infrastructure index is of an extreme. All the districts which are ranked at the bottom – i.e. Kiphire (ranked 80th), Dhemaji (ranked 79th), Chandel (ranked 78th), Longleng (ranked 77th), Churachandpur (ranked 76th), Tamenglong (ranked 75th), Kurung Kumey (ranked 74th) and Karbi Anglong (73rd) are predominately inhabited by tribes.[11] Geographically, all these districts fall under hilly terrain.

Infrastructure in the northeast occupies a special place in overall development. In fact, it is the single-most important component of development from rural/tribal people's perspective. Yet even basic infrastructures are poorly developed or in many places non-existent. There are multiple factors contributing to the poverty of infrastructural facilities, especially in the hills. The politics of dominant communities and states' indifferent attitudes towards rural/tribal people continue to be the major hindrances for infrastructure development. The state is actually in the hands of the dominant communities, and it is these communities that decide when and where to invest and build infrastructure. Manipur echoes this phenomenon even to a greater degree.[12] The Meiteis-dominated districts – i.e. Imphal East, Imphal West, Bishnupur and Thoubal – are far more developed in terms of infrastructure than the hill districts. This reaffirmed the dominant community protecting the centre and denying the rise and growth of alternative centres – i.e. tribal districts.

Besides the politics of dominant communities, the northeast is a landlocked region, marked by difficult geographical terrain and hostile weather conditions. It takes tremendous resources and manpower to lay infrastructure in the hilly region. The non-availability of materials for building infrastructure, say, for laying NHs or even district roads becomes difficult, as all the materials are imported from other parts of the country. This hikes up the financial investment covering the cost of logistics on top of minimal revenue generated within the state. Hence, the state depends entirely on the financial assistance or special grants from the central government and loans from international financial institutions, such as World Bank and ADB. Creating infrastructure without maintenance becomes a liability for the communities rather than an asset. Maintenance of infrastructure in the hilly region is even more expensive than building it. The NEC has estimated that

> for widening of the existing roads to two-lane standard, the cost per kilometre ranges from Rs. 10 to 15 crores depending upon the terrain and location of the project. On the other hand, the cost of maintenance per year for the existing road is around Rs. 8 to 10 lakhs per kilometre per year.[13]

The long gestation, temporalities and suspension nature of public infrastructure in the region is a common phenomenon. Very rarely do infrastructure projects get completed in the stipulated time as per the contract. The roads constructed under the PMGSY is a case in point. The material used for road construction is sub-standard, and in many cases, it fades away even before the completion and inauguration of the projects. These projects are again usually suspended either for a short period of time or indefinitely due to varied factors: land disputes and compensation, rent-seeking behaviour by both state and non-state actors, faulty alignment, non-fulfilment of specificity by contractors, law and order problem, vested interest and cost escalation, amongst others.

The temporalities and poor infrastructure are also due to the non-participation of local communities where the project is being implemented. There is no sense of ownership of public infrastructure being created as it was planned and executed solely by the state over the local communities' historically owned land. Landownership pattern varies from tribe to tribe in the northeast. The Poumai Naga tribe follows the three-tier system: individual land, clan's land and community land. In contrast, amongst the Kuki tribe, it is the chief who owns the land. Local communities have tremendous control over their land and often negotiation with them is a big challenge. However, there are various cases whereby the land rights and transfers have been manipulated by the state and by dominant communities in tribal areas.[14] The state approach to building infrastructure in the hills is more of a future investment than a response to the needs emerging from the communities. The building of AH-1, railway lines and mega-dams, amongst others, are point in this direction. These projects invariably bypassed the tribal land laws and served the interest of the state and neo-liberal agendas. Thévenot noted that infrastructure elicits powerful temporal imaginaries, holding out the promise (or threat) of future connectivity while also articulating the political and material histories that often render these otherwise mundane spaces so controversial. Such controversies arise from the fact that the planning and construction of infrastructure involves the accommodation of many competing interests and expectations (as cited in Dalakoglou and Harvey, 2012: 460).

The project of unilateral modernity in the form of landscape transformation via laying mega-infrastructure can be equated as tribal land destruction, displacement and endangering the eco-system. The concept of modernity framed within the perspective of the state at the behest of the dominant communities amounts to the denial of justice to the tribal communities. 'This, stemming from a dominant (mis)conception that Tribes/Adivasis are mere objects for necessary alteration rather than as thinking reflecting subjects with historical right over their land, culture, and territory' (Bodhi, 2016: 29). Thus, the current state's development paradigm is disempowering tribes and disavowed the agency for an alternative form of modernity which is inclusive.

Above all, most tribal societies in the region are self-contained. The phenomenon of food shortage and death due to malnutrition is uncommon amongst the tribes in the region, with the exception of the famine of 1959–60 caused by bamboo flowering in Mizoram.[15] The notion of total dependence on the state for their livelihood and mobility is somewhat restrained. The state is thus ensnared in a material contradiction. On the one hand, to move tribal communities, it has to manufacture a need in the form of expanding infrastructure. On the other hand, while attempting to do so, it faces resistance because it has to take away land from the very same communities. Each community, no matter how small the population, is a force to reckon with. The characterising feature of the tribal communities in North-east India is marked by a deep sense of connection to their land, and their historical narratives are embedded in the land itself, which they currently inhabit. Thus the political economy of infrastructure development is also the question of land, identity and justice.

Notes

1 For details, see Star, S. and Rudleder, K. 1996. 'Steps Towards an Ecology of Infrastructure: Design and Access for Large Information Spaces.' *Information Technology and Organisational Transformation*, 7 (1).
2 Cabinet Committee on Infrastructure.
3 Mackenzie (1884: 1) stated that 'the North-east frontier of Bengal is a term used sometimes to denote a boundary line, and sometimes more generally to describe a tract. In the latter sense it embraces the whole of the hill ranges north, east, and south of the Assam valley, as well as the western slopes of the great mountain system lying between Bengal and independent Burma, with its outlying spurs and ridges'.
4 The SARDP-NE aims at improving road connectivity between state capitals and district headquarters, as well as remote places in the northeast region. It envisages the two-/four-laning of about, 7530 km of NHs and two-laning/improvement of about 2,611 km of state roads. This will ensure connectivity for 88 district headquarters in the northeastern states to the nearest NH by at least a two-lane road. The program has been planned in three phases (Ministry of Road Transport and Highways. Annual Report 2016–17).
5 The ITBP, apart from guarding the Indo-China border, is also entrusted with strategic road construction. Currently, the ITBP is constructing eight stretches in Arunachal Pradesh (five roads with a total length of 271.04 km). For details, see MDoNER www.mdoner.gov.in/node/ 1269.
6 Kikon and McDuie-Ra (2017) noted, 'Military infrastructure, housing, technology, surveillance and weaponry provide a hyper-modern contrast with state infrastructure. Army bases and barracks are integral to this contrast along with advanced technologies like weaponry (on display in the patrol vehicles and on the bodies of armed forces personnel), telecommunications, and information technology (especially data collected on demography, topography, geology and geography-most of which is unavailable to the public). There are swimming pools, clubs, schools, cafes, movies theatres and medical facilities inside the army garrisons' (:778).
7 For details, see Shakespear, L. W. 1929. *History of the Assam Rifles*. London: Macmillan.
8 This statement issued by the prime minister on 19 January 2014 during the meeting with the CMs of the northeast region to review the progress of infrastructure

projects in the region organised by the Planning Commission. Retrieved from www.thesangaiexpress.com/tseitm-34888-pm-chairs-meeting-of-chief-ministers-of-north-east-states-infrastructure-development-key-element-says-pm/ (accessed on 22 January 2014).

9 India promoted the BIMSTEC, which was formed in 1997 with Bangladesh, India, Myanmar, Sri Lanka, Thailand, Bhutan and Nepal as members; the BCIM Forum for Regional Cooperation; and MGC, which projected the northeast as a gateway to East and Southeast Asia (Srikanth, 2016).

10 MDoNER NER District Infrastructure Index 2009.

11 MDoNER NER District Infrastructure Index 2009.

12 For detail discussion on Manipur's social reality and political economy of development, see Chapter 2.

13 NEC. *Draft North Eastern Council Regional Plan (2017–18 to 2019–20)*. Shillong: North Eastern Council, 2017, p. 19.

14 For details, see Chapter 2.

15 According to Mizo community, the cycle of natural bamboo flowering happens every 50 years, causing food shortages and famine. Using the indigenous calendar, Mizos could predict the cycle of bamboo flowering. The first bamboo flowering (1959–60) in post-independent India in Mizo Hill took place per the prediction. Yet the state government of Assam ridiculed such claims/predictions as unscientific. Mizo/Lushai Hills were then part of Assam state. In 1972, Mizoram was bifurcated from Assam, granted union territory status and in 1987 accorded a full-fledge state with the signing of the Mizo Accord between the GoI and MNF.

References

Ahluwalia, S. M. n.d. *Infrastructure Development in India's Reforms*. Retrieved from http://planningcommission.gov.in/aboutus/speech/spemsa/new/msa29.pdf (accessed on 19 January 2015).

Athreya, V. 2008. 'The Indian Economy Under Economic Reforms, with Special Reference to Food Security'. *The Gokhale Endowment Lectures 2007–08*. Department of Economics, University of Madras, 15 February 2008.

Barua, Alokesh. (ed.). 2005. *India's North-East: Developmental Issues in a Historical Perspective*. New Delhi: Manohar Publishing House.

Baruah, S. 2005. *Durable Disorder: Understanding the Politics of Northeast India*. New Delhi: Oxford University Press.

Bhatia, V. 2016. *China's Infrastructure in Tibet and POK-Implications and Options for India*. New Delhi: Centre for Joint Warfare Studies. Retrieved from https://cenjows.gov.in/pdf/CHINAs_INFRASTRUCTURE_IN_TIBET_Inside_Layout.pdf (accessed on 16 December 2017).

Bhattacharya, R. 2011. *Development Disparities in Northeast India*. New Delhi: Foundation Books.

Bhaumik, S. 2009. *Troubled Periphery: The Crisis of India's North East*. New Delhi: Sage Publication.

Biswas, P. and Sukhlabaidya, C. 2008. *Ethnic Life-World in North East India: An Analysis*. New Delhi: Sage Publication.

Bodhi, S. R. (ed.). 2016. *Social Work in India*. Kolkata: Adivaani.

Brunner, H. P. (ed.). 2010. *North East India: Local Economic Development and Global Markets*. New Delhi: Sage Publication.

Central Statistics Office. 2012. *Manual: Infrastructure Statistics*. New Delhi: Ministry of Statistics and Programme Implementation.

Dalakoglou, D. and Harvey, P. 2012. 'Roads and Anthropology: Ethnographic Perspectives on Space, Time and (Im)Mobility'. *Mobilities*, 7 (4): 459–465. https://doi.org/10.1080/17450101.2012.718426.

Das, P. 2008. 'Evolution of the Road Network in Northeast India: Drivers and Brakes'. *Strategic Analysis*, 33 (1): 101–116. https://doi.org/10.1080/09700160802518635.

Egreteau, R. 2006. *Instability at the Gate: India's Northeast and its External Connection*. New Delhi: Centre de Sciences Humaines.

Elwin, V. 1957. *A Philosophy for NEFA (North East Frontier Agency)*. Berkeley: University of California.

Goswami, N. 2009. 'Looking East Through India's North East: Identifying Policy "Challenges" and Identifying "Responses"'. *Institute of Defence Studies and Analyses, Occasional Paper*, 2.

Goswami, N. 2012. 'Strategic Road-Building along the India-China Border'. *Institute for Defence Studies and Analyses*. New Delhi. Retrieved from https://idsa.in/idsacomments/StrategicRoadBuildingalongtheIndiaChinaborder_NamrataGoswami_070612 (accessed on 16 January 2018).

Government of India. 2007. *The Report of the Working Group on Roads (2007–12) for 11th Five Year Plan*. New Delhi: Ministry of Shipping, Road Transport and Highways.

Government of India. 2009. *District Infrastructure Index for North Eastern Region*. New Delhi: MDoNER.

Government of India. 2010. *Infrastructure Statistics*. New Delhi: Ministry of Statistics and Programme Implementation.

Government of India. 2013. *Basic Road Statistics of India 2011–12*. New Delhi: Ministry of Road Transport and Highways.

Haokip, T. H. 2015. *India's Look East Policy and Northeast India*. New Delhi: Sage Publication.

Haokip, T. T. 2010. 'Searching for a Common Nomenclature: A Study of the Chin-Kuki-Mizo People of Indo-Myanmar Border'. In Th. Tiba (ed.), *Scheduled Tribes of North-East India and Development*. New Delhi, B.R. Publication.

Hassan, M. S. 2006. 'Explaining Manipur's Breakdown and Mizoram's Peace: The State and Identities in Northeast India'. *Crisis States Programme Working Paper* 79. London: London School of Economics.

Higgins, B. 1959. *Economic Development*. New York: Norton.

Hirschman, O. A. 1958. *The Strategy of Economic Development*. New Haven: Yale University Press.

Hussain, W. 2004. *Interaction on the North-East*. New Delhi: Observer Foundation.

Indian Chamber of Commerce and MoDNER. 2011. *Powering Infrastructure in North East India*. New Delhi: Indian Chamber of Commerce and MoDNER.

Kikon, D. and Duncan McDuie-Ra, D. 2017. 'English-Language Documents and Old Trucks: Creating Infrastructure in Nagaland's Coal Mining Villages, South Asia'. *Journal of South Asian Studies*, 40 (4): 772–791. https://doi.org/10.1080/00856401.2017.1373413.

Lall, R. and Rastogi, A. 2007. 'The Political Economy of Infrastructure Development in Post-Independence India'. *IDFC Occasional Paper Series 2007/1*. Retrieved from http://www.idfc.com/pdf/publications/the_political_economy_of_infrastructure_development_in_post_independence_india.pdf.

Lewis, W. A. 1955. *The Theory of Economic Growth*. London: Allen Unwin.

Mackenzie, A. 1884 (reproduced 1979). *The North-East Frontier of India*. New Delhi: Mittal Publication.

Mishra, D. K. and Upadhyay, V. 2017. *Rethinking Economic Development in North-east India*. London and New York: Routledge.

Misra, U. 2000. *The Periphery Strikes Back: Challenges to the Nation State in Assam and Nagaland*. Shimla: Indian Institute of Advanced Study.

Mohan, C. R. 2018. *China Roadmap Is India Wake-Up Call*, 2004. Retrieved from www.phayul.com/news/article.aspx?id=8621&t=1 (accessed on 16 January 2018).

Mohan Rakesh Committee Report. 1996. *Expert Group on the Commercialisation of Infrastructure Projects*. New Delhi: Ministry of Finance.

North Eastern Council. 2017. *Draft North Eastern Council Regional Plan (2017–18 to 2019–20)*. Shillong: North Eastern Council.

Patgiri, R. and Hazarika, O. B. 2016. 'Locating Northeast in India's Neighbourhood Policy: Transnational Solutions to the Problems of a Periphery'. *India Quarterly*, 72 (3): 35–249.

Rangarajan Commission Report. 2001. *Report of the National Statistical Commission*. New Delhi: Ministry of Statistics and Implementation Programme.

Sharma, H. I. 2012. 'Understanding Underdevelopment in Manipur: A Critical Survey'. *Economic and Political Weekly*, XLVII (46): 71–77.

Sharma, S. H. 2011. 'Conflict and Development in India's North-Eastern State of Manipur'. *The Indian Journal of Social Work*, 72 (1): 5–22.

Shimray, U. A. 2004. 'Socio-Political Unrest in the Region Called North-East India'. *Economic and Political Weekly*, 39 (42): 4637–4643.

Shukla Commission Report. 1997. *Transforming the Northeast: Tackling Backlogs in Basic Minimum Services and Infrastructural Needs*. High Level Commission Report to the Prime Minister. New Delhi: Planning Commission.

Srikanth, H. 2016. 'Look East Policy, Subregional Connectivity Projects and North East India'. *Economic and Political Weekly*, LI (47): 45–51.

Star, S. and Rudleder, K. 1996. 'Steps Towards an Ecology of Infrastructure: Design and Access for Large Information Spaces'. *Information Technology and Organisational Transformation*, 7 (1): 111–134.

World Bank. 2006. *World Development Report 2006: Equity and Development*. Washington, DC and New York: World Bank and Oxford University Press.

Xaxa, V. 2018. 'Coercive Development'. *Economic and Political Weekly*, 53 (45).

Ziipao, R. R. 2018. 'Look/Act East Policy, Roads and Market Infrastructure in North-East India'. *Strategic Analysis*, 42 (5): 476–489.

2

POLITICAL ECONOMY OF DEVELOPMENT IN MANIPUR

Social reality of Manipur

Manipur is one of the northeastern borderland states of India. The 2011 census recorded the total population as 2.57 million. Broadly, communities in Manipur can be divided into two distinct categories: tribals and non-tribals or, in other words, hill people and valley people. Tribals constitute nearly 35 per cent of the total population and predominantly reside in five hill districts spread over 90 per cent of the total geographical area of the state. The tribal category comprises 34 STs constitutionally recognised by the GoI. These can be classified into two distinct ethnic groups: Naga and Zo (Kuki-Mizo-Zomi) (Roluahpuia, 2016). Non-tribals, who make up over 65 per cent of the population, consist of Meiteis, Meitei Pangans and immigrants. They are concentrated in four districts covering 10 per cent of the geographical area. What pecularised the state of Manipur is the conglomeration of various ethnic groups spread across nine districts.[1] Each group has its own dynamics of power in relation to others, particularly in relation to the Meiteis who are the dominant ethnic group and key holders of power in Manipur. The state is characterised by layers of contradictions that create space for various ethnic groups to assert their socio-politico-economic aspirations (Table 2.1). This has had bearing on the practice of democracy and on the peaceful co-existence of multi-ethnic communities.

As evident from Table 2.1, Kukis are spread over five hill districts. Paite, Simte, Vaiphei, Gangte, etc., are mainly concentrated in the Churuchandpur District. Nagas, on the other hand predominantly inhabits the districts of Senapati, Ukhrul, Tamenglong and Chandel. Meiteis, Pangans and other non-tribals are concentrated on the four valley districts. The existence of various ethnic groups, each asserting its own political rights, give rise to and sustains numerous insurgent groups. It is not a surprise to find that the number of insurgent groups is proportionate to, or even surpasses, the number of ethnic communities. Table 2.2 provides details of major and active insurgent groups and their areas of operation.

As per the Ministry of Home Affairs, GoI, there are about 35 hill- and valley-based Meitei, Naga and Zo insurgent groups operating in the state of

Table 2.1 Distribution of ethnic groups

District	*Ethnic groups*
Imphal (east and west), Bishnupur and Thoubal	Meiteis, Meitei Pangans, Kom, Zeliangrong and immigrants
Ukhrul	Tangkhuls and Kukis
Senapati	Mao, Poumai, Maram, Thangal and Kukis
Tamenglong	Zeliang, Rongmei, Zeme, Chiru and few settlement of Kukis
Chandel	Anal, Maring, Monsang, Lamkang, Chote, Monyon, Tharao, Paites, Kukis and few Meiteis and Pangans
Churuchandpur	Paite, Simte, Ralte, Mizos, Hmar, Suhte, Purum, Gangte, Vaiphei and Kuki

Source: Shimray (2001)

Table 2.2 Major and active insurgent groups and their areas of operation in Manipur

Ethnic groups	*Insurgency groups*	*Area of operation*
Meiteis	United National Liberation Front (UNLF)	Imphal East
	Peoples' Revolutionary Party of Kangleipak (PREPAK)	Imphal West Bishnupur
	Peoples' Liberation Army (PLA)	Thoubal
	Kanglei Yawol Kana Lup (KYKL)	Churuchandpur
	Kangle Communist Party (KCP)	Chandel
Nagas	National Socialist Council of Nagalim (Isaac-Muivah) (NSCN (I-M))	Senapati
	National Socialist Council of Nagalim (Khaplan) (NSCN (K))	Ukhrul
	Zeliangrong United Front (ZUF)	Tamenglong
	Manipur Naga Peoples' Front (MNPF)	Chandel
Kukis	Kuki National Army (KNA)	Churuchandpur
	Kuki National Front (KNF)	Chandel
	Kuki Revolutionary Army (KRA)	Senapati
Paites	Zomi Revolutionary Army (ZRA)	Churuchandpur
Hmars	Hmars Peoples' Convention (HPC)	Churuchandpur

Source: Shimray (2001)

Manipur. Out of these, 23 insurgent groups come under two conglomerates: United Progressive Front and Kuki National Organisation (KNO), presently under the Suspension of Operation (SoO) with the GoI since August 2008.[2] Insurgency in the state is based on ethnic lines. As evident from Table 2.2, the insurgent groups, belonging to the Naga ethnic group who are fighting for the cause of Nagas are the NSCN (I-M) and (K), the ZUF and the MNPF. Similarly, the UNLF, the PREPAK, the People's Liberation Army (PLA) and the Kanglei Yawol Kana Lup (KYKL) are Meitei-based ethnic insurgent groups. Often these insurgent groups are in conflict with each other. The NSCN (I-M) and ZUF are constantly engaged in low-intensity warfare to edge out each other in the Tamenglong District. The clashes between these two Naga-based ethnic insurgent groups are due to differences in political ideology and control over people, territory and legitimacy over taxes. Conflict amongst the other insurgent groups in the state also stem mainly from similar causes.

Hill-valley divide

Manipur state is plagued by multiple issues, the major one being the hostile relationship between hill and valley people. Roluahpuia posits that one of the common ways of reading Manipur's social reality is

> through the prism of the hill – valley divide. In fact, this has been observed as a significant feature of the northeast itself. In Manipur, the hill – valley divide pierces through all aspects of the state. It is glaringly evident in the everyday social, economic, and political realities of the state.
>
> (2016: 4)

This is most evident in the policy of reservation, infrastructure, educational institutions and medical facilities. Although tribes constitute over 35 per cent of the population, their stipulated share is earmarked at 31 per cent. However, the actual share falls far short of the stipulated 31 per cent. As per the GoM data, only 20.3 per cent jobs are held by tribals in the medical department. Their share in secretariat services stands at only 16 per cent and in the police department at 21.80 per cent. However, in the education department, the share of representation is as low as 8.5 per cent. The imbalance evident in employment is reflected in the budgetary allocation for the hill tribal districts for the year 2004. The allocation earmarked is 26 per cent in the education department, 25 per cent in health, 22 per cent in PWD, 14 per cent in social welfare and 12 per cent in agriculture (GoM, 2014). This points to the dismal implementation of section 4(2)(a) of the Manipur Reservation of Vacancies in Post and Services (For Scheduled Castes & Scheduled Tribes) Act, 1976. Despite the discrepancy in reservation policy and its tardy implementation, the dominant community seems to be dissatisfied with the existing arrangement.

There is, again, a huge disparity between the hills and valley in all key indicators of development. All major infrastructures, such as roadways, power, medical services, banking, educational institutions, telecom services and airways, are mainly located in valley districts. Apart from all department headquarters, institutions such as the Biodiversity Conservation and Sustainable Development, Central Agriculture University, Government Polytechnic,

Indian Council of Agriculture Research, Jawaharlal Nehru Institute of Medical Science, Jawaharlal Nehru Hospital, Manipur Institute of Technology, Manipur Central University, Multi Stadia Complex, National Institute of Technology, Regional Institute of Medical Sciences, Rice Research Centre, Small and Medium Enterprise Development Institute, Soil-Testing laboratory, Sports Authority of India and State Institute of Rural Development, amongst others, are all located in Imphal valley, which makes it quite difficult if not impossible for tribal communities to access and benefit from such developmental services.

Within Manipur state, for decades, there has been an institutionalised mechanism of exclusion, discrimination and denial of agency to tribes in various forms. Despite being denied a fair deal by the Indian state, the dominant communities are themselves guilty of such practices against the tribes. This systemic exclusion is also evident in infrastructure development, which I postulated as injustice in the introduction. This is best encapsulated from the composite districts infrastructure index (Table 2.3).

The composite infrastructure index, as prepared by MDoNER, was based on the following infrastructure indicators: transport, energy, water supply, education, health, communication and banking. As evident in Table 2.3, all the valley district rankings are much higher than those of hill districts, with the disparities being extreme. Interestingly, Chandel District, which has only two legislative assembly members, ranks 78th out of the total 80 districts in northeastern states, whereas Imphal West, which has 15 assembly seats, ranks number 1 in the whole of the northeast. The skewed infrastructure disparities between the hill and valley districts is not just a phenomenon of post-Manipur statehood. Rather, this stemmed from layers of colonial powers imposed upon tribes and varied forms of institutional discriminations

Table 2.3 District-wise composite infrastructure index, Manipur

Name of district	*Rank in northeastern districts*	*Rank district-Wise in Manipur*	*Score*
Valley Districts			
Imphal West	1	1	328.96
Imphal East	6	2	245.00
Thoubal	11	3	189.70
Bishnupur	18	4	151.73
Hill Districts			
Senapati	45	5	114.00
Ukhrul	68	6	83.80
Tamenglong	75	7	73.69
Churachandpur	76	8	73.13
Chandel	78	9	70.49

Source: MDoNER (2006)

after Manipur signed the merger agreement. Suan's (2011) riposte to dominant rumination of Manipur's integrity claimed by unravelling the hill-valley divide in the state is embedded in a socio-cultural historical contingency which informs the trajectory of the stateness-democracy continuum. This invariably has an implication on economic development, as demonstrated in the district infrastructure index.

The hill-valley divide continues to be a defining political space for laying infrastructure in Manipur. 'Imphal, the capital of the state, is located within the valley and is therefore the seat of governance of the state' (Roluahpuia, 2016: 6) and the power house. Hence, this attributes to the imbalance in governance and power in terms of decision making (where, when, how and for whom infrastructure investment). This merits the discussion of the political economy of development in Manipur. Though tiny in size (22,347 sq km – i.e. 0.67 per cent of India's total geographical area) on the map of India, it presents one of the most challenging and cross-cutting issues in India. The state is faced with political instability, law and order problem, layers of corruption, systemic loopholes in implementation of various programmes, contradictions between different ethnic communities, issues with uniform land laws, ethnic fusion and fission, deeply imbedded hostility between the hills and valley, increasing securitisation, highest number of insurgent groups in India, nexus between politicians-militants-bureaucrats-contractors,[3] frequent bandhs and blockades and high rate of extrajudicial killing, amongst others. All these add up to the complexities of issues in the state, and they have indelible bearing on infrastructure development.

Political economy of development

The trajectory of development in Manipur echoes a clear picture whereby those who hold power also control development activities and projects. This concentration of decision-making power in the hands of a few individuals and by the dominant community results in the exclusion of those communities that actually require development. Development thus becomes a political question necessitating a political solution. Kurtz (2001) succinctly demonstrated how political agent-leaders and others enter and influence development processes through their acquisition and manipulation of economics and ideological instruments of power as they pursue political goals. Echoing from this perspective of the political economy as a framework of analysis, Manipur's development experience illuminates how the unequal power relations of various ethnic communities led to social unrest, development disparities, deep hostilities and structural inequality. The agent-driven politics of the dominant community – i.e. the Meitei and the subordinate social category, such as tribes with deeply embedded hostilities and polarisation of the hill-valley divide – formed the basis of the political economy of development. Often, the voices of the tribes are subsumed by the dominant power structure. Hence the voices from the margins, in shaping the decision-making process with respect to different developmental activities, are hardly heard. The dominant perspective, especially the elites' perspective, legitimises all the decision making, be it politically, socially or economically.

It is interesting to note that most of the hydropower projects, such as the Tipaimukh hydroelectric multipurpose project, Khoupum irrigation project, Khuga Dam and Mapithel Dam, amongst others, are located in the hills. Ironically, it is in the hill areas that electricity is most irregular and displacement of people, loss of agricultural land and livelihood are most rampant. This resonates with Xaxa's (1999) argument that tribes are progressively being dispossessed of control over land, forests, water, minerals and other resources in their own territories and are increasingly subjected to inhuman misery, injustice and exploitation. Savyasaachi (2012) echoed a similar perspective and pointed out that 'several Adivasi struggles, across the length and breadth of India, are today opposing the regimes emerging from a combination of forces of the state, the market, and corporate organisations. They are resisting the repression and the violence unleashed by these regimes, which destroys Adivasi livelihood systems and pushes Adivasis towards seeking employment in these regimes' (27). Bhatia (2010) observed that tribes in Manipur are also wary of land being taken away in the name of public purpose, as is happening in many other parts of the country, often without any compensation. Already, large development projects are located or planned to be located in the hills, and inroads have been made by contractors into their forests.

Manipur's sluggish and dependent economy

The key variables that political economists employ to comprehend social realities include population, economic size, per capita income, economic growth and poverty. These are the popular indicators to measure development. No doubt, one needs these indicators to understand where the state stands in development indicators, especially in comparison with other states and at the national level. And yet endorsing these indicators without contextualising and bypassing the dynamics and politics of identity, ethnicity, landownership pattern, political demands and structural inequality, amongst others, in a state like Manipur would disentangle only a myopic view of the larger social reality.

The economy of Manipur as a whole depends heavily on central government fund allocation. The revenue generated from the state is minimum. Hence it cannot even meet the basic requirement for maintenance of infrastructure already created by the central government pool of funding and other international financial institutions. The plan expenditure of Manipur during the first three five-year plans (1951–66) was entirely funded by the central government. Similar trends continued. During the sixth five-year plan period, the total expenditure of the state plan was Rs. 243.32 crores, out of which the central assistance was to the tune of Rs. 240.50.[4] During the tenth five-year plan period (2002–07), the central assistance went up to Rs. 3166.42 crores as opposed to the state plan outlay of Rs. 2,804 crores. Such economic arrangements make the state more vulnerable and subject to paternalistic treatment by the centre. In the words of an ex-minister, 'people's representative from the state particularly ministers often go to the central government like a *beggar with begging bowls* seeking for more funds. They hardly discussed an alternative framework nor innovative strategy to overcome such problems besides money'.[5] The dependency nature and inability of the state government to address the persistent issues, such as frequent bandh and economic blockade by various ethnic communities, adds up to the sluggish economy and rampant corruption.

Manipur's development strategy could be well placed as a measure for counter-insurgency and valley centric. The recruitment of youth into state armed forces[6] has increased threefold over a period of time and so too the number of insurgent groups.[7] The total strength of the police force in Manipur during the year 1992–93 was only 13,061 personnel. But this has increased to 25,674 personnel in the year 2013–14.[8] It is interesting to note, the total police per 100 sq km in Manipur (as on 1 January 2013) stood at 109.73, whereas the overall India average was only 52.45.[9] The state is experiencing militarisation of employment with funding from the central government (Ishworchandra, 2008). The underground economy operating in the processes of recruitment is itself a big scam. It is an open secret in Manipur, without bribing concerned ministers, members of the legislative assembly, bureaucrats and respective department heads, amongst others, one cannot get into any government jobs. Every government job in the state has its own price tag. The cycle of corruption flows uninterrupted. Say a police constable paid a sum of Rs. 4 lakh to a minister to get his/her job. Once his/her training is over and the person is posted at a police station, he/she starts collecting illicit taxes on vehicles on the highway and taking bribes to recover that capital with interest, which they borrowed from money lenders. As a result, the prices of goods and vehicle fare shoot up. Ultimately, it is the common citizens who bear the high cost on top of poor infrastructure such as roads/highways. 'Militarisation of employment can create conflict among social actors and more importantly between those who benefit from it and those who do not, but nonetheless bear some of its cost' (Sharma, 2012: 76). Suan (2011) emphasised that

> one of the fundamental problems engendered by the increasing militarisation of the state is deinstitutionalisation. This is further accentuated by the absence of legitimate local democracy, at least in the

> hill areas, which in turn generates an unseemly pendulum of such institutions paving the way for collusion with certain vested interests.
> (: 284)

The following section will look at Manipur's key resource and attempt to understand its bearing on the question of income, poverty, education and infrastructure.

Landownership and use pattern

Geographically, Manipur covers an area of 22,327 sq km, much of which is hilly terrain.

> The central valley with an elevation raging between 700 and 800m above along with the Jiribam situated at a lower altitude of 400m in the south west part of the state outside the western hill ranges of Manipur, together covers 2,238 sq km and the rest belong to hilly terrain.
> (Singh, 2009: 174)

In the valley districts, the human settlement accounts for more than 10 per cent. In contrast, hill districts settlements account for less than 1 per cent. Of the total land in the state, only 2.44 per cent of the land is under human settlement. In the valley, agricultural land accounts for about 48.37 per cent of the total land, whereas in the hills, it accounts for only 2 per cent. The total agricultural land in Manipur is less than 3 per cent (ibid.).

The landownership pattern between the hills and valley differ significantly. And so has been the land-use system. The landownership pattern thus determines the land-use system in the state. Land in the four valley districts were under the provision of the Assam Land and Revenue Regulation, 1886 and the rules framed therein were applied in Manipur by the state dabar resolution no. 5 of 23.5.47 until the Manipur land revenue and land reforms (MLR&LR) Act, 1960 (Guite, 2000). Amongst the tribes of Manipur, two types of landownership systems prevail. They are the Naga and the Zo (Kuki-Mizo-Zomi) system. The Nagas follows a three-tier landownership pattern: village community land, clan land and individual land. However, even amongst Naga tribes, landownership varies from tribe to tribe. In the Tangkhul Naga tradition, the village chief is the nominal owner of village land. In practice, the land belongs to the whole village community. Community land is called *yarui lam*, clan's land is *shangnao lam* and private land is known by its owner's name (Shimray, 2009). Land use amongst the Tangkhul tribe can be divided into the following categories:

a Land for village site;
b Land for cultivation, both shifting and terrace;

c Forest for housing materials, fuel, hunting, and collection of wild fruits, and roots;
d Land for public utility such as burial grounds, bachelors' houses, cattle grounds, etc.

(Horam, 2000: 79)

No land is to be sold, mortgaged, leased, bartered, gifted or otherwise transferred to an outsider except with the sanction of the village chief. Every individual Tangkhul Naga has to follow the tradition while transferring land property. The land to which they are born is their basic institution and defines their identity. It is sacrosanct and immutable in every circumstance. Its uniqueness lies in the traditional land-use system, which sustains the cultural roots and the politics of the community (Shimray, 2009). The Mao and Poumai Naga tribes follow similar landownership (three-tier system) and use patterns. Community land is called *maisou deih*, clan's land is *khel deih* and private land is usually prefixed with the name of the owner followed by *deih*. No individual is entitled to either buy or sell *maisou deih* or *khel deih*. In the case of individual land, it can be sold and transferred only to its villagers. Landed property is neither transferable nor sold to neighbouring villages nor any other tribes.

The Zo (Kuki-Mizo-Zomi) landownership and use pattern is different from that of the Naga system. Chieftainship prevails above all others. The chief of a village enjoys the rights over the land within the specific jurisdiction bestowed upon him. He also enjoys rights over his subjects who would pay him tributes out of the annual harvest, forelegs of wild animals killed and four days of free labour from the villagers every year. The chief, in return, helps the villagers with paddy whenever famine breaks out or there is a shortage of food in the village.[10] According to Sitlhou (2015),

> Landownership under the chieftainship system is different from other land systems. There are those who procure permanent ownership rights to their land from the chief. In a very few cases, the chief actually sells the land to the villagers. Some were given rights to the land because they assisted the chief at the time the village was settled. These two types of landownership can be termed permanent ownership: the landowners can dispose and transfer the land at the will and inheritance laws apply to such ownership. The chief can also gift land. In theory, such land is temporarily owned and cannot be sold. If the family migrates, the land goes back to the chief. However, such ownership assumes a kind permanency after years of occupation and inheritance laws may also apply in this case.
>
> (:71)

Land in the hill districts is regulated under the customary laws of respective tribes. However, with the introduction of the MLR&LR Act, 1960, and subsequent amendments, many hill villages have come under the purview of the act bypassing the customary laws and paving the way for land transfer to non-tribals. To date, the GoM has amended the act for the seventh time to extend it to hill areas. Sub-section (2) of section 1 of the act empowers the GoM to extend the act to hill areas by notification in the official gazette. On the one hand, tribes in Manipur are protesting the extension of the MLR&LR Act. On the other hand, Meiteis have been demanding uniform land laws in the state. Sitlhou (2015) posited that

> the existence of both customary laws and government's laws create complexities in land relation in Manipur. This has resulted in the emergence of various discourses in the form of demands and negotiation for a land law that respects the customs and culture of the locale and enable self-rule in hills of Manipur.
>
> (: 70)

The competing interests of tribes viz-à-vis the state and Meitei illuminate the complexities of landownership and use patterns. This has a bearing on development and identity in the state. Tribes, as the organic and historical communities, have a deep sense of attachment to their land. Their identity, culture, tradition and livelihood stem from and end with land. A Naga proverb read as follows:

> It is mother Earth which give life to everything;
> It is man that makes heaven or inferno of it;
> She keeps time to end Herself and everything dwelling therein shall perish.
>
> (As cited in Yonuo, 1974)

Forest

Land and forest are the two main sources of tribal livelihood in the state, as elsewhere in other parts of the country. The forest in Manipur, besides serving as a repository of flora and fauna and mega diversity, meets a higher percentage of energy needs of the state. The extent of support for the tribal economy from the forest ranges from 15 per cent to 84 per cent, depending on the community and region. The forest provides tangible products, such as fuel, wood, fodder, timber and countless non-timber forest products (Singh, 2009). The richness of Manipur's forest caught the attention of colonial administrators. As Pemberton (1835) noted,

> The surrounding mountains in most instances, covered with the noblest varieties of tree common to both tropical and colder climate. I know no spot in India where products of the forest are more varied and magnificent but their utility is entirely local, as the nature

of the country precludes the possibility of transportation to foreign markets.

(:48)

Brown (1873), describing Manipur's forest, noted that the whole of the hill ranges lying between the valleys of Kachar and Manipur, and by far to the north and south, are densely close to their summits with the tree jungle. Almost the only exception to this has been hill slopes facing Manipur valley. These slopes have been steadily cleared of their timber; consequently, they present a denuded appearance. The forest in Manipur accounts for 77.12 per cent of the total geographical area covering 17,219 sq km. The dense forest constitutes 720 sq km, while it is moderately dense with 5,818 sq km and open forest covers 10,681 sq km (GoI, 2003). The Churuchandpur District has the highest forest coverage area in the state with 4,157 sq km. Over the years, the forest coverage in Manipur has declined due to the shortening of the shifting cultivation system, the developing on megaprojects and the diverting of 1,028 ha of forest land for railway projects.[11] The revenue collected from all forest products in the state from 2001 to 2002 to 2007 to 2008 was just Rs. 661.09 lakh.[12]

Invariably, all forests are in the hill districts; valley is free from forest coverage. Hill areas during the colonial period were administered disparately and remained outside the preview of Meitei monarch. Yet the colonial policy of classifying forests into different categories under the Forest Act of 1878 was applied. For the first time in the history of tribes, their forests were classified into three categories: village-reserved forests, state-reserved forests and open-reserved forests in 1891 directly controlled by durbar (Sitlhou, 2015). Today, tribes are experiencing the ramification of a colonial panoply of forest laws and other policies. Various forest acts and rules[13] were made applicable to tribal territories, and this has a bearing on livelihoods. The state forest department directly controls and regulates all those forests declared as reserved forests. In a protected forest, even the cutting of firewood by the inhabitants is restricted. Tribes in the state are left with no other option but to confront the state's forest laws and policies to reclaim their traditional rights over their forests for sustainable livelihoods and to maintain their intrinsic age-old relationship with nature. According to economic survey in 2007–08, reserved forests in the state constitute 1,467 sq km, protected forests constitute 4,171 sq km and unclassed forests constitute 11,780 sq km (GoM, 2009). Thus tribes are barred from accessing 5,638 sq km of their own forest resources.

Water

Water is the basic necessity for all forms of life and a site of conflict and contestation.

> Availability of water in an area for meeting human needs and demands is governed by the terrestrial parts of the natural hydrological cycle and the level of human ability to use the water that comes as a gift of nature.
>
> (Bandyopadhyay, 2009: 1)

The largest freshwater lake in the northeast, the Loktak Lake, is located in Manipur. The state normally receives good rainfall with an average of 1,454 mm, which adds to the richness of surface water. The state is also prone to flooding, particularly in the valley due to heavy rains during the monsoon. Yet both civil society and the government pay scant attention to flooding and encroachment of land on human settlements.

Water resources in the state have become a bone of contention between the state and tribes. The state caters to the needs and aspirations of the dominant community, as does its policy towards harnessing water resources for supplying drinking water, irrigation and generation of electricity. The major multipurpose dams are located in the tribal areas, but the benefits of those dams flow in another direction. The controversial Mapithel Dam located in the Ukhrul District is to provide irrigation for 17,500 ha of land, generate 7.5 MW of electricity and supply 10 million gallons of water in a day for the state capital, Imphal, and other valley districts (Chakravarti, 2015) at the cost of the local community's land and its people. The Khuga Dam in Churachandpur failed to generate a single unit of electricity, even though it has a component to generate 4.5 MW of power. The Khoupum Dam in the Tamenglong District is yet another example of a failed project where tribes were dispossessed of their land and livelihood. The GoM has given a green signal to the Tipaimukh Dam[14] in Churachandpur and at the Chapkpi River in the Chandel District despite the locales' protests over its implication to the water body. Such is the political economy of water in the state.

Minerals

The mineral reserve in Manipur is mostly found in the hill districts of Ukhrul, Churachandpur and Chandel. As per the geological survey of India, considerable quantities of valuable mineral deposits, such as limestone, copper, lignite, nickel, chromite, asbestos and salts, amongst others, are available in these three districts. Limestone, an essential raw material for manufacturing cement, is mainly found in Hundung, Mata, Khangoi, Sokpao, Lambui and Kasom in the Ukhrul District. It is also found in the Chandel and Churachandpur Districts. The total inferred deposit of limestone has been estimated at 6.35 million tonnes and 5.76 million tonnes at Phugyar and Meiring, respectively (GoM, 2009). Asbestos, copper and chromite are found in the Chandel and Ukhrul Districts. Nickel associated with the serpentine rock has been located in the Nampesh and Kwatha areas of the Chandel District, while the metallurgical grade chromite is found north of the Sirohi peak in Ukhrul (Bareh, 2001). The total mineral production in Manipur in 1993–94 and 1994–95 were 642 and 784 tonnes, respectively. The production had decreased from 470 in 1995–96 to 62 tonnes in 1996–97 (ibid.).

The GoM has granted a licence to Jubilant Oil and Natural Gas Limited (JONGL) for drilling rich oil deposits in Tamenglong, Churachandpur and Jiribam. There was (is) stiff opposition from locals and tribal civil societies against the exploration and drilling of oil.[15] The land grabbed by the GoM bypassed the tribal culture, tradition and customary laws and even the constitutional provision under Article 371 (C). It is estimated that Manipur has nearly 5,000 billion cubic feet of oil. As per the agreement signed between the GoM and JONGL, 3,850 sq km of land was given to the company for drilling oil. The company envisaged drilling oil from 30 oil wells identified by the Alpha Geo company, Hyderabad.[16] There was no informed consent before the leasing agreement was signed by the GoM. The locals were not informed about the terms and conditions. Villagers were duped into signing no objection letters. There was no detailed environmental impact assessment. This was a clear case of the violation of the right to free, prior, and informed consent of communities under national and international law, especially the UN Declaration on the Rights of the Indigenous Peoples, 2007. This has bearing on poverty, income, education and infrastructure in the state.

Poverty

The high incidence of poverty is fundamentally a reflection of deprivation, malnutrition, illiteracy and low human development (GoM, 2013). Manipur has a high poverty ratio. Half of the total population of Manipur lives below the poverty line. In 1973–74, the total population living below the poverty line was as high as 5.86 lakhs. Two decades later – i.e. 1993–94 – the poverty ratio declined to 33.78 per cent. In the same year, the urban poverty ratio was reduced to 7.73 per cent. This means rural poverty remained high. The poverty ratio in the state, which had a poverty ratio of 37.9 per cent in 2004–05, increased to 47.1 per cent per the estimates of 2009–10 (see Table 2.4)

There is significant disparity in the poverty ratio of various categories in the state. STs in Manipur constitute 80 per cent of the total rural poor, Other Backward Classes (OBCs) 18 per cent and general only 2 per cent. Even in the urban area, ST constitutes as large as 86 per cent of the poor and the OBC 14 per cent. In the urban area – i.e. mostly valley districts – there is no record of people living below the poverty line per data released by MDoNER. This is presented in Table 2.5. Though poverty in the state is highly concentrated in the hill districts, the major development projects and

Table 2.4 Percentage of population below poverty line

Year		*Manipur*	*Northeast*	*All India*
1973–74	Rural	52.67	54.09	56.44
	Urban	36.92	36.92	49.01
	Combined	**49.96**	**50.79**	**54.88**
1983–84	Rural	42.60	–	45.6
	Urban	26.38	–	42.2
	Combined	**38.08**	–	**44.8**
1993–94	Rural	45.01	45.01	37.27
	Urban	7.73	7.73	32.36
	Combined	**33.78**	**34.60**	**35.97**
1999–00	Rural	40.04	40.04	27.09
	Urban	7.47	7.47	23.62
	Combined	**28.54**	**29.16**	**26.10**
2004–05	Rural	39.3	28.9	42
	Urban	34.5	20.6	25.5
	Combined	**37.9**	**26.8**	**37.2**
2009–10	Rural	47.4	26.8	33.8
	Urban	46.4	21.6	20.9
	Combined	**47.1**	**25.1**	**29.8**

Source: Compiled from basic statistics of NER 2006, economic survey 2008–08 Manipur and MDoNER

Table 2.5 Percentage share of poverty by social group in Manipur

State	*Rural*			*Urban*		
Manipur	ST	OBC	General	ST	OBC	General
	80	18	2	86	14	0

Source: MDoNER

facilities continue to be confined to the valley districts. Sharma (2012) has pointed out that

> large-scale construction projects have so far benefited ministers, bureaucrats and contractors more than the people at large. Moreover, most of the construction projects are confined to a small area in Imphal city. This urban bias has given rise to a valley-hill dichotomy and generated a debate on urban-rural disparity. In short, the urban tilt of development has both stratified the population and converted Imphal into a very congested, polluted and disorganised city
>
> (76)

The poverty in tribal society is very high when compared to the general category. The average per capita income of Manipur for the year 2013–14 was estimated at Rs. 40,909 (at current prices),[17] but this phenomenon did not really capture the dynamics of the economic status of various ethnic groups. Valley-centric development approach, disproportionate representation in the assembly, non-extension of the sixth schedule and ineffective implementation of development schemes, amongst others, are some of the factors which are attributed to the wide variation of poverty in the state.

Per capita income

The per capita income gives the quick overview of the development level of an economic unit, even though it has its limitations. It estimates the mean income per person but does not give income distribution of different strata of the society. With Manipur being a multi-ethnic state, to measure development in terms of per capita income would be just one sided. Nevertheless, in absence of a single standard indicator which captures absolute development in the state, per capita income is taken as one of the indicators of development to ascertain the economic welfare of the state and average size of income. The per capita income of Manipur vis-à-vis that of all India for the year 1980–81 (at 1993–95 prices) stood at Rs. 4,901 and Rs. 5,966, respectively. The pace of development in terms of per capita growth of Manipur lagged behind that of all Indian levels. The per capita income in 1993–95 was Rs. 8,963, whereas all Indian levels stood at Rs. 12,596. On the other hand, the net per capita income of Manipur was estimated to be Rs. 18,640 at current and constant prices (2004–05), whereas the all Indian levels average was Rs. 24,143 for the same period (GoM, 2005).

Education

Despite Manipur being a chronic conflict-ridden state where educational institutions are often forced to close down due to bandh, blockades and law and order problems, it continues to fare well in the educational sector. In 1921, the literacy rate of Manipur was merely 3.82 per cent. It steadily increased to 11.41 per cent in 1951. The tremendous improvement in the literary rate was witnessed after Manipur was elevated to a full-fledged state in 1972. The number of educational institutions has increased from 538 in 1950–51 to over 4,222 by 2004–05. Out of this total of 4,222 institutions, 4,089 were schools, 62 colleges and 2 universities (GoM, 2009). According to the 2011 census, the Manipur literacy rate of 79.21 per cent is above the national average and is ranked third amongst the northeastern states.

Unlike other development indicators, where there is a wide disparity between hill and valley districts, the literacy gap between the two categories is at a minimum. The average literacy rate for the hill districts stands at 73 per cent and for the valley districts at 79.58 per cent.[18] Nevertheless, there is a variation in educational status between the two categories which has an element of historical roots. As Horam (2000) noted, the dichotomy between the educational system in the hills and the valley is that the former has a well-developed universal system of imparting basic skills for social and economic survival, such as weaving, hunting, dancing, martial arts and warfare, which relies entirely on an oral tradition in dormitories, while the latter has an exclusive but highly developed literacy and scholarly tradition for the nobility and elite. The other factor is the uneven distribution of educational institutions across the districts. Both of the central universities are located in the valley. Out of 27 government colleges, only 7 are in the hill districts. Similar trends follow in primary and high schools.

Amongst the tribes in Manipur, there is a correlation between Christianity and education. Wherever there are Christians one can find functional schools in villages and small towns. Historically, along with the wave of British colonisation in the state, proselytisation of tribes into Christianity with the introduction of modern education took place. Pukhrambam posits that amongst tribes in Manipur, Tangkhuls were the first to embrace Christianity. Hence, they were more educated and better adapted to the modernity and western cultures than other tribes (as cited in Reimeingam, 2013). However, this thesis can be contested from lived experiences, and one needs to critically analyse the impact of Christianity amongst tribes rather than generalising it. There exists a wide variation of literacy rates amongst tribes. According to 2001 census, the literacy rate of the Maring tribe was 46.2 per cent, whereas for Ralte tribe, it was as high as 80 per cent and for Koireng above 72 per cent.[19] The intra-/inter-tribe variation of educational attainment is mainly due to differential accessibility to physical infrastructure, non-availability of trained teachers and practice of proxy teachers, amongst others. Leo has pointed out that 'Rashtriya Madhyamik Shiksha Abhiya (RMSA) teachers posted in the hill areas are all busy engaged in coaching institutes at Imphal and they hardly come to their place of posting'.[20]

Infrastructure

Infrastructure continues to be, by far, Manipur's biggest hindrance to growth and development, and it is the most politicised. The state lacks in coverage of roads and highways for the connectivity of its citizens to services and markets (GoM, 2013). Within the state, valley districts are well connected with networks of roads and other infrastructure facilities when compared to those districts in the hills. It is true that the development of infrastructure in the hilly terrains (the case of hill districts) is costlier when compared to their counterpart valley districts. Partly because of this reason and partly for political reasons, these areas also tend to get limited administrative and political attention for building infrastructure to improve their connectivity and reduce inaccessibility (Papola, 2017). Disparities of infrastructural facilities are another crucial dimension of injustice.[21] Table 2.6 echoes this disparity of infrastructure distribution across the nine districts in Manipur.

Table 2.6 unearthed the infrastructure disparities and echoes the valley-centric development approach by the state. It supports the argument of how the dominant community appropriates development for the centre and

Table 2.6 District-wise infrastructure index of Manipur

Indicator	*IW*	*IE*	*TBL*	*BPR*	*UKL*	*TML*	*SPT*	*CCP*	*CDL*
Road length per 100 sq km	120	120	144	84.68	24.47	22.77	24.73	21.23	19.32
Surface road as per cent of total road	85	93.9	92.16	88.81	70.56	68.21	77.65	70.01	71.53
Village electrified	84.33	95.59	84.47	87.76	91.41	81.87	77.92	73.08	82.27
Household having tap water connection per cent	44.63	25.32	10.84	17.75	20.53	12.24	50.7	16.84	11.77
School per 1,000 population	1.42	1.56	1.37	1.55	2.33	2.48	1.91	1.91	2.35
School per 100 sq km	121.97	86.74	97.28	65.32	7.22	6.29	16.6	9.52	8.39
Post and telegraph offices per 10,000 population	0.32	0.13	0.11	0.19	0.21	0.09	0.32	0.18	0.51
Post and telegraph offices per 100 sq km	2.7	0.71	0.78	0.81	0.07	0.02	0.28	0.09	0.18
Telephone exchange per 1000 population	0.29	0.2	0.19	0.29	0.07	0.18	0.35	0.18	0.34
Telephone exchange per 100 sq km	2.50	1.13	1.36	1.21	0.02	0.05	0.31	0.09	0.12
Hospital beds per 10,000 population	16.60	16.60	3.9	5.38	9.52	9.87	5.04	7.99	6.25
Hospital beds per 100 sq km	142.12	92.44	27.63	22.58	2.95	2.51	4.37	3.98	2.23
Bank branches per 10,000 population	0.72	0.28	0.27	0.38	0.28	0.36	0.42	0.22	0.42
Banks per 100 sq km	6.17	1.55	1.95	1.61	0.09	0.09	0.37	0.11	0.15

Source: Planning Department, Manipur, 2013 and MDoNER

IW = Imphal West, IE = Imphal East, TBL = Thoubal, BPR = Bishnupur, UKL = Ukhrul, TML = Tamenglong, SPT = Senapati, CCP = Churachandpur, CDL = Chandel denies the growth of alternative centres. The hospital beds per 100 sq km for Imphal West (142.12), Imphal East (92.44), Thoubal (27.63) and Bishnupur Districts (22.58). In contrast, those of the hill districts are Ukhrul (2.95), Tamenglong (2.51), Senapati (4.39) and Churachandpur (3.98); for Chandel, there are merely 2.23 beds per 100 sq km.

Power dynamics and politics of representation

The vast hill areas of Manipur are endowed with rich natural resources and yet they continue to lag behind the valley districts in development indicators. Development disparity between hill and valley districts has grown to such an extent that the valley become crowded and congested. The centre of power and governance which are crucial for development remain in the valley. There is a correlation between the number of constituencies in a district and infrastructure development. The greater the number of constituencies the better the infrastructure, as demonstrated by the difference between hill and valley districts, with the Chandel and Imphal West Districts being the two extremes (see Table 2.3). The details of political representation in the state assembly for the valley and hills are presented in Table 2.7.

The ratio of valley to hill members of legislative assemblies (MLAs) in Manipur is 2:1; that is, Meiteis have double the number of representatives in the legislative assembly as compared to STs who hold a total of 20 seats. For instance, The Senapati District, with an area of 3,271 sq km and a population of 354,972, has only six legislative constituencies. In contrast, the Thoubal District in the valley with a total area of 514 sq km and a population of 420,517 has 10 constituencies. The difference in voter population is only 65,545, but there is a difference of four assembly seats (see Table 2.7).

Table 2.7 Representation of districts in Manipur state assembly

Districts	*Area in sq km*	*Population**	*No. of assembly constituencies*
Chandel	3,313	144,028	2
Senapati	3,271	354,972	6
Tamenglong	4,391	140,143	3
Ukhrul	4,544	183,115	3
Churachandpur	4,570	271,274	6
Tribal districts (Total)	**20,089**	**1,093,532**	**20**
Imphal East	709	452,661	9
Imphal West	519	514,683	15
Thoubal	514	420,517	10
Bishnupur	496	240,363	6
Valley districts (Total)	**2,238**	**1,628,224**	**40**

*Population as per the 2011 census.

Source: 2011 census

The imbalance in representation to the assembly is the key element of development disparity and hostility in the state, as policies, laws and acts are formulated in favour of the dominant ethnic groups. During the financial year 2010–11, a sum of Rs 3,000 lakh was released under the MLA local area development programme, out of which Rs 2,000 lakh went to valley districts and Rs. 1,000 lakh for hill districts (GoM, 2014). In 2015–16, a sum of Rs 70 crore was allocated under the state's own fund for the maintenance of roads in the PWD. This amount was distributed to the 60 assembly seats, a sum of Rs 1 crore each for the 40 valley district MLAs and Rs 1.5 crores for each of the 20 hill MLAs was allocated.[22] However, the average area of administration by one MLA in the hill areas is 1,004.45 sq km in contrast with just 55.95 sq km in the valley. Thus the factors of geographical area and backwardness of a district have not been taken into consideration while allocating funds for infrastructure development in the state. Rather, the consideration is population size. According to Vungzamawi of Churachandpur College, this imbalance between the number of people's representatives, geographical area and flow of funds in the districts of the state gave rise to a '*democratic deficit state*', and the imbalance in the socio-politico-economic development of various ethnic groups led to deteriorating law and order and a '*misfit state*'.[23]

Manipur's development approach has failed to address the historical discrimination and structural inequality imbedded deeply within the power structure of the state. This is also clearly reflected in development indicators and the continued forms of oppression by the dominant communities over the ethnic minorities. In the words of Paul Leo, former United Naga Council (UNC) president, 'The rivalry among tribal MLAs/Ministers led to underdevelopment in the hill districts. Once they are elected, they become the puppet of the dominant Meiteis and act against the interest of the larger tribal society'.[24] However, Soso Lohrii, former deputy chief minister (CM) of Manipur, offered a different perspective from his personal experience. According to Lohrii,

> Tribals in Manipur know very well that they are the minority in the assembly. If they don't assert their rights, nothing will work out. It is not a question of majority versus minority but the assertion of rights that prevails.

He stated, 'Most of the tribal MLAs and Ministers are just busy begging rather than voicing their rights in the assembly'.[25]

Towards a new perspective of development and assertion

The development approach of the state, particularly in tribal areas, is caught in a dichotomy. The state neither follows nor respects the existing tribal institutions and governances, nor does it pay heed to constitutional provisions. This situation combined with state apathy towards the development of tribal areas further widened the infrastructure gap between the hill and valley areas and fostered deep hostility, deepening the contestation of varied ethnic communities.

The usage of the terms 'democratic deficit' and 'misfit' state in the context of Manipur has socio-politico-economic dimensions not limited to the practice of democracy alone. The everyday experience of development deficit and disparity, injustice, marginalisation, unbalanced political representation, deteriorating law and order and various laws and acts bypassing tribal customary laws and tradition, amongst others, are some of the indicators that have led tribal people to feel that they are misfits in the state of Manipur. It is evident from their political movements that they want separate a political administration for their region and to part peacefully from their neighbours in the valley.[26] The failure of the state to address the particularities of tribal rights/demands in Manipur has established an 'institutional pendulum and democracy deficit' – to borrow from H. Kham Khan Suan (Suan, 2011).

The concepts of *democratic deficit* and *misfit state* are produced and articulated by the reality of Manipur. During the course of my ethnographic fieldwork, when trying to unravel the different social and political processes of building infrastructure, this was exactly the kind of language being used by the people I met. It is intriguing, as it opens up new research questions – i.e. what makes them speak in such a language and what are the dimensions/indicators of such concepts? Interestingly, these concepts originate from the Churachandpur District where the Zos are predominate. The reality of Churachandpur is not unique but can be found across the tribal areas in Manipur at different points in time. However, the recent incident in Churachandpur after the passing of three controversial bills in 2015 distinguished it from other cases.[27] Nine martyrs' dead bodies were kept at the Churachandpur District mortuary for 632 days,[28] and the state did not even try to negotiate with or listen to the voices of the tribes. Rather, it responded by creating five new hill districts and two new valley districts. The dead were put to rest only after the president of India rejected the three bills and thereafter a memorandum of understanding (MoU) was signed between the state government and the joint action committee against anti-tribal bills (JACAATB).

So when one articulates the concept of democratic deficit in the context of Manipur, it actually means that there is no democracy; the tribal people are not being heard; they are treated as second-class citizens; their lives are less important than the lives of Meiteis in Manipur. In this context, they feel they are misfits in the state and begin to question, 'Is this our state?' 'Can the state really accommodate us and give us equal treatment?' While the Zos in Churachandpur in particular and across the state in general have felt neglected as a result of more recent events, the Nagas in Manipur have experienced such a feeling for over 60 years, as they never felt part of the state at all. Hence, tribal societies have been asserting their political right to a peaceful co-existence in the form of either a separate state or total autonomy from that of the dominant community.

Notes

1 The GoM in December 2016 created 7 new districts in the state, totalling 16 districts. The newly created districts are Tengnoupal, bifurcated from the Chandel District; Kangpoki, bifurcated from the Senapati District; Jiribam from the Imphal East District; Kakching from the Thoubal District; Kamjong from the Ukhrul District; Pherzawl from the Churuchandpur District; and Noney from the Tamenglong District. However, to date, separate development indicators pertaining to new districts are not available. Hence my analysis follows the nine old districts of Manipur.
2 *Lok Sabha Unstarred Question No. 604*. Retrieved from https://mha.gov.in/MHA1/Par2017/pdfs/par2017-pdfs/ls-19122017/604.pdf (accessed on 1 October 2018).
3 For details, see Chapter 6 (social and political processes of building infrastructure).
4 Data pertaining to budgetary allocation by the central government to its states is extracted from the *basic statistics of NER, 2000 and 2006*. NEC, Shillong.
5 Extracted from the personal interviews with ex-ministers about tribal development, veterinary and animal husbandry, education and GoM on 13 September 2014.
6 These include Manipur rifles, Manipur police, Manipur commandos, IRB, village defense force and deployment of large number of Indian army.
7 As per the Ministry of Home Affairs, there are 34 active insurgent groups operating in the state of Manipur. However, if we take into account all insurgent groups formed in the state, the number could more than double.
8 GoM, Directorate of Economic and Statistics (2014).
9 Ministry of Home Affairs, GoI. Data extracted from IndiaStat.
10 For details, see Haopik (2000) and Ngaihte (2013).
11 Lok Sabha unstarred question no. 2232, dated 10 March 2010. Retrieved from IndiaStat.
12 Compiled from Economic Survey, GoM.
13 This includes, the Forest Act of 1927, the National Forest Policy of 1952 and the Manipur Forest Rules, 1971, amongst others.
14 Tipaimukh Dam is to generate 1,500 MW of electricity and will involve felling 2,700 ha of forest land.
15 The production-sharing contract for Manipur oil block I (AA-ONN-2009/1) was signed on 30 June 2010, and the petroleum exploration license was granted by the Manipur government on 23 September 2010. The contract for Manipur block II (AA-ONN-2009/2) was signed on 19 July 2010, and the license was granted by the Manipur government on 20 September 2010. And the deeds for the exploration licenses were signed on 15 November 2010. Retrieved from www.change.org/p/stop-oil-exploration-and-drilling-in-manipur (accessed on 2 February 2016).
16 Letter to the Honuorable Prime Minister of India Dr. Manmohan Singh. Retrieved from www.change.org/p/stop-oil-exploration-and-drilling-in-manipur (accessed on 2 February 2016).
17 Data per the GoM, Economic Survey (2004–05).
18 Data as per the 2011 census.

19 As calculated by Reimeingam (2013) based on the 2001 census.
20 Extracted from the personal interview with Paul Leo (Social Leader) at Karong on 19 September 2014.
21 For details, see Chapter 6 (social and political processes of infrastructure development).
22 Staff Reporter, 'Anomalies Galore in PWD Works'. *The Sangai Express*, 18 October 2015. Retrieved from www.thesangaiexpress.com/page/items/58248/anomalies-galore-in-pwd-works (accessed on 19 October 2015).
23 These terms were used by Vungzamawi during my personal interview with him on 20 May 2014.
24 Excerpt from a personal interview with Paul Leo (social leader) at Karong on 19 August 2014.
25 Excerpt from the personal interview with Soso Lohrii (former deputy CM) at Imphal on 20 August 2014.
26 The case of Naga, Kuki and Zomi movement point in this direction.
27 For details, see Chapter 3 (state of contestation and negotiation).
28 For details, see Barooah Pisharoty, 2017. 'Bodies of Churuchandpur "Martys", Kept in Morgues Since September 2015, Will Finally Be Buried.' *The Wire*. Retrieved from https://thewire.in/politics/churachandpur-martyrs.

References

Bandyopadhyay, J. 2009. *Water, Ecosystems and Society: A Confluence of Disciplines*. New Delhi: Sage Publication.

Bareh, H. M. 2001. *Encyclopedia of North East India: Manipur Vol. III*. New Delhi: Mittal Publication.

Bhatia, B. 2010. 'Justice Denied to Tribals in the Hill Districts of Manipur'. *Economic and Political Weekly*, XLV (31): 38–46.

Brown, R. 1873 (reproduced 2001). *Statistical Account of Manipur*. New Delhi: Mittal Publication.

Chakravarti, S. 2015. *Dignity for the Displaced*. Retrieved from www.livemint.com/Opinion/DaD1SKQPZm3HD7GUDXDl3J/Dignity-for-the-displaced.html (accessed on 28 October 2015).

Government of India. 2003. *The State of Forest Report, 2003*. Dehradun: Forest Survey of India.

Government of India. 2006. *Basic Statistics of NER*. Shillong: North Eastern Council.

Government of Manipur. 2005. *Economics Survey, 2004–05*. Imphal: Directorate of Economics and Statistics.

Government of Manipur. 2009. *Economic Survey 2008–09*. Imphal: Directorate of Economics and Statistics.

Government of Manipur. 2013. *Annual Report 2013*. Imphal: Planning Department.

Government of Manipur. 2014. *Economic Survey 2013–14*. Imphal: Directorate of Economics and Statistics.

Guite, K. C. (2000). 'MLR & LR Act, 1960 and Sixth Schedule in Relation to Hills Areas'. In M. Horam (ed.), *The Rising Manipur: Including other North Eastern States*. New Delhi: Manas Publication.

Haopik, P. T. Y. 2000. 'Land-Use System of the Kukis of Manipur'. In M. Horam (ed.), *The Rising Manipur: Including other North Eastern States*. New Delhi: Manas Publication.

Horam, M. (ed.). 2000. *The Rising Manipur: Including Other North Eastern States*. New Delhi: Manas Publication.
Ishworchandra, H. 2008. 'Deconstructing Development Politics in Manipur'. *Alternative Perspective*, 3 (3): 5–17.
Kurtz, V. D. 2001. *Political Anthropology: Paradigm and Power*. USA: Westview Press.
Ngaihte, S. 2013. *Elite, Identity and Politics in Manipur*. New Delhi: Mittal Publication.
Papola, T. S. 2017. 'Globalisation and the Indian Himalayan States'. In Deepak K. Mishra and V. Upadhyay (eds.), *Rethinking Economic Development in Northeast India*. London and New York: Routledge.
Pemberton, B. 1835. *Report on the Eastern Frontier of British India*. Calcutta: Government of India.
Reimeingam, M. 2013. 'Educational Development Among the Scheduled Tribes of Manipur'. *Journal of North East India Studies*, 3 (1): 1–17. Retrieved from www.asthabharati.org/Dia_Jan06/Gul%20.htm (accessed on February 6, 2014).
Roluahpuia. 2016. 'Media in Conflict or Conflict in Media: Examining Media Coverage of Conflict in Northeast India'. *Asian Ethnicity*, 19 (4): 488–504. https://doi.org/10.1080/14631369.2016.1219224.
Savyasaachi. 2012. 'Forest Rights Act 2006: Undermining the Foundational Position of the Forest'. *Economic and Political Weekly*, XLVI (15).
Sharma, H. I. 2012. 'Understanding Underdevelopment in Manipur: A Critical Survey'. *Economic and Political Weekly*, XLVII (46): 71–77.
Shimray, U.A. 2001. 'Ethnicity and Socio-Political Assertion: The Manipur Experience'. *Economic and Political Weekly*, 36 (39): 3674–3677.
Shimray, U. A. 2009. 'Land Use System in Manipur Hills: A Case Study of the Tangkhul Naga'. In F. Walter and S. Barbora (eds.), *Land, People and Politics: Contest Over Tribal Land in Northeastern India*. Guwahati: North Eastern Social Research Centre.
Singh, J. 2009. 'An Account of the Natural Resources of Manipur: Management and Sustainability Issues'. In B. Singh and J. Singh (eds.), *Challenges of Economic Policy in Manipur*. New Delhi: Akansha Publishing House.
Sitlhou, H. 2015. 'Confronting the State. Land Rights Discourse in the Hills of Manipur'. *Economic and Political Weekly*, L (30): 70–77.
Suan, H. K. K. 2011. 'Hill-Valley Divide as a Site of Conflict: Emerging Dialogic Space in Manipur'. In S. Baruah (ed.), *Beyond Counter-Insurgency: Breaking the Impasse in Northeast India*. New Delhi: Oxford University Press, pp. 263–289.
Xaxa, V. 1999. 'Transformation of Tribes in India: Terms of Discourse'. *Economic and Political Weekly*, 4 (24): 1519–1524.
Yonuo, A. 1974. *The Rising Nagas: A Historical and Political Study*. Delhi: Vivek Publishing House.

3

STATE OF CONTESTATION AND NEGOTIATION

Ever since its formation as a union territory/state, Manipur has been constantly confronted with contestations. Hence the state is marked by the process of negotiation of one kind or another. Of the many contestations and negotiations, the dominant form has been that of the hills versus the valley, state versus non-state actors, and between various ethnic communities. The process of contestation and negotiations has continued till today. Historically, the state of Manipur has always put the interests of the dominant community at the forefront, while the tribal minority remains marginalised. A recent example is the creation of 7 new districts on 8 December 2016, an increase from the existing 9 for a total of 16 districts. This has been the cause of opposition and protest, especially by Nagas, leading to an economic blockade which went on for 139 days. The GoM, instead of consulting with the agitating United Naga Council (UNC), which objected to the proposed creation of two of the new districts – i.e. Sadar Hills and Jiribam – went ahead and created seven new districts.

A related issue was the passing of three bills during the special assembly session held in August 2015. The special session was held in light of the agitation by the Meiteis for the introduction of an ILP that would control the entry of non-Manipuris into the state. The three bills enacted during the special session were (1) the Manipur Land Revenue and Land Reform Act (MLR&LR; Seventh Amendment) 2015, (2) the Protection of Manipur Peoples' Bill 2015 and (3) the Manipur Shops and Establishments (Second Amendment) Bill 2015.[1] Soon after the bills were passed, there were agitations, protests, bandhs and violence all over the hills, resulting in the killing of nine tribals in the Churachandpur District (the epitome of protest) by state forces.

The nine dead bodies were kept in the Churachandpur District mortuary for 632 days. The tribals in the state refused to carry out the last rites of the dead unless the GoM withdrew the three controversial acts. Following the passing of the bills, the tension between the hills and valley – that is, between the Meiteis and hill communities – intensified. The tribal communities interpret these three bills as a direct infringement on their rights over their land, forests and other resources, as well as over their customary laws and identities. In contrast, the bills move in the direction of uniform land laws for which the dominant community has been articulating a need for. The nine martyrs were buried only after the president of India rejected the bills and thereafter a MoU was signed between the GoM and JACAATB on 10 May 2017. The state's indifferent attitude towards the tribal protest led by JACAATB and that of the ILP movement led by the Meiteis under the aegis of a Joint Committee on Inner Line Permit System (JCILPS) represents the fact that the state is in the hands of the dominant community. In the case of the protests, the state responded with the use of force, leading to the deaths of the nine protesters. The state passed the three bills in congruence with JCILPS's demands by calling a special assembly session. It is interesting to note that the contestation over the three bills by the tribal and non-tribals (Meiteis). The tribals asserted that the bills would jeopardise their rights over their historically own land and bypass the Hill Area Committee (HAC) mandated by the Constitution of India Article 371 (C). Hence, they opposed the three bills. In contrast, the JCILPS posited that the bills would protect the indigenous people of Manipur and regulate outsiders/non-Manipuris, locally called *mayangs*. Roluahpuia (2017) stated that the claim and counter-claims made by both sides were a manifestation of the long-standing division between the hills and the valley.

This merits some discussion on the broad features of the social organisation and administration that divides the hills and valley in the state. However, I shall merely highlight this in relation to tribes as they fell outside the preview of major agreement signed between Meitei monarchs and British, such as the Anglo-Manipuri Treaty of 1762, the Treaty of Yandabo 1826 and the Manipur Merger Agreement 1949, amongst others. The present turmoil is linked both to the historical process of the formation of the state and the relationship between tribes and the Meitei rulers of the past.

Locating tribes in Manipur: pre-and post-independence

Tribes in India have a social structure which is different from that of the caste society. So in this book, the term tribe has been used not in the definitional sense but as a category opposed to that of caste, a pervasive feature of the larger Indian society. In Manipur, the people described as tribes/STs[2] are in the minority and inhabit the hill areas of the state. Hence the term tribes or hill people or ethnic minority are used synonymously in this book. The use of the term 'tribe' is fraught with certain difficulties in Manipur and elsewhere in India, as it tends to generalise communities that are distinctly different from each other in respect to language, culture, tradition, customs and so on. And yet for the purpose of this study, as many as 34 communities that constitute tribes in Manipur have been subsumed under two distinct social categories: Naga and Zo (Kuki-Mizo-Zomi). Geographically, the tribal population in Manipur occupies 90 per cent of the land, though it constitutes only 35 per cent of the total population.

Historically, tribes in Manipur were neither ruled by the Meitei monarch nor under the direct control of the British during colonial rule. They were independent with their own self-rule and a deep sense of attachment to their land. It is important to note that tribal identities, such as Poumai, Mao, Paite and Kuki, amongst others, cannot be understood if one removes land and territory from these people. Hence land is the key to defining their identity, culture, tradition, custom, and so on. Before the advent of British rule in Manipur, the Meitei ruler had no control over the people of the hills; he was unable to even protect the inhabitants of the valley against aggression from the hills and from Burma (McCulloh, 1852). Kamei (2012) unravelled the historicity of Manipur and observed that the Meitei monarchs carried out occasional expeditions and raids on the tribal villages located in the surrounding mountains. The Meiteis exploited the forests and gathered timber for making their houses and boats. The Meitei rulers even compelled tribes to accept the suzerainty of the Meitei state by invading the tribal villages from time to time. However, once the Meitei forces withdrew, the tribes continued with their lives uninterrupted in the hills, independent of the control of the Meitei rulers of the valley. McCulloh's (1852) observation is pertinent in this context:

> With the internal government of the *Koupooees*[3] or of any of the hill tribes, the *Munnipore* Government does not interfere, they are left entirely to themselves and looking at them casually they appear individually to be under no control . . . each village has become a small republic, the safety of which, experience has taught members, is only to be gained by strictly observing the rights of person and property, individuals infringing the laws or usages of the community are punished by fine, or even expelled.
>
> (:42)

Shimray (2007) evoked similar observations and noted that

> prior to the event of the colonial intervention, there was little interaction between the valley and hill areas of the present Manipur. The interaction was also confined to the adjoining foothills areas. There was an occasional raid by the Meitei in the Hills and vice versa. However, such occasional raids literally did not present territorial expansion or invasion. Neither did they carry out regular administration nor imposed tax except occasional tribute.
>
> (: 57)

Thus the early relationship between the Meitei monarch and the hill people during the precolonial period was in the form of trade, service and occasional raids. Over time, however, the military supremacy of the Meitei monarch began to impose stringent measures on tribals. The imposition of *Lallup*[4] feudal service upon the hill tribes by Maharaja Garibniwaz in 1735 was strongly resented, and the congenial relationship between the hill and valley people became strained. The reign of Garibniwaz was also a period when Hinduism was formally made a state religion. This contributed to the further fracturing of the relationship between the valley and hills (Ziipao and Kamei, 2016). With the conversion of the ruling families and the people of the valley to Hinduism and the introduction of the caste system, social relations between the Hindu Meiteis and the tribal groups living in the vicinity of the valley underwent a great change. Social barriers cropped up due to caste and differences in dietary habits; the tribes were looked down upon by the Kshatriya Meiteis, as they were outside of the Hindu varna system. The liberal social policy of the ancient Meitei kings was abandoned and replaced with an orthodox caste-oriented attitude towards the hill tribes (Kamei, 2004, 2008). Meitei expeditions to the hill areas intensified[5] after Maharaja Bhagya Chandra signed a friendly alliance with the British East India Company in 1762.

The hill tribes of Manipur came under the British political agent after the conquest of the state in 1891. It is interesting to note Shimray's (2007) argument about the manner in which the hill areas came to be administered:

> It may be re-called that on 24 March 1891, five British officers of high standing [in the] British Indian Government were murdered by the Meiteis. Following this, Manipur was brought under British management and later on given the status of a native ruler to conduct. Manipur State was forced to pay a fine of Rs. 2,50,000 and annual penalty of Rs. 50,000. It was under the British rule that the Darbar was set-up, giving enough powers to the Manipuri King, who was also the President of the same.
>
> (:58–59)

Following the annexation of the hills and the valley into the British territory, Manipur saw a dual administration. The hill territory was separated from the general administration. This led to the view that 'the hill people are not Manipuris and have entirely different customs and languages' (Laldena, 1990: 81). The hill areas were administered by the vice-president of the Darbar who was the British political agent, whereas the valley was administered by the Meitei raja. Nevertheless, the British Government devised a policy of indirect rule when it came to the hill areas.

The repressive measures and policies adopted by the British towards the hill areas, such as imposition of tax and reimposition of *Lallup*, amongst others, led to a series of uprisings and revolts. These included the Kuki Uprising (1917–19) and the Zeliangrong Revolt led by H. Jadonang and Rani

Guidinliu (1927–33). Subsequently, the government framed rules for the management of hill tribes in 1935. In the course of the British Empire's withdrawal from the Indian subcontinent, the inevitable political turmoil took place in Imphal valley (Shimray, 2007). Maharaja Bodh Chandra Singh constituted a Constitutional Making Committee (henceforth CMC) for Manipur. Thereafter, the maharaja passed the Manipur State Constitution Act in May 1947 just months before India gained its independence. In the words of Kamei (2008), this act provided a 'democratic constitutional monarchy' in Manipur.

Within the CMC there emerged a huge difference in political ideologies between the valley and the hill people's representatives. The hill areas representatives – namely Mr. A. Daiho and Mr. Tiankham – made it clear that unless a clause such as

> the principal of equality and freedom as applied to all without distinction of caste, creed, and race shall include the right of any section of the Hill Peoples to secede at the end of the five years period should condition within the Constitution not be satisfactory was incorporated into the Manipur State Constitution Act, they would not be part of the CMC (as cited in Shimray, 2007).

However, their demand was not considered by the committee. This was also the phase where Naga leaders, such as R. Suisa, Athiko Daiho, T. Kilong and others, advocated for the integration of the Naga areas of Manipur with the Naga hills (Nagaland). This was spearheaded by A. Daiho with the formation of the Naga National League in 1946. These political differences between the hills and valley continue to this day without any amicable solution.

> It is this historical baggage, these dissenting voices that echoes in the wilderness of the hills and the valley of Manipur. They now seem to have indelible bearing on all developmental or non-developmental trajectories of the state encompassing socio-economic, cultural, and political spheres.
>
> (Suan, 2011: 274)

With the signing of the Merger Agreement, 1949, Manipur ceded and became part of the Union of India. Thus Manipur became a Part 'C' state (later as a union territory) under the Constitution of India. It was elevated to full-fledged statehood in 1972. The hill-valley divide continues to be a marker of socio-politico-economic development of the state. Administratively, the hill areas in Manipur came under the preview of Article 371(C)[6] of the Constitution of India. Under the provisions of this Article, the president of India approved the Manipur Legislative Assembly (Hill Areas Committee (HAC)) Order, 1972.[7] Theoretically, this constitutional provision is a powerful tool for safeguarding the rights and development of tribes in Manipur. Yet the practice at work has generally been contrary to the spirit of the Constitution. This is not unique to the tribal reality of Manipur alone but across the tribal belt. Xaxa argued that despite 'constitutional provisions, indigenous/tribal peoples remain amongst the poorest and most marginalised sections of the Indian society' (Xaxa, 2016: 146) The dominant Meitei legislators have at regular intervals aborted/thwarted the function and power of the HAC. According to an ex-minister of the Manipur government,[8] this committee, formed under the provision of the Constitution of India, Article 371 (C), 'is a supreme form of legislation as it has been ordered by the President of India but the consecutive government failed to implement [it] in totality due to power dynamics within the government'.

The HAC comprises all elected members from the hill area constituencies. The committee includes a chairman[9] and vice-chairman who are appointed by the ruling party in the state government.[10] The committee has been unable to function per the clauses of administration, as its function is generally manipulated by the government. There are two factors which contribute to the ineffective functioning of the HAC. One is that the government-appointed officials and elected members are not adept at political manoeuvring. Hence, they get easily manipulated by the politicians and officials from the valley. The second is that all bills, as well as annual plans for the state government, have to be tabled in the HAC before they are taken up in the state legislative. However, the members of the HAC are unable to understand the nuances of the bills and usually approve them without any discussion or deliberation.[11] Besides, in many cases, the government has bypassed the HAC. The passing of the three controversial bills, as discussed earlier and the case of the newly created seven districts, are a few recent examples. The list goes on.

The GoM has passed many acts which encroach on local customary laws and practices.[12] Amongst several statutory acts passed by the GoM which bypass tribal customary laws and practices are (1) the Manipur (Village Authorities in Hill Areas) Act, 1956; (2) the Manipur Hill Areas (Acquisition of Chiefs' Rights) Act, 1966; (3) the Manipur Land Revenue and Land Reforms Act, 1960; and (4) the Manipur (Hill Areas) District Council Act, 1971. When one examines these acts, and especially their bearing on tribals, one gets a grim picture; each of the acts has disempowered rather than empowered the hill people. Tribes have been deprived of their rights, contrary to what is guaranteed in the Constitution of India.

The Manipur (Village Authorities in Hill Areas) Act, 1956, imposed rules and structure that went against the customary practices, traditions and usages at work in tribal villages. The act introduced bureaucratisation and nullified the traditional tribal system of governance. With its implementation in 1957, the number of village authorities was determined on the basis of tax-paying houses.[13] The act also limits the traditional power of the village chief. In many parts of hill areas, village authority elections still take place in consonance with the act without any financial power and autonomy.

The Manipur Hill Areas (Acquisition of Chiefs' Rights) Act, 1966, was an attempt to strip the traditional rights of the chief in a village. It empowered the state government to transfer all rights, titles and interests held by the chief a village's land and vest the same in the government free from encumbrances by a mere notification in the official gazette. Shimray (2007) pointed out that 'this was a deliberate attempt of the state to have control over land, customs, traditional political practices of justice etc., which was under the village chiefs' (:69). This act was vehemently opposed by chiefs and tribal communities. And yet the government went ahead with the act, though it was not effectively implemented.

Sub-section (2) of section (1) of the Manipur Land Revenue and Land Reforms (MLR&LR) Act, 1960, says 'except the hill areas,' which means that this act is not applicable in the hill areas. However, the GoM made conscious efforts to extend the act to hill areas through several amendments. It deliberately attempted to remove section (1) so as to have uniform land laws in the state. After the Sixth Amendment to the act in 1989, certain clauses were inserted that allowed the state government to extend the act in full or in part to any of the hill areas by notification of gazette. In the process, the MLR&LR Act, 1960, has been extended to 89 villages in the Churachandpur District in 1962 (vide notification no. 142/12/60, dated 22/02/1962), 14 villages in Sadar Hills of the Senapati District (vide notification no. 138/4/64, dated 25/02/1965) and 14 villages in the Khoupum Valley of the Tamenglong District (vide notification no. 3/12/83, dated 14/11/1987). The latest of such amendments was the MLR&LR (Seventh Amendment) Act, 2015, which was rejected by the president of India. The unrest in Churachandpur, where nine tribals were killed by the state forces as discussed earlier, is linked to this act.

Since the 1970s, tribes in Manipur have been demanding the status of the Sixth Schedule of the Constitution.[14] However, they have been denied this status even after Manipur's attainment of the full-fledged statehood in 1972. What they have been granted is the autonomous district council (ADC) outside the purview of the Sixth Schedule, i.e. under the Manipur (Hill Areas) District Council Act, 1971 and the Manipur (Hill Areas) District Council (Third Amendment) Act, 2008. This is contrary to what tribals in the state have been demanding. The act provides local governance without any autonomy to the hill districts. In view of this, tribals in Manipur have refused to hold district council election for more than two decades. It is worth noting the statement of the president of the UNC:

> Nagas and other tribals did not object to the inclusion of Meiteilon in the 8th Schedule, neither the extension of Panchayati Raj to Imphal valley under the 11th Schedule and implementation of the Municipality Acts in Imphal valley under the 12th Schedule.

> However, when tribals have been demanding for the extension of the 6th Schedule in the hill areas, the successive Manipur state governments have opposed it and have sabotaged the rights of the tribals ever since the Merger Agreement.[15]

The ADC election was held in 2010, after a gap of nearly two decades, the devolution of powers as promised by the government has not taken place till date. In the words of the Chairman, ADC (Senapati):

> Tribal ADC members or for that matter MLAs are like beggars without asserting their rights. It is the dominant community who actually control and rule over the tribals in the state even when it comes to matters pertinent to tribes. Moreover, all 20 MLAs who constitute HAC are against the devolution of power (ADC) and do not want to share power with ADC members.[16]

The joint secretary of the Department of Tribal Affairs and Hills, Manipur, admitted that 'once we have power, we don't want to share it'[17] (referring to the context of the present ADC). The administration of hill areas had been locked on the one hand within the dominant structure of the Meiteis, and on the other hand the continuous internal power struggle amongst tribal leaders. This echoes to what Hassan argued that state power vested in an exclusivist Meitei elite severely reduced the state's legitimacy in the eyes of the minority tribal communities in the state (Hassan, 2006). Given the gravity of problem and issues faced by tribes in the state and persistent demands by the Sixth Schedule demand committee, the GoI constituted a committee to study the feasibility for the extension of the Sixth Schedule to hills areas. Subsequently, the national commission to review the workings of the Constitution recommended the extension of the Sixth Schedule provisions to the hill areas of Manipur (GoI, 2002). It is interesting to note how the dominant community opposed the extension of the Sixth Schedule provision to the hill area, citing the question of Manipur integrity. In 2001, the GoM gave consent to the Ministry of Home Affairs for the extension of the Sixth Schedule to the hill areas with 'certain local adjustment and amendment.' Yet, to this date, the GoM has not clarified nor amended any provision for the same. This echoes the perspective of the dominant community and elicits how the state works in the interest of the dominant ethnic group. The state of contestations, contradictions and varied political assertions by different ethnic communities stems from this baggage of historical injustice meted out to tribes.

Issues of contradiction and contestation

In an ethnically polarised state like Manipur, the issues of land and autonomy are key features of contestation and contradiction. The gravity of this problem can be gauged from the fact that there are several distinct lines of discourse and articulation by varied communities in the state. The fight for ethnospace, be it the valley dwellers majority or the tribes from the hills, continues unabated in different forms and strategies. Yet the hill-valley divide is visible in this ethnospatial assertion. Disparately, the Meitei-based insurgent groups in the valley struggle to restore Manipur's sovereignty or the Kangleipak kingdom. This stems from the Manipur's merger agreement signed in 1949 between the governor general of India and the maharaja of Manipur. Since then, Manipur merged into the Indian union.

The political demands of the tribes, on the other hand, can be couched in two different discourses: the Naga and the Zo. The Nagas in Manipur articulate their political rights in the form of an alternative arrangement (AA) pending the Indo-Naga political issue – i.e. unification of all Naga-inhabited areas led by NSCN-IM. This they demand as a form of interim arrangement for the Nagas in Manipur led by the UNC. Ngaihte (2013) succinctly pointed out two forms of Zo's political demand:

> While one group, coming under the KNO, demands a separate Kuki state to be sliced off from Manipur, the other group, coming under the anodyne name of United People's Front (UPF), demanded an autonomous hill state for the tribal hill areas, loosely based on Article 244A of the Constitution of India.
>
> (: 21)

However, the difference in their political articulation includes the ethnic line as well within the board nomenclature of Zo. The former is predominantly spelled out by the Kukis, whereas the latter is spelled out by the Paites.

Disparately, the GoM stood upfront for the territorial integrity of Manipur state. Against this background, the Manipur legislative assembly has unflinchingly passed many resolutions to uphold and safeguard the territorial integrity of the state. It may be recalled that on 14 March 1997, the Manipur Assembly unanimously passed a resolution to safeguard the territorial integrity of Manipur that existed at the time of the merger of the state of Manipur with the Indian union in 1949. It is pertinent to note that in the same year, the GoI and NSCN-IM signed a second ceasefire agreement on 25 July 1997. The GoM reiterated its stand and further passed a resolution on 17 July 1998 to urge the GoI to make suitable amendments of Article 3 of the Constitution of India or to insert appropriate provisions in the Constitution of India for the territorial integrity of the State of Manipur. The latest of such resolutions was passed on 23 July 2018.[18] The apprehension on the part of the GoM and the Meiteis in light of the Indo-Naga peace talk, particularly following the framework agreement signed on 3 August 2015, invigorated such resolutions. The bone of contention is ethnic territoriality vs. territorial integrity of the state.

Broadly, one could chart out political contestations in Manipur as (1) territorial integration movement (NSCN-IM, KNO, Meitei-based insurgent groups), (2) state within the state or autonomous hills state (UPF) and (3) AA (that of the UNC) Manipur state territorial integrity (GoM and that of the valley-based civil societies). The genesis of the integration movements stems from the Indian state formation process, whereas the autonomous movement is the resultant and by-product of the failure to grant meaningful autonomy to the hill areas in particular (Roluahpuia, 2016). The GoM, United Committee Manipur (UCM; Meitei-based civil society) and Coordination Committee (CorCom; conglomeration of seven Meitei-based insurgent groups) echo the totalising project of the state. Their stand is antithetical to that of the Nagas and Zos (tribals) political demands. Suan's (2011) observation is pertinent to this wherein he infers that the demands of the Naga and the Zo peoples for carving autonomous homelands for themselves have posited uneasy questions and challenges to the Meitei's totalising project.

Amidst the differences and opposing political stands regarding all the competing and varied ethnic communities and their insurgent groups, the commonality or the central issue is the question of land and territoriality. Irrespective of the Naga or Zo or Meitei or the GoM, the core issue revolves around land and who has the right over their historical/ancestral land. Nagas and Zos struggle for territorial integration – i.e. the right to self-determination of their ancestral land and the right to govern their own land per their tradition, customary laws, culture, etc. Similarly, the Meitei-based insurgents fight to restore Manipur's sovereignty, which was lost after the merger agreement. The GoM reverberates the right to govern and administer Manipur's territory. Hence the state assembly has passed several resolutions, as discussed earlier. The political situation in Manipur is fraught with certain difficulties due to competing ethnic community assertions over land. The slogan for the Naga Peoples' Movement for Human Rights (NPMHR) is '*our land is the only space from where our freedom springs. We are slaves without it.*' It resonates with my thesis that land is the fundamental issue of their movement. Sitlhou (2015) argued the relationship between land and identity in the hills of Manipur as encompassing both 'geographical territory' and 'cultural territory', and changes in land relation lead to a redefinition of identity (: 70). Tribal culture, identity, religious practices, customary laws and territories and territoriality, amongst others, are intricately linked to land. In the words of Leo, 'Without land, our culture, religious practices, and our identity as Nagas, we are nothing. Our struggle is to claim what is rightfully ours i.e. our ancestral land.'[19]

Against this backdrop of varied competing interests, it is interesting to note the response of the state and the ongoing negotiation with different stakeholders in Manipur. The GoI and the state GoM, taking the cognisance of tribal assertion from the hills, has invited the Nagas and Zos to the negotiation table. In the case of Nagas, the tripartite talk involving the GoI, GoM and UNC has entered into the tenth round. The latest of such talks/negotiations was held on 1 September 2018 at the Senapati District headquarter. Despite ten rounds of negotiations, there has not been any amicable solution agreed upon. Similarly, for the Zo, there are two parallel negotiations led by KNO and UPF. Both organisations are now under SoO since August 2008 and have held rounds of negotiation with the GoI and GoM. Yet the number of talks held has not resulted in any positive political development in the state. The seven Meitei rebel groups under the nomenclature CorCom have not entered into any formal political negotiations either with the GoI or with GoM. It may be noted that all seven rebel/insurgent groups were declared as unlawful activities under the Unlawful Activities (Prevention) Act, 1967.

The cross-cutting issues in Manipur are coupled with the contestation of varied ethnic communities. The major contestations or the fault lines can be chart out between the Meitei and Naga, the Naga and Kuki, the Kuki and Paite and, above all, between tribals and non-tribals. I will dwell into these contestations in the following section. However, Honray's observation is pertinent to these contestations where he posited that the dominance of a particular ethnic group has always aroused ill feelings on the part of others. In every respect, the various ethnic groups contest keenly amongst themselves, whether it is over jobs, politics, resources, land, etc. This has often aroused mutual jealousy and hostility and thus widened the gaps in their relationships. Every community, whether it is the Meitei or the Naga or Kuki or Zomi, is very much conscious and aware of its identity (as cited in Shimray, 2001). These contestations entail a profound socio-politico-economic manifestation in the state. The ramifications of such assertions are experienced by the common citizens.

Meitei and Naga

The contestation between Meitei and Naga stems from the colonial period. The contestation escalated with the rise of the Naga movement and the subsequent formation of the Naga National Council (NNC) in Nagaland and the NNL in Manipur. Since then, the notion of a cordial relationship or the so-called historical brotherhood between the Meitei and Naga has not yielded a fructifying relationship. Rather, the relationship is marked by contestation and sporadic opposition to each other's ethnic assertions in the state. The allegiance of the emerging literate Nagas was with their brethren in the Naga Hills, and the fast-rising consciousness of shared ethnicity manifested in the demand for a merger with the Naga Hills. The Meitei did not take kindly to this demand and their actions since 1947 and more so post-1990s; legally or otherwise, their actions are indicative of their hostile intentions to continue domination of the tribes (Ziipao and Kamei, 2016: 34–35) or, in other words, the totalising project of the dominant community.

In the wake of the Indo-Naga peace talk, which subsequently led to the signing of a second ceasefire agreement in 1997 between the GoI and NSCN-IM, the Meitei-Naga relationship has been hostile. For Meiteis, the Naga political movement and its assertion for a 'Greater Nagalim' is a direct threat to their dominance in the state, as Nagas predominantly inhabit the four hill districts. As the peace talks or, rather, political negotiations between NSCN-IM and GoI progress, both parties mutually agreed to extend the ceasefire agreement without territorial limits[20] in 2001. This did not go over well with the Meiteis or the GoM. They vehemently opposed the extension of the Naga ceasefire without territorial limits. The Meitei-based civil society known as the People's Solidarity for Peace and Democracy responded to the Naga ceasefire agreement, which was encapsulated in a booklet titled *Ceasefire or Setting the North East on Fire? Peace in Jeopardy*. The booklet lambasted the ceasefire agreement as an 'historical appropriation' which is ignorant or dismissive of people's historical mooring's (as cited in Suan, 2011: 276). In the aftermath of the ceasefire extension without territorial limits, there was a widespread protest led by all Manipur United Club organisations, which are a part of the Meitei-based civil society in the valley. They set ablaze public properties, including the Manipur Assembly and CM secretariat, amongst others, as a sign of blatant protest against the NSCN-IM ceasefire agreement with the GoI. It is unfortunate to note that during the peak of the protest, 18 lives were lost. The GoM responded to the Meitei civil societies and protesters from the valley by requesting that the GoI withdraw the ceasefire agreement without territorial limits with the NSCN-IM. Hence the GoI withdrew its agreement, colluding with the interests of the Meitei protesters in Manipur. The GoM also declared June 18 as state integrity day in honour of the 18 lives lost during the protest against the extension of the Indo-Naga ceasefire.

With the latest framework agreement[21] signed between the GoI and NSCN-IM on 3 August 2015, the Meitei-Naga relationship became further strained and tensions and apprehensions renewed in different forms. The GoM took extra precautionary measures by adopting a resolution in the state legislative assembly. During the special assembly session held in August 2015, the house unanimously adopted the following resolutions: to urge the central government that the Naga Framework Agreement of 2015 does not compromise Manipur territorial integrity and to amend Article 3 of the Constitution of India.[22] It suggested a measure to incorporate a clause that the prior consent of the state legislature of the affected state(s) shall be mandatory while forming a new state.[23] Shri. K. Ranjit, a Meitei legislator, went to the extent of declaring on the floor of the assembly that 'there were no Naga in Manipur'.[24] This echoed the political domination of the Meitei legislatures in the state assembly, the highest decision-making body in the state. Similar resolutions were adopted and declared by the Meitei civil societies against the Indo-Naga framework agreement. Such statements ignite the already polarised ethnic communities in Manipur. One could infer from this political development and competing interest that the state is in fact in the hands of the dominant community and always subjugates the minorities.

Naga and Kuki

The Naga-Kuki contestation gave birth to the bloodiest and longest ethnic conflict in the state, resulting in the loss of thousands of lives and immovable properties. The difference in political orientation and assertion of rights as claimed by both of the communities led to contradictions and confrontations. The primary contestation of Naga-Kuki was over land, political territoriality and resources. The Naga-Kuki ethnic conflict (1992–96) stemmed from a small town known as Moreh, located in the Chandel District, Manipur. Moreh is a border town located between India and Myanmar. It is fast emerging as an international trade centre/spot. The highest revenue generation for any insurgent group in the state is by imposing tax from various sources. Moreh is one of the important locations for revenue generation for insurgent groups. Both Kuki and Naga insurgents operate actively in this area and maintain their de facto rule over the small tribal towns. They tried to dominate and control trade activities and maximise their tax collection, which eventually led to a clash in interests and hence ethnic conflict. Moreh was the epicentre of Naga-Kuki ethnic conflict, which escalated to other hill districts. The Senapati and Ukhrul Districts witnessed maximum displacement of people and loss of lives and livelihood due to the conflict.

The spillover of the ethnic conflict took the form of tension, stale political relations and hostile social interactions, amongst others. Even though the ethnic conflict came to a halt in 1996, the political contestation between the two ethnic communities intensified in the form of political demands. The Kukis in the Senapati District have been demanding the upgrade of the Sadar Hill subdivision into a full-fledged revenue district. This movement has been led by the Sadar Hill District's demand committee and backed by the Kuki Inpi.[25] In contrast, Nagas are against such demands by the Kukis. The UNC, a Naga civil society, asserted that their ancestral land[26] cannot be bifurcated at any cost, as it will have grave repercussions on the ongoing Naga movement for the integration of all Naga-inhabited areas. The common strategy used by Nagas and Kukis to further their demands is resorting to economic blockade and bandhs on NHs. This they do to draw the attention of the government and express their grievances. In 2011, the state witnessed the longest economic blockade (123 days) – i.e. perpetual halt of any vehicles carrying goods on both NH-2 and NH-37. The economic blockade and bandh were first imposed by Kukis in pursuance of its demand. This was followed by Nagas, imposing a counter-economic blockade on the contentious issue over the Sadar Hill District's demand. It is interesting to note that the GoM in December 2016 created seven new districts. This included the

Kangpokpi District, which was bifurcated from the existing Senapati. It may be recalled that the government, instead of using the nomenclature Sadar Hill as demanded by the Kukis, named it the Kangpokpi District, which otherwise remained the same. The Nagas, led by UNC, still demand the roll back of the new districts, and hence they are holding a tripartite talk with the GoI and GoM.

Kuki and Paite

The Naga-Kuki conflict led to a demographic reorganisation of the Churachandpur District. Many Kuki settlers from the Senapati, Ukhrul, and Chandel Districts fled to Churachandpur to escape the violence unleashed during the peak of the Naga-Kuki ethnic conflict. The Thadou Kuki and Paite share a common cultural and linguistic heritage (Kumar et al., 2011). The attempt to unify Kuki and Zomi people in Manipur led to ethnic conflict (1997–98) over the use of nomenclature. The contestation revolves around the legitimacy of the category of Kuki or Zomi.

> The Zomi nomenclature is accepted by the Zou, the Simpte, the Vaiphei, the Paite and the Tedim-Chin tribes; the Thadou-speaking groups of tribes deny it and want to keep the term Kuki. The armed factions of the KNF (P) forces the Zomi to accept the name Kuki, justifying this by stating that the term Zomi is a misnomer.
>
> (Ibid.: 30)

The contestation and imposition of the category of Kuki over other tribes led to the Kuki-Paite clash in 1997. Shimray (2004) encapsulated the intra-ethnic politics stemming from the Churachandpur District. He noted,

> The recent ethnic politics and consolidation movements brought the smaller ethnic groups coming together for a larger identity among the Kuki-Zomi-Chin groups in Churachanpur district of Manipur. The ethnic groups like Zous, Simtes, Vaipheis, Paites, Ralte, Suhtes, Gante, and Tedim-Chin identify themselves with the nomenclature Zomi, disowning the Kuki. The Kuki groups like the Haokip, Kipgen who speak Thadou maintains the Kuki identity. The process of adopting the nomenclature Zomis among the above-mention groups began in 1993. Under the common nomenclature, Zomi, they formed a social forum called Zomi Re-Unification Organization (ZRO).
>
> (: 4640)

The formation of the ZRO subsequently gave birth to an armed wing known as ZRA. Ever since the ethnic conflict, the ZRA and KNF are in dissension with each other. Hence their political articulation also differs sharply.

The Kuki groups demand a Kuki state, whereas the Paite or the Zomi groups struggle for an autonomous hills state. Unlike the Naga insurgent groups where NSCN-IM and NSCN-K are in loggerheads and oftentimes engage in low-intensity warfare with each other. The case of Zo ethnic-based insurgents in contemporary times hardly engage in armed conflict with each other, even though their area of operation at times falls under the same territory. It is interesting to note that both the Kuki and those who subscribed to the category of Zomi have entered into an agreement for negotiations with the GoI by signing the SoO in August 2008. The Kuki ethnic-based insurgents came under the umbrella group known as KNO, whereas Paite, Hmar and others came under UPF. The talks with the GoI have not progressed as expected. The parliamentary committee reviewing the security situation in the northeastern states is taking note of the ongoing talks with KNO and UPF, which are under the SoO recommends 'that the Ministry of Home Affairs should make sincere effort to expedite the talks and hold them more frequently' (Parliament of India, 2018: 9).

Tribes and non-tribes

There are 34 societies in Manipur recognised as STs by the GoI. As discussed, these societies in the state can be broadly categorised into the Naga or the Zo ethnic communities. Meitei and Meitei Pangan are non-tribes that are the majority in the state, even though their geographical area is confined to only 10 per cent of the total geographical area of the state.

> The Meiteis occupy a dominant position in the political and economic systems of Manipur. They comprise a majority of the State's population, occupy the most productive and fertile lands of the State and play an influential role due to their historical association with the former monarchs of Manipur.
>
> (Parliament of India, 2018: 9)

The primary contestation between tribes and non-tribes or, in other words, the hill-valley divide is on the question of land and identity. As noted earlier, tribes occupy more than 90 per cent of the land in the state. Tribal land cannot be sold or transferred to non-tribals. Hence the GoM and the dominant community in the state make a conscious effort to bring uniform land laws in the state. This effort has been contested and challenged by tribes.

> On one hand the inhabitants of hill areas, Nagas and Kuki, oppose the assimilation and integration of hill and valley areas, while on the other hand, the valley people, the Meiteis are against any policy measures that will lead to a distinction between the two areas.
>
> (Ibid.: 10)

The Seventh Amendment of the MLR&LR Act, which was returned by the president of India in 2016 to further re-examine the act, echoes how the GoM in close proximity with the dominant community regulates the land laws and bypassed the HAC. The intricate hostility that characterises the socio-political processes in Manipur is deeply imbedded in the structure of ethnicity and landownership patterns. Echoing this perspective, Shimray (2001) observed,

> Ethnic-based social manifestations capture the overall socio-political processes in the state. Ethnicity as well as insurgency based on it is very much alive and mobile. The current popularity of the principle of 'self-determination' based on ethnicity too came into centerstage in the state's socio-cultural scenario. Even the people's representatives are compelled to incline towards their ethnic bases; at the same time those more aware remain fearful of being assimilated to dominant socio-cultural and political groups.
>
> (:3677)

The Meitei hegemony over tribes is manifested in political, social and economic spheres and the demographic relations between the two. The totalising project or the effort to establish a pan-Manipuri identity for all ethnic communities residing in the Manipur state by the Meitei is outrightly rejected by tribals. For tribes, identity as Manipuri is confined only to the Meiteis ethnic community and not to tribals. Poumai, Mao, Tangkhul and Maram, amongst others that belong to the Naga ethnic group, are known as Nagas and not as Manipuri. Similarly, Kuki, Paite, Hmar, Vaiphe and Gante, Ralte, amongst others, identify as Zo and not what the Meitei community would want them to identify as: Manipuri. Besides identity, the dimension of Manipuri language imposition is another sphere of contestation between the two. The opposition by the Meiteis to the extension of the Sixth Schedule provision in tribal areas displays the politics of denial by the dominant community. This is just one of such instances. The list continues. The binary opposition between tribes and non-tribes in the state is manifested in every domain. Reading Manipur's social reality from the lens of the hill-valley divide or contestation between the two categories will deepen our understanding of the political economy of the state. Tribes in Manipur invariably fit into Scott's argument about Southeast Asia; the tribes (Naga and Zo) in his terms would form a non-state space – an 'illegible space' from the perspective of the states in the lowlands – i.e. the Meitei (Scott, 1999). The parliamentary committee reviewing the security situation in northeastern states made an interesting observation in regard to tribes in Manipur. They note that

> the Autonomous District Councils (ADC) in Manipur have remained ineffective due to various reasons. The Committee notes that the

> Ministry of Home Affairs is considering a proposal to amend the Sixth Schedule to the Constitution to improve the working of ADCs. The Committee is of the view that the functioning of the ADCs needs to be strengthened through sufficient devolution of funds and functions. The Committee, therefore, recommends that the Ministry should take an early decision on the proposal to amend the Sixth Schedule to the Constitution of India.
>
> (Parliament of India, 2018: 23)

The contemporaneous contestation between tribes and non-tribes is on the issue of ST status demands by the Meitei. The Scheduled Tribe Demand Committee of Manipur Valley (STDCM) rather than the Meitei demand for STs status was operationalised by submitting a memorandum to the governor of Manipur on 30 November 2012. One of the many reasons the committee cited for the inclusion of the Meitei on ST list is that it will bring about the integration of hill and valley people or, in other words, remove the hill-valley divide. Piang's (2014) riposte to the Meitei's assertion dismissed their claims, citing empirical evidence. He posited that the Meitei's claims are 'illogical, as development gap between the valley and hill people cannot be bridged by merely changing the social category of the dominant caste group, residing in the plains, to that of the marginalised hill tribes' (: 1). However, the vested interest of the Meitei's demand for ST status echoes the words of the vice-president of the committee. He said,

> Meitei becoming ST will pave way for ILP, all kinds of loss of the future of the youth and loss in the service career will be protected, MLR&LR Act of 1960 will automatically implement all over Manipur and the most important and biggest benefit will be safeguarding of own land, own community and own culture.[27]

This demand by the Meitei continues today in a more stringent manner by staging protests and blockades and submitting memorandums, etc. Tribes, on the other hand, responded to the Meitei's assertion for ST status as a blatant manipulation and strategy to further deprive tribes of their land and its resources. The latest of such opposition is well reflected when the three tribal bodies from Manipur – the UNC, the Zomi Council and the Hmar Inpui – apprised the union government and submitted a memorandum to the union minister of tribal affairs on 11 October 2018.[28] The volatile ethnic relations between tribes and non-tribes in the state led to binary opposition and often staled the development processes. Bhatia (2010) made an interesting proposition for a peaceful co-existence of varied ethnic communalities in Manipur. She elicited that conflict or contestation can be addressed if (1) there is political will, (2) the government respects the rule of the law, (3) there is a willingness to treat all of its citizens equally, (4) the government does not resort to militarisation, (5) rights are fulfilled and historical injustices corrected.

Manipur is in fact one of the most difficult states in the entire northeastern region to govern and amicably solve the existing cross-cutting issues and layers of power imposed on the minorities. Thomas, one of the Zomi leaders, humorously captured the intricate and persistent contestation prevailing in the state by saying, 'If one can understand the cross-cutting issues in Manipur and resolves with an amicable solution acceptable to all ethnic communities then one can easily become an international consultant'[29] His statement unravelled the befuddled nature of Manipur's social reality. Having problematised the political economy of development, conflict, ethnic contestation and negotiations, I shall now turn to their effect on roads and electricity infrastructure in the state.

Notes

1 The first bill is concerned with the landownership and use system, the second pertains to identity – i.e. who can be considered to be Manipuris and the third concerns the economy. These are discussed later in this chapter.
2 Constitutionally, ST in India is used as a politico-administrative term.
3 Koupooees means people and refers to the people of Rongmei (Pemberton, 1835). Koopooee: Kabui = Rongmei (Kamei, 2004: 85).
4 Lallup was a feudal service rendered by the subjects of Manipur between the ages of 16 to 60. They would render their labour as soldiers during wartime and as workers in peacetime.
5 The consequence of such expeditions by the Meitei maharaja along with British forces was that the tribals were forced to pay house taxes and natural resources were exploited.
6 Article 371(C) stated, '(i) Notwithstanding anything in this Constitution, the President may, by order made with respect to the State of Manipur, provide for the constitution and function of a committee of the Legislative Assembly of the State consisting of members of that Assembly elected from the Hill Areas of that State, for modifications to be made in the rules of business of the Government and in the rules of procedure of the Legislative Assembly of the State and for any special responsibility of the Governor in order to secure the proper functioning of such committee'.
7 The order provides that all bills, other than the Money Bill, affecting wholly or partly the hill areas shall, after their introduction in the assembly, be referred to the HAC for consideration and report to the assembly. All 20 elected members from the hill constituency form the HAC.
8 Ex-minister of tribal development, vet and animal husbandry, and education, GoM.
9 Protocol-wise, the chairman of the HAC is next to the CM of Manipur.
10 Often, it is the CM who appoints the chairman and vice-chairman.
11 Extract from the personal interview with an ex-minister at Imphal on 13 September 2014.
12 The local customary laws and practices provided autonomy for self-governance to tribes.
13 According to the Manipur (Village Authorities in Hill Areas) Act, 1956, every village with 20 or more tax-paying households is to have a village authority.

14 The Sixth Schedule of the Constitution of India primarily aims to protect hill and other tribal communities from the control and power of the groups in the plains. It gives provision under Article 244 (2) and 275 (1) to the administration of tribal areas in the state of Assam, Meghalya, Tripura and Mizoram by constituting an autonomous districts and autonomous regions with financial power.
15 Excerpt from the personal interview with Mr. Paul Leo, former president of UNC at Karong on 2 September 2012.
16 Excerpt from the personal interview with the chairman of the Senapati ADC at Imphal 20 August 2014.
17 Excerpt from the personal interview with Mr. Mungliu (it is a pseudonym), joint secretary of the Department of Tribal Affairs and Hills, GoM at Imphal on 18 June 2014.
18 For details, see Year Wise List of Resolutions. Retrieved from https://manipurassembly.net/Resolutions-Adopted.
19 Excerpt from the personal interview with Mr. Paul Leo at Karong on 9 August 2014.
20 This literally means that there would be a ceasefire in all Naga-inhabited areas, which includes four districts in Manipur.
21 The framework agreement has not made it public as of today, but the apprehension and tension it generated can is visible in different forms from Manipur, Assam, and Arunachal Pradesh, as well.
22 Article 3 of the Constitution of India provides a provision for the creation of new states, alterations of the existing state boundary or names of the existing states through a bill tabled in the Parliament of India.
23 The Economic Times. 2015. 'Centre Urged Not to Infringe Manipur Territory in Naga Peace Accord,' 31 August 2015. Retrieved from http://articles.economictimes.indiatimes.com/2015-08-31/news/66070578_1_manipur-assembly-territorial-integrity-state-legislature (accessed on 20 November 2015).
24 Statement of Shri. K Ranjit during the assembly season held on 31 August 2015. After condemnations from various Naga-based organisations, he issued a statement that claimed it was a slip of the tongue and what he meant was that 'there were no Nagas of Nagaland in Manipur'.
25 Kuki Inpi is the apex civil society of the Kuki tribe.
26 Nagas claimed that Senapati belonged to their ancestral land.
27 The Sangai Express. 2014. 'The Scheduled Tribe Demand Committee of Manipur.' Retrieved from www.thesangaiexpress.com/scheduled-tribe-status-for-meitei-meetei/ (accessed on 8 March 2016).
28 Imphal Free Press. 2018. 'Hill Based Bodies Apprise Centre Against Meitei ST Demand.' Retrieved from www.ifp.co.in/page/items/52785/hill-based-bodies-apprise-centre-against-meitei-st-demand/ (accessed on 16 October 2018).
29 Excerpt from the personal interview with Mr. Thomas (it is pseudonym), leader of ZRO on 24 May 2014.

References

Bhatia, B. 2010. 'Justice Denied to Tribals in the Hill Districts of Manipur'. *Economic and Political Weekly*, XLV (31): 38–46.

Government of India. 2002. *National Commission to Review the Working of the Constitution. Volume II. Ministry of Law and Justice.* New Delhi. Retrieved from http://legalaffairs.gov.in/sites/default/files/EMPOWERING-AND-STRENGTHENING-OF-PANCHAYATI%20RAJ.pdf (accessed on 13 October 2018).

Hassan, M. S. 2006. 'Explaining Manipur's Breakdown and Mizoram's Peace: The State and Identities in Northeast India'. *Crisis States Programme Working Paper 79*. London: London School of Economics.

Kamei, G. 2004. *The History of the Zeliangrong Nagas: From Makhel to Rani Gaidinliu*. New Delhi: Spectrum Publication.

Kamei, G. 2008. *Ethnicity and Social Change: An Anthology of Essays*. New Delhi: Akansha Publication.

Kamei, G. 2012. *Lecture on History of Manipur*. New Delhi: Akansha Publication.

Kumar, A., et al. 2011. 'Situating Conflict and Poverty in Manipur'. *CPRC-IIPA Working Paper no. 37*. New Delhi: Indian Institute of Public Administration.

Laldena. 1990. *History of Manipur (1762–1949)*. Imphal: Reliable Books Centre.

McCulloh, M. 1852 (reproduced 2016). *Account of the Valley of Munnipore and the Hill Tribes*. New Delhi: Akansha Publishing House.

Ngaihte, Th. 2013. 'Manipur and Its Demands for Internal Autonomy'. *Economic and Political Weekly*, 48 (16): 20–21.

Parliament of India. 2018. 'Rjya Sabha. Security Situation in the North Eastern States of India'. *Report no. 213. 2018*, p. 9. Retrieved from http://164.100.47.5/committee_web/ReportFile/15/101/213_2018_7_17.pdf (accessed on 15 October 2018).

Pemberton, B. 1835. *Report on the Eastern Frontier of British India*. Calcutta: Government of India.

Piang, L. K. 2014. 'Moving Backwards: Meitei's Demand for Scheduled Tribe Status'. *Economic and Political Weekly*, 49 (15): 1–5.

Roluahpuia. 2016. 'Media in Conflict or Conflict in Media: Examining Media Coverage of Conflict in Northeast India'. *Asian Ethnicity*, 19 (4): 488–5041. https://doi.org/10.1080/14631369.2016.1219224.

Scott, C. J. 1999. *Seeing Like a State: How Certain Schemes to Improve the Human Condition Have Failed*. New Haven: Yale University Press.

Shimray, U. A. 2001. 'Ethnicity and Socio-Political Assertion: The Manipur Experience'. *Economic and Political Weekly*, 36 (39): 3674–3677.

Shimray, U. A. 2004. 'Socio-Political Unrest in the Region Called North-East India'. *Economic and Political Weekly*, 39 (42): 4637–4643.

Shimray, U. A. 2007. *Naga Population and Integration Movement*. New Delhi: Mittal Publication.

Sitlhou, H. 2015. 'Confronting the State. Land Rights Discourse in the Hills of Manipur'. *Economic and Political Weekly*, L (30): 70–77.

Suan, H. K. K. 2011. 'Hill-Valley Divide as a Site of Conflict: Emerging Dialogic Space in Manipur'. In S. Baruah (ed.), *Beyond Counter-Insurgency: Breaking the Impasse in Northeast India*. New Delhi: Oxford University Press, pp. 263–289.

Xaxa, V. 2016. 'Tribes and Indian National Identity: Location of Exclusion and Marginality'. *Brown Journal of World Affair*, XXIII (I): 223–237.

Ziipao, R. R. and Kamei, A. 2016. 'Revisiting Exclusion and Oppression Within the Marginalised: Implications for Indigenising Social Work Practice in North East'. In S. R. Bodhi (ed.), *Social Work in India: Perspective from Within*. Kolkata: Adivaani.

4

POLITICAL HIGHWAY AND ITS TRIBUTARIES

Political highway

The colonial legacy of roads known as a 'political path'[1] in post-independent India has taken the form of political highways in Manipur. The NH-2, also known as AH-1, is the most politicised highway in Northeast India. This highway is the lifeline of Manipur, as it is the only viable means for the movement of both people and goods. However, NH-2 is often in the limelight for reasons other than transportation. Various ethnic communities, civil society groups and student organisations have been using this highway as a means to negotiate and draw the attention of the state government to issues affecting them. They do so by calling for economic blockades and bandhs, which invariably translate into blocking the highway. Almost every ethnic community in the state has resorted to the strategy of highway blockades to voice their demands and political aspirations. In the words of a student leader, 'The government of Manipur invites us for talks only when we resort to economic blockade of the highway. We use this as a last resort to place our agenda before the Government of Manipur and India (GoM)'.[2] This suggests that the GoM listens and responds only when people adopt extreme forms of agitation, which implies that democratic forms of protest do not work in a state like Manipur. Blockades, counter-lockades and bandhs, then, have become part of the system.

The Sadar Hill District Demand Committee of the Kuki community, for example, imposed an economic blockade on 1 August 2011 which continued until 31 October 2011, affecting movement on NH-2. This was done to put pressure on the GoM for the upgradation of the Sadar Hill subdivision into a full-fledged revenue district. The Nagas[3] imposed a counter-blockade from 21 August 2011 to 28 November 2011 in opposition to the Kuki's demand. The economic blockade lasted for 120 days. Apart from being the focus of blockades and bandhs, NH-2 is also a money-spinning highway for both state and non-state actors who collect illegal taxes from vehicles plying on the highway. No goods or passenger vehicles can escape the tax imposed by these self-appointed collectors. NH-2 is, therefore, repeatedly turned into a *political highway*, reaffirming the colonial construction of a road as a *political path*. It is also worthwhile to mention that the two great forces during the Second World War used this road when heading to the Battle of Kohima in 1944. Roads apart from connectivity also form a space of conflict and contestation, besides political and social spaces of patronage and power (Sinha, 2017).

Due to frequent bandhs and blockades by different ethnic communities, common men have gone to the extent of preparing a *bandh calendar* in Manipur, taking into account the dates of all the proposed strikes so that they can be prepared for the shortages that will ensue. From January to August 2009, Manipur witnessed as many as 79 bandhs and 10 highway blockades.[4] In May 2016 alone, as many as 17 different bandhs and blockades were called by different organisations. This culture of economic blockades, bandhs and protests, which is peculiar to the state of Manipur, is one of the indicators of poor governance and a volatile state, or is it a case of a misfit state? While resorting to economic blockades on the highway has turned out to be a most effective political strategy, it is the public that bears the brunt of this extreme step. Even though NH-2 is the lifeline of Manipur, it is poorly maintained in comparison to other highways in the northeastern states. Most of the highways in Manipur meet the NH-2 at the point of entry into the state capital Imphal; they include NH-150 (Imphal-Ukhrul), NH-37 (Imphal-Tamenglong) and NH-102 (Imphal-Moreh). These and other state highways form tributaries of NH-2.

Ontology of roads

In an ethnically volatile, militant prone and landlocked state like Manipur,[5] roadways are the only form of physical connectivity for the circulation of goods and services. And yet they are inadequately developed with uneven networks across the state. The state heavily depends on the goods imported from other parts of the country. Whenever any non-state actors[6] resort to blockading the highways, which is the order of the day, the prices of essential commodities shoot up. Often, blockades of highways amidst poor maintenance become a point of negotiation between the state and non-state actor/civil society. It is being argued that the state only listens or calls for negotiations when the civil societies resort to extreme forms of agitation – i.e. economic blockades on the highways or total shut down. Every ethnic community in the state makes effective use of this strategy to draw the attention of the state. Hence the black economy operating during this blockade period inversely affects the common citizens due to the exorbitant rise in price of essential commodities.[7]

Roads in Manipur, as elsewhere in the country, are primarily constructed as public works by the PWD, National Highway Authority of India (NHAI) and BRO. 'The realisation of such works involves financial, regulatory and technical relations that often fold international, national and local regimes into a single and specific location' (Dalakoglou and Harvey, 2012: 460). However, the fundamental question remains: what is a road? For Thevenot, what qualified as a road is a joint characterisation of human and non-human beings with conventionalised capacities. Accordingly, he detailed the typologies of roads. Thus a *market road* supports human beings qualified as customers who seek to make market relations and facilitates relations between customers and goods that qualify as transactions. An *industrial road* is an efficient infrastructure designed by long-term planners and engineers and is competently utilised by professional drivers with reliable vehicles. A *domestic road* is customarily used by locals and other domestic beings, including cattle. A *civic road* is a potential vehicle for equality and solidarity amongst citizens in spite of territorial inequalities (Thevenot, 2002: 69). Articulating roads in the context of mobility, Dalakoglou and Harvey (2012) wrote,

> Roads could arguably be taken as the paradigmatic material infrastructure of the twenty-first century, supporting both the information society (in the ever-increasing circulation of commodified goods and labour), and the extractive economies of developing nations on which the production and reproduction of such goods and labour depends.
>
> (:459)

According to the Poumai Naga[8] narratives, the route of their migration from Makhel[9] to their present habitat refers to a bridle path. Roads were constructed for the purpose of movement of people and their livestock. As evident from the location of terraced fields in and around the villages of the Poumai Naga tribe, the roads thus constructed were not meant for wheeled traffic. While exploring for a plot of land for cultivation, the foremost step is the construction of a pathway/country road. Those roads are collectively constructed with the labour from family members, relatives, neighbours and fellow villagers. Even today, Phiivayu[10] is observed and practised every year. On this occasion, the whole village collectively contributes labour for the repairing of roads, pathways and routes in and around the village and especially roads leading to the terraced fields. The philosophical foundation of Phiivayu is embedded in the principles of (1) egalitarian society, (2) interconnected and interdependent ecology and culture, (3) environmental conservation and (4) creation of sustainable roads (Bodhi, 2014). The construction and maintenance of roads for livelihoods, sustenance of economy and maintaining the ecological balance of people and nature has been an integral aspect of tribal lived reality.

Before the introduction of wheeled traffic in tribal society, the only form of inter-village communication involved travelling by foot. Such communication was a crucial aspect of maintaining cordial relationships and also helped in building alliances to fight common enemies. Roads thus served both as a way to get to the battlefield and a means for peace building between villages/tribes. The process of peace building or conflict resolution between villages was known as *Shoutoyu*.[11] In this ritual, two former warring villages took a vow not to fight each other again by exchanging their weapons and celebrating together as a sign of peace. During this ritual celebration, all the adults had to travel by foot to each other's villages and celebrate together and make friends through the process known as *kho*.

Roads are systematically constructed and maintained in tribal society. Amongst the Naga tribes, construction of roads varies depending on the types of soil and topography. Their in-depth knowledge of their ecology and close relationship with nature help them to construct roads that withstand all weather. R. G. Woodthorpe (British Army engineer) made an interesting observation in reference to the Ao tribe's art of constructing roads. He called them 'road engineers' and wrote,

> Their [Ao Nagas'] roads are constructed with due regard to the easiest gradients, and are not carried up and down over every little hillock. The steeper parts are stepped and paved to prevent the rain washing channels in them, and in the gentle gradients cuts are made across the roads at every change of inclination or direction in the most scientific manner to carry off the water down the hill side.
>
> (As cited in Dzuvichu, 2013: 484)

Amongst the Mao Nagas, the preference was to construct rough and steep roads so as to impede the progress of any invading party. The Angamis would usually prefer a steep ascent while laying their roads, based on the idea that an easy path made their home too accessible. Amongst the Poumais, roads were constructed depending on their site and usage: whether leading to wet rice cultivation/terraced fields, or to jhum cultivation sites, neighbouring villages or dense forests for collecting timber. Roads leading to terraced fields were constructed using layers of stone according to the gradient in such a manner that ensured easy movement and durability. Bridges, on the other hand, were carefully connected from one end to the other using timber with stone abutments to withstand the monsoon. In case of streams, the two banks were connected by large stones, often carried from long distances and dexterously crafted to suit the particular site.

Poumais, or, for that matter, hill people, treasured the infrastructure they created. Roads and bridges were collectively maintained and repaired on a regular basis. There was shared responsibility for maintaining roads amongst the tribes. For roads connecting two or more villages and different tribes, each village/tribe would maintain and repair the roads up to the boundary line as demarcated by their foreparents. Tribal knowledge and age-old skills for the construction of roads and bridges have been kept alive and passed on orally in the form of lived experiences and shared narratives. However, this invaluable knowledge is on the brink of extinction, as tribal reality has intersected with the inexorable waves of political-economic forces and various rules and regulations framed by the state. The old roads are dismantled in the pretext of new and modern inter-village and district roads by the state. And yet those modern roads hardly see the light of completion as envisaged and promised.

Echoing from the perspective of mobility, roads become road infrastructure and public assets only when they are constructed, regularly maintained and motorable. In this sense, roads are not in any positivist lens 'simply out there' (Larkin, 2013). The landscape per se is not a road, but when that landscape changes permanently in relation to construction by levelling using asphalt/bitumen and other materials, only then does it become a road: facilitate the circulatory regime of goods, people and ideas. As Larkin noted, *road* infrastructure centres on built things, knowledge things or people things and suggested that one could analyse all these things from the actor-network lens as disparate elements of a single system (Larkin, 2013: 320). However, it is inadequate to purely analyse from the lens of the actor-network theory the social reality emanating from Manipur without taking into account the power dynamics vis-à-vis inter- and intra-ethnic communities' power play in the state while embarking on road infrastructure. Nevertheless, roads entail the intersection of science and technology, society and material relations to build networks which facilitate the movement of other matter.

Roads, though a non-human material of network, have social, political and economic dimension which has impacted upon the human relationship and everyday politics. Socially, roads evoke the building of social relations as they bridge the communication gap. Politically, the development of roads constitute the key element of control over land and its resources, administration, political ideology, expansion of territory and what James Scott called 'distance demolishing technology' (Scott, 2009). Economically, roads connect and provide an easy movement from farms to the market for both goods and people. They facilitate the flow of capital and ideas across the globe. Road infrastructure is, therefore, an important marker of development.

The colonial roads or roads for colonising?

The traditional means of communication between villages, hill-valley and trade, prior to the introduction of wheel traffic was via pathways either on carts or by foot. The construction and maintenance of bridle paths or small routes amongst tribes in Manipur was part of their tradition and culture. Johnstone (1896), a colonial administrator, enunciated his lived experience while engaging in Naga Hills and Manipur. He observed that 'there was a footpath all round the hill, which after a little alteration of level here and there, and a little repairing, where landslips had made it unsafe, was delightful for a morning walk' (: 14). He further pointed out that roads in the hill were in fair condition for men and elephants but did not admit wheeled traffic, had there been any carts to use (ibid.).

The valley or the Meitei territory was connected to other countries, such as Burma and the British Province in Cachar, by roads. However, these roads were, again, in the form of pathways, and there was no concept of surface roads until the British colonised Manipur. Brown's account unravelled road infrastructure in Manipur. He wrote,

> The most important of the roads is that leading from the Manipur Territory to the British province of Cachar. Before the construction of this road by Government, communication with the British provinces was chiefly carried on by two routes, the Kala Naga, along which the road was constructed, and the Aquee route lying to the north of the above and still used, through unfrequently, by the hill-people. The distance of the road is calculated to be 103 miles from the Sudder station of Silchar to the capital of Manipur.
>
> (Brown, 1873: 97)

The colonial state-building process, or rather control over the region and its resources, was streamlined with the construction of roads. Roads for territorial expansion and resource extraction were the core agenda of the British East India Company (Ziipao, 2018). This same principle was applied to Manipur. The expansion of colonial rule into Manipur was actualised by developing an efficient line of road communication. The Kala Naga Range Road was constructed under the supervision of Capt. Guthrie between 1837 and 1844. This was a joint venture in which the total expenditure was born by the British and the Manipuri government (Johnstone, 1896).

The politics of physical access and new roads by the British served threefold objectives in Manipur: (1) political control and administration, (2) control over land and its resources and (3) easy mobility for colonial administrators and its armed forces. The Imphal-Cachar Road points in this direction. It was constructed after the first Burmese War by the British in consonance with the Manipur Raja. The journey from Imphal-Cachar takes approximately ten days (Brown, 1873). The most crucial road which the British constructed was the Assam-Burma Road. This road connects Manipur with Kohima and Dimapur with Assam. The present NH-2, or the AH-1, which connects three states – i.e. Assam, Nagaland Manipur – to Myanmar, is the modern Assam-Burma Road. Today, some of the old bridges and inspection bungalows constructed by British engineering corps are visible, even though they are no longer in use. The British were instrumental in laying the basic modern road infrastructure in the state.

The (un)making of highways and other roads

Manipur has only 1.5 km of railway line as of today.[12] The Imphal International Airport[13] has limited service due to poor infrastructure facilities. Development of waterways as a means of connectivity is out of the question since Manipur is a landlocked state. The only viable mode of connectivity that remains are roadways. Roads are the veins and arteries of transportation. The GoM follows the classification of roads on criteria evolved by the Indian Road Congress. Apart from state highways, district roads and village roads, Manipur has eight NHs. They are

1 NH-2 (Mao-Imphal-Moreh)
2 NH-2 (Imphal-Tipaimukh)
3 NH-202 (Imphal-Jessami)
4 NH-37 (Imphal-Jiribam)
5 NH-137 (Tamenglong-Khongsang)
6 NH-102B (Churachandpur-Tuivai)
7 NH-102A (Tadubi-Ukhrul)
8 NH-155 (Jessami-Melori)

And yet only two highways – namely NH-2 and NH-37 – are functional, that is motorable. NH-37 is only used as a detour route for emergency when NH-2 is blocked due to various economic blockades and bandhs imposed by different agencies until recently. Moreover, NH-37 is much longer with weak bridges unfit for transportation of goods and commodities during the monsoon. The upgradation of NH-37 into two lanes is in process. Suresh (2015) pointed out that a sum of Rs.225 crore was earmarked for this road. This meant an allocation of Rs. 1 crore per km and Rs. 70 crores per year for its maintenance for the last four years. Despite the high investment, this road is impassable during the monsoon, leaving aside the transportation of goods. The NH-102(A), 102 (B), 202 and 155 are yet to be operational since their construction/upgradation work is either incomplete or poorly developed. The NH-102 (A) was recently elevated to the status of NH from state highway, which is supposed to connect the Ukhrul and Senapati Districts. Ironically, this state highway remained in the form of highway alignment only on paper. The construction work began only after its upgradation to NH, and contract work was given to BRO from state PWD. Hence NH-2 remains the only functional highway in the state of Manipur, which connects other parts of the country.

Non-maintenance of NHs and other roads in Manipur is the order of the day. Of all physical infrastructures, roads continue to be in the most deplorable condition. One dimension of infrastructure as put forth by Start and Rudleder is infrastructure 'becomes visible upon breakdown' (Start and Rudleder, 1996). Often roads in Manipur, particularly those stretch out in hill territory, are much more prone to breaking down due to the poor quality of construction and non-maintenance. Apart from breaking down, the phenomena of temporality and suspension of work, as argued by Akhil Gupta (2015), are ably visible in the case of road infrastructure in the state. Roads constructed under PMGSY and those receiving sporadic repairs hardly withstand a single monsoon season.

The portion of NH-2 from Mao to Dimapur (Nagaland) is regularly repaired throughout the season as opposed to the portion from Mao to Imphal (Manipur). Even though it falls under the same highway, the differences in quality and frequency of maintenance of the highway is clearly observable. This seems to be due to differences in governance systems in the states of Nagaland and Manipur. To illustrate this point, the portion of NH-2 which falls under the jurisdiction of Manipur is entirely controlled by the state PWD. In opposition, the portion in Nagaland state is maintained by BRO. This explains the differences in the maintenance work. One of the several factors responsible for poor quality of highways in Manipur is the issue of multiple contractors and the use of sub-standard materials. For repairing the portion of NH-2 from Senapati to Maram, more than eight sub-contractors were involved in 2014. And yet the repairing of this road executed by different contractors and supervised by GoM did not withstand the 2015 monsoon. Such is the scenario of NHs repaired under the direct supervision of state PWD in Manipur. The following observation of the Senapati District Students' Association (SDSA) makes for interesting reading.

> It has become an annual affair of public demanding for repairing the poor condition of one of the lifelines of the State although the demand has failed to capture the attention of the authorities concerned to maintain the said highway. . . . The highway is blacktopped for the name sake and deplorable condition returns as usual every year. Poor drainage system coupled with landslide and continuous plying of overloaded trucks without any regulation has worsened the condition of the highway.[14]

During his visit to Manipur in 2006, the prime minister of India announced the upgradation of NH-2 from the existing two lanes to four lanes between the Maram-Imphal stretch (78 km). The estimated cost for the upgradation was Rs. 300 crore. As of 2018, after 16 years, there was no sign of any work on this highway besides sporadic repairs. The construction and maintenance of key highways or the lifeline of Manipur are under the jurisdiction of PWD, whereas BRO is responsible for those highways which either involve new cutting or those state highways elevated to NHs. Table 4.1 provides the length of highways under PWD and BRO, respectively.

As evident from Table 4.1, the BRO takes responsibility of 840.280 km of highway, whereas PWD takes responsibility of 467.465 km of highway.

Table 4.1 NH under PWD and BRO in Manipur (in km)

Name of NHs			*Road Length*		
Portion	*Old*	*New*	*Under BRO*	*Under State PWD*	*Total*
Mao to Imphal	NH-39	NH-02	–	106.515	106.515
Imphal to Moreh	NH-39	NH-02	–	111.560	111.560
Imphal to Tipaimukh	NH-150	NH-02	262.000	62.750	324.750
Imphal to Jessami	NH-150	NH-202	171.000	23.250	194.250
Imphal to Jiribam	NH-53	NH-37	218.780	3.220	222.000
Newly Declared NH					
Tamenglong to Khongsang		NH-137	39.500	–	39.500
Churachandpur to Tuivai		NH-102B	–	160.170	160.170
Tadubi to Ukhrul		NH-102A	144.000	–	144.000
Jessami to Melori	NH-155		5.000	–	5.000
	Grand Total		**840.280**	**467.465**	**1307.745**

Source: PWD, Manipur

There is a sharp difference in quality and durability of the roads maintained by BRO and those by the PWD. NH-2 from Mao to Moreh via Imphal is under the PWD. Hence this explains why this highway is in a deplorable and at times impassable condition during monsoon, even though it is the only lifeline for the state. The BRO and PWD contractors face same challenges in the construction and maintenance of roads: hilly terrain, hostile weather, non-availability of materials, law and order problems and topography. Yet the quality and durability of roads and people's trust are accredited more to BRO than PWD. The difference in work quality stems mainly to the difference in organisational set ups and governance systems. BRO is under the GoI and directly commanded by the Indian Army. It has its own border roads engineering service and task force. Hence, they execute all kinds of work by the organisation. In contrast, PWD is under the GoM and commanded by the work minister. The department is headed by a chief engineer. All road construction and repairs are executed through tendering and contracting to government registered contractors. This illustrates the differences in the two organisations and their governance systems.

Manipur falls under the category of resource constraint state and is unable to meet the growing demands of its citizens for all-weather roads. The strategy often used by the GoM is to request that the GoI give the existing state highways NHs status.[15] Hence there are eight NHs in the state. It is interesting to note that while other parts of the country are moving towards building super and express highways, Manipur is still struggling to maintain its existing roads. One of the many factors leading to the high cost of construction and other goods are the bad roads, resulting in high transportation costs. On average, all goods vehicles (carrying above 10 tonnes) take more than 16 hours[16] to cover a distance of 201 km – i.e. from Dimapur[17] (Nagaland) to Imphal (Manipur). Table 4.2 gives the lane-wise length of NHs in Manipur.

NHs in Manipur cover a total length of 1,317 km. Yet only 23 km of highway are four lanes, as shown in Table 4.2. This four-lane highway is confined within the vicinity of Imphal city. More than 850 km of NHs are less than two lanes, which implies that there is one way traffic. Moreover, NHs keep deteriorating with an increasing number of potholes and huge craters as they move from the plains towards the hill districts. A good example is NH-2. As one drives from Imphal to Senapati,[18] the highway is in good condition until it reaches Sekmai (entry point of the hills). The quality and riding condition changes drastically from the Sekmai stretch onwards, which extends to Mao, the border between Nagaland and Manipur. A similar trend is visible in the case of NH-37. The stretch from Imphal to Noney is in fair condition, but the quality declines as it goes further into the interior of the Tamenglong District.[19] The only exception in regard to the uniformity of quality is the stretch of NH-2 connecting Imphal to Moreh.[20] This is due to the fact that Moreh is projected as an international market, sharing a border with Myanmar. Thus the GoM attaches importance to the development and maintenance of this highway. And moreover, it is this highway that connects India with Southeast Asia.

The Ministry of Shipping, Roads, Transport and Highways has classified road quality into two categories: fair and poor condition. Accordingly, the report of working groups on roads for the 11th five-year plan gave an overview of road conditions in the northeast which stated,

> The riding quality and condition of main roads is generally fair to poor. Only 10 percent of these roads are reported to be in good condition. About 50 percent of the network has poor riding quality. The position is much worse in case of State Highways and Major District Roads. . . . Only about 10 percent of the state highways can be said to be structurally adequate to carry the legally permissible single axle loads of 10.2 tonnes.
>
> (GoI, 2007)

Table 4.2 Lane-wise length of NHs in Manipur

State	*Total Length*	*Less than Two Lanes*	*Two Lanes*	*Four Lanes and Above*
Manipur	1,317	850	444	23

Source: Basic Statistic of Road, 2013

In Manipur, more than 60 per cent of the total roads are in the category of poor, which is far higher than the northeast average of 48.4 per cent (ibid.). One of my respondents pointed out, 'If this is the state of national highways, one could imagine what could be the status of other categories of roads in the hill districts'.[21] His observation is in consonance with my experience during my 13 months of fieldwork in Manipur. The density of the roads is again very low, with just 739.11 km. In contrast, the average density of the roads in the northeast stand at 1,154.85 km (GoI, 2009). The state is not only marked by the poor quality of roads but also falls into the category of a state with low road networks. Table 4.3 provides the road mileage of Manipur from 1956 to 2010.

The total road network in Manipur, as shown in Table 4.3 (at the end of the first five-year plan), was 959.77 km. Out of the total road length of 959.77 km, 216.41 km are of NHs whereas 743.36 km of length constitutes district roads. Before 1956, there were no state highways or any major district roads. By 1960, the total road length increased to 1,705.38 km. The major addition of roads during this period were the state highways (849.55km). This was followed by a village road with 296 km. However, there was no addition of NHs in the state. What is interesting is that in 1970, the state highway was drastically reduced to merely 8.8 km from 849.55 km. One can infer that during this period, an additional category of road was added – i.e. the municipal road. Hence a municipal road constitutes 223.2 km and other district roads consist of 629.6 km, respectively, in 1970. What was significant in 1980 was the rapid increase in village roads from 296.06 km in 1960 to 1818 km in 1980. This went up to 9,008 km by 2010, and the total road length in the state stands at 13,827 km. The rapid increase in village/rural roads in the state, as elsewhere in the country, can be attributed to the fact that GoI implemented various rural connectivity programmes. This includes the PMGSY and the Mahatma Gandhi National Rural Employment Scheme (MGNREGS), amongst others.

Table 4.3 Road mileage of Manipur (1956–2010) in km

Classification of Roads	*1956*	*1960*	*1970*	*1980*	*1990*	*2000*	*2010*
NHs	216.41	216.41	208.8	214.5	434.3	957	1,101
State Highways	–	849.55	8.8	480	557	675	1,228
Major District Roads	–	336.28	432.8	545	978.1	964	1,272
Other District Roads	743.36	7.08	629.6	290	443	1013	1,218
Village Road	–	296.06	1,247.3	1,818	2,507	3,563	9,008
Municipal Roads	–	–	223.2	193.8	122	139	–
Total	**959.77**	**1,705.38**	**2,750.5**	**3,541.3**	**5,034.4**	**7,172**	**13,827**
Surfaced Roads	959.77	588.09	961.9	1,874.1	3,684.3	4,427	–
Unsurfaced Roads	–	1,117.29	1,788.6	1,667.2	1,359.1	2,745	–

Source: Compiled from PWD, Statistical Handbook, Economic Survey, GoM

Over the decades, road mileage in Manipur has increased threefold – i.e. from 959.77 km of road in 1956 to 13,827 km in 2010. Yet the total of surface roads, or those roads categorised as in fair condition per the GoI norms, remain a point of contention. Infrastructural creation without the provision of maintenance becomes a liability rather than a public asset. Construction of roads is not an exception to this phenomenon. Suspension and temporality of road projects occur on a regular basis, this is more so with state highways and district and village road projects. The oddity of such projects is that the surface road (bitumen) fades away even before its official inauguration or completion. To cite an example, the Senapati-Phaibung (state highway) project had stopped midway; a shortage of funds was cited as a reason for incompletion of this highway. The Maram-Purul (20 km) Road project provides a case where bitumen faded away even before its completion, and there was no maintenance or provision for repairing the road. Local commuters from neighbouring villages mobilised to repair the road from time to time without any government support. The SDSA pointed out that the 'contractors responsible for construction and repairing of roads in hill district do not follow to the prescribed specification. The work that is executed is more of a *cosmetic work*. It is carried out haphazardly to enable the contractors to withdraw the final bill'.[22] This gives the impression that the state is not in a position to supervise work executed by PWD, even with full budgetary support from GoI and other development agencies.[23]

Rural road: the case of PMGSY

The GoI launched the PMGSY in December 2000. Its objective is to provide all-weather roads to unconnected habitats in the country which have populations of more than 500 inhabitants. However, in the case of hill and tribal villages, the population criterion is 250 inhabitants. Rural connectivity is a key component of rural inhabitants for trade and economic growth, access to markets, school, health centres and banks, amongst others. Yet many remote villages remained unconnected and hence excluded from markets and the fruits of economic growth in the country. Rural roads continued to be the single-most important factor in rural development, as accentuated by local communities in Manipur. Villagers from the hills of Manipur, time and again, reiterate the pitiable state of their roads. In the words of an elderly man from Hiimai village, 'All I want is good road in my village. For us, rural development is all about road development and I wish, one day, I could travel in a surface road, free of potholes and craters to reach Senapati'.[24] This echoes the larger sentiments of the villagers from remote locations and resonates with the Leninian notion of infrastructure development as a form of revolution. Given the large number of unconnected villages in India, PMGSY is a welcome initiative of the government.

Manipur, as in other states, also implements the cent per cent funding of PMGSY. It is executed by the Manipur State Rural Road Development Agency (MSRRDA) under the department of rural development, GoM. Roads constructed under PMGSY are supposed to be surface/all-weather roads with the provision of maintenance up to five years by the concerned contractor. From the inception of the programme, 'the state has been able to construct approximately 500 km of rural roads every year' (GoM, 2016b: 3). Effectively, if Manipur continues at the same pace of rural road construction, then by 2020, it will have 7,500 km of rural roads. This implies that every village in the state will be connected by all-weather roads. Strangely, however, many rural roads constructed under PMGSY do not last even for a single season in the hill districts.[25] Hence, defeating the very notion of surface/all-weather roads.

> It is important to note that while it is the centre which provides 100 per cent finance for construction of rural roads under the PMGSY, the primary responsibility to ensure the quality of the construction works and maintenance of roads lies with the state.
>
> Lalvani (2010)

The inability and inefficiency of the GoM, coupled with poor infrastructural governance and injustice meted out against the hill people, are the key factors responsible for the poor, crumbling rural roads in Manipur. PMGSY, as part of the rural development and rural roads transformation, needs to address the unequal power relations and historical deprivation in tribal society. Predominantly, all hill districts come under the category of rural, with the exception of small towns located within the vicinity of each district headquarters. A comparison of budgetary allocation under PMGSY of valley districts (10 per cent geographical area) versus hill districts (90 per cent geographical area) is presented in Table 4.4.

PMGSY in Manipur was first implemented in the financial year 2005–06. In its maiden year of implementation, valley districts were allocated a sum of Rs. 7.06 crores. In contrast, the hill districts received Rs. 13.89 crores in total (Table 4.4). Taking into account the total geographical area, rurality and unconnected villages between valley and hill districts, the former districts received much more funding than that of the latter. This amounts to budgetary discrimination and breeds injustice. It is the state government which initially sent the proposal and works to be included under PMGSY. Accordingly, the ministry of rural development recommends and releases the approval list and funding to the respective states. Had the GoM taken into account and addressed the historically deprived society inhabiting in the hill districts then PMGSY's focus should have been nine times on those areas than on the valley districts, which already have a well-connected network of roads.

Table 4.4 Budgetary allocation under PMGSY (district-wise)

District	*2005–06*	*2006–07*	*2007–08*	*2008–09*	*2009–10*	*2010–11*	*2011–12*	*2012–13*	*2013–14*	*Total*
Valley districts										
Thoubal	2.13	0.86	11.68	5.22	16.78	10.50	8.24	4.2	2.39	**62.01**
Imphal West	1.68	3.07	4.90	2.41	15.92	15.70	9.34	2.97	1.73	**57.71**
Imphal East	1.84	1.32	1.60	1.91	6.32	5.03	4.49	2.85	0.78	**26.14**
Bishnupur	1.41	0.85	5.64	2.05	3.94	3.95	3.60	5.23	1.42	**28.08**
Hill districts										
Senapati	3.12	1.39	12.08	5.3	17.09	21.18	40.81	13.29	34.17	**149.05**
Ukhrul	1.77	1.53	7.85	5.23	8.66	15.14	29.82	16.6	39.22	**125.83**
Tamenglong	2.21	1.89	4.92	3.27	8.37	12.23	17.05	13.94	20.36	**84.34**
Churachandpur	2.47	0.18	11.65	10.90	31.42	13.17	32.85	7.51	13.89	**124.04**
Chandel	4.32	1.28	8.19	2.9	13.69	14.62	15.16	12.89	18.38	**91.44**

Source: MSRRDA

Amongst the hill districts, Senapati received the highest total funding with Rs.149.05 crores from 2005 to 2006 to 2013 to 2014 (Table 4.4). This is followed by Ukhrul district (Rs. 125.83 crores), Churachandpur (Rs.124.04 crores), Chandel (Rs.91.44 crores) and Tamenglong (Rs.84.34 crores). During my fieldwork (2014–15) and subsequent yearly visit to my field site (Manipur), I observed that some roads under PMGSY in the hill districts were reflected only in terms of sign boards and not surface roads. The sign boards thus erected gave the following information: (1) name of the road, (2) length of the road, (3) year of starting and completion, (4) detail layers, (5) name of the contractor and (6) total budget of the project. Echoing this, Thomas, a social activist opined, 'Manipur is a funny state as everything finishes in office and there is nothing in reality. This motivated us to fight for the cause of our people with whatever means available'.[26] When Thomas asserted that everything *finishes in office*, he was referring to a rampant form of systemic corruption operating at the centre of power and governance – i.e. Imphal, the capital of Manipur. Loopholes in the implementation of development programmes and schemes are common across the districts. Yet the overarching structural and power inequality between the hills and the valley disallowed the growth of an alternative centres – i.e. hill districts. I shall further demonstrate this form of infrastructural inequality in the following section where I analyse road disparity between the hills and the valley.

Road disparity: hill-valley divide

The hill-valley divide continues to be a detrimental factor for the poverty of infrastructure in tribal districts. The ramifications of such a divide as reflected in the economic development and road disparity is one such indicator. The Manipur Development Report 2016 echoes the same. It stated,

> Since non-surfaced roads can be used only for a short period largely during the dry season, all weather roads are required in the hill districts to improve connectivity and transportation around the year. There is also a big divide with regards to connectivity of villages with all-weather roads across the hill and valley districts. The pathetic condition of the existing roads in the hill districts has been detrimental for development.
>
> (GoM, 2016a: 67)

The polarisation of infrastructure further deepens the hill-valley divide. The density and total surface of roads in valley districts are far higher than those in the hill districts. This is ably demonstrated in Table 4.5. Per the NEC district infrastructure index, all four valley districts ranked above the hill districts (Table 4.5). It is important to note that all the valley districts in the state are placed within the top-ten ranking out of the total 80 districts

Table 4.5 Road density vis-à-vis surface road

District	*NER Rank*	*State rank*	*Road length per 100 sq km*	*Surface road as % of total Road*
Valley districts				
Thoubal	3	1	143.97	92.16
Imphal West	7	2	120.6	85.4
Imphal East	8	3	120.6	93.6
Bishnupur	10	4	84.68	88.81
Hill Districts				
Senapati	62	5	24.73	77.65
Ukhrul	63	6	24.47	70.56
Tamenglong	65	7	22.77	68.21
Churachandpur	70	8	21.23	70.01
Chandel	71	9	19.32	71.53

Source: MDoNER, 2009

surveyed in the northeastern states. In contrast, hill districts in the state are all at the bottom of the ranking. The extreme polarisation of road infrastructure in the state is that of the Thoubal and Chandel Districts. The road length per 100 sq km in Thoubal stands at 143.97, whereas Chandel is merely 19.32 (Table 4.5). Similarly, 92.16 per cent of the total roads in Thoubal are of surface roads, whereas in Chandel it is just 70.01 per cent. The average road length per 100 sq km of valley districts stands at 117.46 whereas for hill districts its merely 22.50. This echoes what I have argued on the concept I positioned in this book, infrastructure of injustice. One can further infer and contest from the existing data the notion of an infrastructure deficit state. The all-India average road length per 100 sq km is 115.30 (GoI, 2011), whereas the valley districts of Manipur stand at 117.46 and hill districts at merely 22.50. This implies that the infrastructure deficit is applicable only in the context of hill districts.

The government servants I interviewed during my fieldwork often cited the issue of insurgency, corruption, law and order and hilly terrain as major factors for the poverty of road infrastructure in the hills.[27] It is true that these factors also contribute to the crumbling road infrastructure, but they are not the key factors. What government officials often ignored is the aspect of structural inequality between the hill-valley divide and the systemic deprivation, which should be embedded in the planning stage. Statistically, the number of active insurgent groups in the valley is more than in the hills. Likewise, the cases of law and order problem in the valley is more than in the hills. Yet as evident from Table 4.5, road length per 100 sq km in the valley is five times longer than in the hills. This raises an interesting question: why is poverty of road infrastructure experienced only in the hill districts? A comparative analysis of the Senapati and Imphal

Districts[28] further reveals wide disparity of road infrastructure, as presented in Table 4.6 (A) and (B).

Table 4.6 (A) and (B) reveal that the hill-valley divide in terms of road infrastructure is historically rooted and the trend continues today. By 1974 (three years after Manipur was elevated to full-fledge statehood), Imphal had a total of 1,385.23 km of road. This includes NHs (71.87 km), state highways (238.74 km), major district roads (115.25 km), other district roads (73.90 km) and inter-village roads (885.47 km). In contrast, the Senapati District has only 263 km of road in total: NHs (78 km), state highways (51 km), major district roads (48 km), other district roads (19 km) and inter-village roads (67 km). What is striking in 1974 is that Senapati has only 67 km of inter-village road, whereas Imphal has 888.47 km. This implies that Imphal villages already had a well-connected network of inter-village roads since 1974. Non-surfaced roads, or what is commonly called mud roads, can only be used during the dry season. Construction of new mud roads without the provision of maintenance is equivalent to building bridle paths, both are

Table 4.6 (A) Road length in km (Imphal district#)

As on 31st March	*NHs*	*State highways*	*Major district road*	*Other district road*	*Inter-village road*	*Total*
1975	71.87	238.74	115.25	73.90	885.47	1385.23
1983*	83.57	138.80	44.75	144.34	516.00	892.46
1995	53.00	152.00	113.00	328.00	746.00	1392.00
2002	109.00	183.00	185.00	243.00	751.00	1481.00
% of Surface Road as of 2001	100	100	92.25	93.10	52.32	87.53

#Imphal (East and West)
*It also includes Thoubal and Bishnupur districts

Source: PWD and Development Profile of Manipur, GoM

Table 4.6 (B) Road length in km (Senapati district)

As on 31st March	*NHs*	*State highways*	*Major district road*	*Other district road*	*Inter-village road*	*Total*
1975	78.00	51.00	48.00	19.00	67.00	263.00
1984	93.83	106.20	7.25	54.25	178.00	439.53
1995	115.00	128.00	35.00	180.00	235.00	693.00
2002	106.00	107.00	20.00	54.00	522.00	809.00
% of Surface Road as of 2001	100	100	53.29	13.57	6.64	38.02

Source: PWD and Development Profile of Manipur, GoM

impassable for wheeled traffic. According to 2001 data, the Senapati District had only 6.64 per cent of total inter-village roads that were surfaced roads, whereas Imphal's surfaced roads amounted to 52.32 per cent (Table 4.6 (A) and (B)). The national rural road development committee observation on the lack of rural roads is pertinent for planning in Manipur. The report (GoI, 2011) identified the following symptoms due to a lack of road accessibility:

- Death of pregnant women on a daily basis as they fail to reach health centres on time.
- Lakhs of rural children cannot reach schools during the rainy season.
- Perishable agricultural produce cannot reach the markets on time, leading to heavy losses for the farmers.
- A large number of cattle die in epidemics, especially during the rainy season, because timely help cannot reach them.
- Water tankers cannot reach several thousand drought-prone villages, leading to the migration of the rural population in total despair.
- The public distribution system fails to penetrate to thousands of villages, leading to malnutrition and infant mortality.
- Poor connectivity has a high correlation with high levels of illiteracy, unemployment and poverty.
- Low levels of accessibility have deprived a large number of villagers of equality of opportunity as compared to the urban population.

Remote and unconnected villages from hill districts have been experiencing the aforementioned symptoms on a daily basis. The valley- and dominant community–centric development approach of the state further widened the gap between the state and tribes and polarised the hill-valley divide. The current infrastructure development approach disempowered tribes and breed injustice. This is reflected in Tables 4.5 and 4.6. Hence it is imperative that infrastructure development take into account the geo-specific approach – i.e. prioritising roads and other physical infrastructure wherever there is poverty of such facilities.

Budgetary allocation of roads and the transport sector

Examination of five-year plans indicates heavy investment in the transport sector for the first four five-year plan, even though the plan outlay was relatively small. In the first five-year plan, 72.33 per cent (Rs. 74.17 lakh) of the total expenditure was on the transport and communication sectors (Table 4.7). The second, third and fourth five-year plans followed the similar trend of expenditure in the transport and communication sectors. There was, however, a gradual decline from the fifth five-year plan. Yet the actual budgetary allocation increased exponentially, even though there was a decline in total expenditure. During the fourth five-year plan, an outlay of Rs.1260 lakh out of Rs.3100 lakh was spent on this sector. In the fifth five-year plan

Table 4.7 Five-year plan expenditure of the transport sector in Manipur (Rs. in lakhs)

Plan period	*Total expenditure*	*Expenditure on transport sector*	*% to total expenditure*
1st Plan (1951–56)	102.56	74.17	72.33
2nd Plan (1956–62)	596.93	208.90	34.99
3rd Plan (1961–66)	1,281.28	503.23	39.28
4th Plan (1969–74)	3,100.00	1,260.00	40.65
5th Plan (1974–78)	6,661.91	1,480.60	22.22
6th Plan (1980–85)	24,312.32	3,706.51	15.25
7th Plan (1985–90)	50,485.69	7,466.83	14.79
8th Plan (1992–97)	122,450.97	20,111.14	16.42
9th Plan (1997–02)	184,865.10	25,638.15	13.87
10th Plan (2002–07)	279,777.00	26,332.00	9.41
11th Plan (2007–12)	9,21,894.00	53,021.31	4.94
12th Plan (2012–17)*	2,045,791.00	110,505.00	5.40

Note: In the first six five-year plans, transport and communication were under one head of development. *Projected plan outlay

Source: Statistical Handbook of Manipur, 1992, Statistical Abstract Manipur, 2005, and Economic Survey Manipur, 2007–08 and 2014–15

(1974–78), the total outlay for this sector was to the tune of Rs.1480.60 lakh (see Table 4.7). And yet there was merely an addition of 25.90 km of road during the fifth five-year plan (GoM, 1992). Similarly, during the eighth five-year plan, a sum of Rs. 20111.14 lakh was spent on transport. However, there was only an addition of 5.70 km of road.

During the 11th five-year plan (2007–12), the actual expenditure was Rs. 53,021.31 lakh, and yet there was no additional road constructed during this period. A sum of Rs. 9321 lakh was spent on widening roads in Imphal areas alone and Rs. 1138.26 lakh on wayside amenities, which is non-existent in most of the roads. The projected outlay for 12th five-year plan (2012–17) is Rs. 110505 lakh for transport and target for physical achievement is nil. Out of this total outlay, a sum of Rs. 7,500 lakh have been earmarked for the construction of a city bus terminal, directorate of transport office building and district transport offices in Imphal (GoM, 2015).

To address the infrastructural gap in Manipur, various development agencies, apart from central ministry, are continuously supporting the state. The major infrastructure funding includes a non-lapsable central pool of resources (NLCPR), NEC, National Rural Road Development Agency (NRRDA), border area development programme (BADP), special plan assistance (SPA) and international financial institutes, such as World Bank and ADB. All of this funding is independent of the state annual plans.

The Ministry of DoNER introduced the NLCPR in 1998–99. The funding under this head is reserved for the infrastructure development of northeastern states. GoM has received a sum of Rs. 843.86 crore[29] since its inception, out of which a sum of Rs. 149.14 –i.e. 18.72 per cent – was spent on roads and bridges alone. Manipur, like other northeastern states, has been getting funding for infrastructure development from the central government since 2001–02 in the form of SPA. The allocation under SPA during the 11th five-year plan was Rs. 2,720.50 crore. Often, high dignitaries visiting Manipur announce special economics packages. To illustrate, during his visit to Manipur in 2004, the prime minister announced a reconstruction plan of Rs. 641.59 crore for upgradation of district roads and other major infrastructure development. The BADP has been implementing its programme in Manipur since 1997–98. The priority of the programme is the construction and maintenance of link roads. During the 11th five-year plan, BADP received Rs. 87 crore which was spent in Manipur. Another important development cum planning body in the region is NEC, which funds all eight states' development projects, especially when a state is not in a position to implement a project due to resource constraints. NEC particularly supports the construction of bus terminals, maintenance of roads in the border areas and construction of inter-state roads. From 1972 to 2014, the GoM received Rs. 526.94 crore[30] from NEC for road development alone. Against this background, the argument of state PWD officials that a lack of funding led to wide variation in road infrastructure between the hills and the valley can be contested and nullified. An analysis of five-year plans shows that a sum of Rs. 250,307.84 lakh (Table 4.7) has been spent on the road and transport sectors alone. There is a cost differential[31] in infrastructure creation in northeastern states, but a lack of funding is not an appropriate conclusion. There are various factors which lead to poor road infrastructure and wide disparity in the state. One of the key factors is structural inequality. The other factors include layers of stakeholders, vicious cycle of corruption, power dynamics, systemic loopholes, landownership patterns and land-use systems, political negotiation, political instability, dynamics of contracting, historical process, issues of contradiction and contestation amongst major ethnic groups, changes in internal needs and demands and demography.[32]

Notes

1 The roads constructed using tribal labour and control by the British during their rule in the region were termed political paths by Capt. Johnson (political agent of Manipur from 1870 to 1886).

2 Personal interview with Mr. Shoho (it is a pseudonym) in Senapati on 21 May 2014.

3 Led by the UNC, the apex body of Nagas in Manipur.

4 *The Northeast Today*, 2019. Retrieved from http://thenortheasttoday.com/10-bandhs-that-crippled-manipur-this-year/ (accessed on 10 December 2016).

5 Manipur has the highest number of active insurgent groups and has faced imposition of president rule ten times. Every ethnic community have its own insurgent groups.

6 Student organisations, ethnic civil societies and insurgents, amongst others.
7 The price of essential commodities, such as LPG price, goes up to Rs. 1,800 per cylinder, petrol to Rs. 280 per litre, rice to Rs. 120 per kg and the list goes on.
8 Poumai Nagas are one of the 34 tribes recognised as STs by the GoI in Manipur.
9 Makhel is considered sacred and the dispersal site of the Tenyimi (Mao, Poumai, Angami, Maram, Chakhesang, Inpui, Pochury, Rengma, Thangal and Zeliangrong tribes).
10 Phiivayu usually takes place a few weeks before the harvesting of terraced paddy fields. This day is set and announced by the Veoh (the nominal head of the village in rituals who would traditionally be the first person to sow the seed and to harvest the paddy field).
11 Shoutoyu is a festival celebrated by Naga tribes.
12 The Jiribam-Tupul-Imphal railway line (111 km) project was conceived in 2004. Even though the construction work had begun, the Ministry of Railway said, 'No timeline can be set for completion of this project'. For details, see www.theapolitical.in/india/no-timeline-can-set-completion-jiribam-imphal-railway-project-security-reasons-says-centre (accessed on 21 May 2018).
13 Even though Imphal Airport was declared Tulihal International Airport, international flights are yet to be operationalised.
14 The Sangai Express. 'Many Senapati Denizens Expressed Concern Over Poor Repairing Works Executed by Contractors.' Retrieved from www.thesangaiexpress.com/page/items/57413/nh-2-in-deplorable-condition-public-decry (accessed on 3 October 2015).
15 This they do since the GoM cannot maintain the existing highways without full budgetary support from GoI. When a highway is elevated to NH status, the onus is with the Ministry of Road Transport and Highways.
16 This was noted when I was doing my ethnographic fieldwork and accompanied a truck carrying 14 tonnes of cement in July 2018.
17 Dimapur is the nearest commercial hub and railway station where all goods for construction and other materials are transported from.
18 Imphal is in the valley, whereas Senapati is the hills.
19 I have travelled on these highways many times during my fieldwork, as well as whenever I come to Manipur, and I am aware of the difference in quality of highways between the stretch in the hills and valley.
20 Moreh is the international border commercial hub in the Chandel District, Manipur.
21 Excerpt from the personal interview with Mr. Thomas (it is a pseudonym), activist from Hmars' tribe at Lamka on 12 May 2014.
22 The Sangai Express. 'SDSA Highlights State of NH-2'. Retrieved from www.thesangaiexpress.com/page/items/60927/sdsahighlights-state-of-nh-2 (accessed on 21 December 2015).
23 For details, see Chapter 6 on social and political processes of infrastructure development.
24 Excerpt from the personal interview with Mr. Peihmeh at Hiimai village on 30 June 2018.
25 During his fieldwork, the author came across many such cases of rural roads under PMGSY. In some cases, there were only the sign boards with details of work orders, name of the roads, contractors, and total budget but no roads. This implies that the roads exist only on the sign boards.
26 Excerpt from the personal interview with Mr. Thomas (it is a pseudonym), activist from Hmars' tribe at Lamka on 12 May 2014.
27 Excerpt from the personal interview with Shri. Singh (name changed), additional chief engineer and Shri. Choaba (name changed) chief engineer, GoM at Imphal on 28 July 2014.

28 Imphal (valley) and Senapati (hill) districts were taken for comparison due to the non-availability of uniform base year data for other districts in the state.
29 All data cited in this section are calculated from state annual plans unless mentioned otherwise.
30 As per the right to information replied from NEC filed by the author.
31 An interview with the advisor (Transport and Communication), NEC pointed out that per the CPWD rate, if the cost of construction is Rs. 100 in Delhi, then it will cost the same amount of work in Manipur Rs. 200, Rs. 160 in Nagaland, Mizoram and Tripura, Rs. 150 in Arunachal Pradesh and Rs. 127 in Assam.
32 All of these factors are analysed in Chapter 6 (social and political processes of infrastructure development) and their linkages is demonstrated in Figure 7.1 in Chapter 7.

References

Bodhi, S. R. 2014. 'Tribal Social Work: Reflection on Its Philosophical Foundation'. *Indian Journal of Dalit and Tribal Social Work*, 2 (6): 64–74.

Brown, R. 1873 (reproduced 2001). *Statistical Account of Manipur*. New Delhi: Mittal Publication.

Dalakoglou, D. and Harvey, P. 2012. 'Roads and Anthropology: Ethnographic Perspectives on Space, Time and (Im)Mobility'. *Mobilities*, 7 (4): 459–465. https://doi.org/10.1080/17450101.2012.718426.

Dzuvichu, L. 2013. 'Roads and the Raj: The Politics of Road Building in Colonial Naga Hills, 1860s–1910s'. *The Indian Economic and Social History Review*, 50 (4): 473–494. https://doi.org/10.1177/0019464613502416.

Government of India. 2007. *The Report of the Working Group on Roads. Ministry of Shipping, Road Transport and Highway*. New Delhi, p. 47. Retrieved from http://planningcommission.nic.in/aboutus/committee/wrkgrp11/wg11_road.pdf (accessed on 15 September 2015).

Government of India. 2009. *Economic Survey 2008–09*. New Delhi: Ministry of Finance.

Government of India. 2011. *Basic Road Statistics of India 2010–11*. New Delhi: Ministry of Road Transport and Highways. Retrieved from www.indiaenvironmentportal.org.in/files/file/basic%20road%20statistics%20of%20india.pdf (accessed on 24 October 2018).

Government of India. 2011. *Working Group on Rural Roads*. New Delhi: Ministry of Rural Development.

Government of Manipur. 1992. *Statistical Handbook of Manipur, 1992*. Lamphelpat: Directorate of Economics and Statistics.

Government of Manipur. 2015. *Economic Survey Manipur 2014–15*. Lamphelpat: Directorate of Economics and Statistics.

Government of Manipur. 2016a. *The Manipur Development Report 2016*. Imphal: Planning Department.

Government of Manipur. 2016b. *Manipur State Rural Roads Maintenance Policy 2016*. Imphal: Department of Rural Development and Panchayati Raj.

Gupta, A. 2015. 'Suspension. Theorizing the Contemporary'. *Cultural Anthropology*. Retrieved from https://culanth.org/fieldsights/722-suspension (accessed on 7 March 2018).

Johnstone, J. 1896. (reprinted 2002). *My Experience in Manipur and the Naga Hills*. Delhi: Gyan Publishing House.

Lalvani, M. 2010. 'Bharat Nirman: A Stocktaking Exercise'. *Economic and Political Weekly*, 45 (17): 19, 21–24.

Larkin, B. 2013. 'The Politics and Poetics of Infrastructure'. *The Annual Review of Anthropology* 42: 327–342. https://doi.org/10.1146/annurev-anthro-092412-155522.

Scott, C. J. 2009. *The Art of Not Being Governed: An Anarchist History of Upland Southeast Asia*. New Haven: Yale University Press.

Sinha, N. 2017. 'Infrastructural Governance and Social History: Roads in Colonial and Postcolonial India'. *History Compass*, 1–10. https//doi.org/10.1111/hic3.12401.

Star, S. and Rudleder, K. 1996. 'Steps Towards an Ecology of Infrastructure: Design and Access for Large Information Spaces'. *Information Technology and Organizational Transformation*, 7 (1): 111–134.

Suresh, Th. 2015. 'Hand Over NH-37 to the Army and Save Manipur'. *The Sangai Express*, 3 June 2015.

Thevenot, L. 2002. 'Which Road to Follow? The Moral Complexity of an Equipped Humanity'. In J. Law and M. Nnnermarie (eds.), *Complexities: Social Studies of Knowledge Practices*. Durham and London: Duke University Press.

Ziipao, R. R. 2018. 'Roads, Tribes, and Identity in Northeast India'. *Asian Ethnicity*, 1–22 https://doi.org/10.1080/14631369.2018.1495058.

5

ELECTRICITY

Regularly irregular

Electrified without electricity

Tingsong village in the Senapati District of Manipur is located 45 km away from NH-2. According to the 2011 census, the village has 246 households, with a population of 1,377 persons. The following is a case of blatant corruption in rural electrification programmes and was learnt from interactions with members of the Tingsong village[1] at the Senapati headquarters, after which I personally visited the village. The village headman and his team managed to obtain electricity poles in order to get their village electrified after running from pillar to post for five years. Through community labour, an appropriate path was laid out for the electricity lines amidst terrain with ravines. The community erected all of the electricity poles en route to their village with the hope that it would finally get electricity.

Strangely enough, the electricity wire for distribution lines were not provided, even after the electricity poles were erected. Consequently, many electric poles either got rusted or damaged. After following up, the headman and his team came to learn that the electricity wires meant for their village had already been sold on the black market by a section officer in the concerned department. The Tingsong village was officially recorded as an electrified village much before it even got electricity wires for the distribution line. Against this background, it is interesting to note what constitutes an electrified village according to the GoI. A village would be declared as electrified

> if (1) basic infrastructure such as distribution transformer and distribution lines are provided in the inhabited locality; (2) electricity is provided to public places like school, panchayat office, health centres, dispensaries, community centres, among others; (3) the number of household electrified be at least 10 per cent of the total number of households in the village.
>
> (GoI, 2004)

In this case, Tingsong village does not qualify to be declared an electrified village since it neither possessed basic infrastructure nor distribution lines.

Rather, it echoes the case of manipulation by concerned officials and the politics of rural electrification.

The villagers placed the matter before the concerned minister. After his intervention, the Tingsong village got new electricity poles in 2014. However, only modicum wires to connect the lines were provided. To make matters worse, the department was reluctant to work with the villagers to construct the necessary electricity infrastructure. Since the village did not have technical expertise and resources, the process of village electrification got held up once again. Tingsong village lost faith in the government after struggling for ten years. The science and technology department supports electrification programmes in remote areas with non-conventional energy sources, such as solar, wind energy and biomass. The Manipur Renewable Energy Development Agency (MANIREDA) implements this scheme in Manipur. Tingsong village thus applied for this scheme. They even made a deposit for solar lighting of their village. Once again, an agent manipulated this scheme, and Tingsong did not see any light. In fact, their deposit got refunded after a span of two years. The only alternative left for the villagers was to buy solar lights from Imphal that cost, on average, Rs 10,000 per panel. However, only a few households could afford this. The majority of households were excluded, as they did not have the monetary resources and continue to live without electricity. This case is a classic example of layers of corruption inherent in the system of governance and the processes involved in village electrification in Manipur.[2]

Against all of these odds, the community has demonstrated the effectiveness of collective labour for village development where the state has failed miserably. Corruption and the nexus between different stakeholders and systemic loopholes continue to cast a shadow over development projects in Manipur. Following the corporatisation of electricity (in 2014) in Manipur – that is, from postpaid to prepaid energy metres in urban areas – many tribal villages in the state continue to live without electricity and basic infrastructure facilities. Tingsong village is one of many such cases where there is neither electricity nor motorable roads. Thus the village experiences the temporality of electric infrastructure on the one hand and the political economy of rural electrification on the other hand. This echoes what Schnitzler (2013) posited as the politics of metres, poles and wires, wherein infrastructure itself becomes a political terrain on which such questions are negotiated and contested. Thus Tingsong village represents the case of being electrified without electricity.

Electric infrastructure, as much as a circulatory regime and network of connectivity, effectively disconnects the rural populace due to an irregular power supply coupled with inadequate infrastructure. This reminded me of Lenin's approach to infrastructure development following the Russian Revolution, where he emphasised building infrastructure as a form of social revolution. This is evident from his address to the eighth All Russian Congress of Soviets on the critical importance of electrification: *Communism is Soviet power plus the electrification of the whole country* (Lenin, 1920). The GoI initiated various programmes, such as Deendayal Upadhyaya Gram Jyoti Yojana and Bharat Nirman, amongst others, with the aim of universalising electricity access or electrifying all un-electrified villages in India. According to the GoI, this was achieved on 28 April 2018 with the electrification of Leisang village. It is interesting to note the last village in India to be electrified – i.e. Leisang is located in the hill district of Manipur. On the same day, the prime minister of India declared that every single village in India now has access to electricity with 'powered and empowered'.[3] Given the lack of rural infrastructure, this is a welcomed initiative. Yet the mere presence of physical infrastructure disempowered rural inhabitants and public assets became liabilities – for example, electricity without a power supply, unmotorable roads, schools without teachers, hospitals without doctors and nurses, rural banks without banking, offices without staffs and the list goes on. A reliable and affordable power supply in rural habitats could be a way forward to address the infrastructural gap and bridge the hill-valley divide. As Richmond and Patwardhan noted, electricity has clear multiplier effects for development outcomes, including health, education and living standards generally. Hence the provision of adequate and affordable electricity is paramount to the country's long-term development strategy (Richmond and Patwardhhan, 2018). This chapter charts the historiography of electricity in Manipur. It delves into the politics of billing electricity and analyses the hill-valley divide of electrification. The chapter unearths electricity reform or, to borrow what Schnitzler called 'techno-political device', prepaid electricity metreing. The chapter concludes by investigating failed hydropower projects and how tribes negotiate with the state in the form of resistance. Overall, the chapter argues that electricity, like road infrastructure, breeds injustice and widens the hill-valley divide.

Electrifying Manipur and its trajectory

Reliable energy is indispensable for development. The primary mode of energy in India and Manipur is electricity. Electricity is the versatile form of energy, which is crucial for agricultural development, industrial progress, housing chores, etc. However, electricity is an intangible (invisible) homogenous product characterised by high capital intensity and riskiness, hazardous in handling and proneness to high transmission and distribution (T&D) losses after generation. Electricity is an instantaneous product; it cannot be stored. Generation and use must be simultaneous (Neog, 2009). Thermal and hydroprojects are the major source of electricity generation in India. This involves massive investment, long gestation periods, environmental hazards and displacement. Sustainable development requires energy and climate security at the same time. Ensuring a basic minimum supply of electricity for all inhabitants is a basic requirement. Roads and electricity are two crucial infrastructures for rural development. However, these two basic infrastructures in Manipur are disproportionately distributed across the state, coupled with poorly maintained and irregular supply of electricity. The Human Development Report, 2007 observed that 'living without electricity affects many dimensions of human development'. Energy services play a crucial role not just in supporting economic growth and generating employment but also in enhancing the quality of people's live (UNDP, 2007). Manipur is one of the least non-performing states in terms of meeting energy security amongst the northeastern states.

Electricity in Manipur is not as old as roads. In fact, the first power generation began at Leimakhong in 1930. The Manipur State Hydro Electric Board constituted by the British initiated two mini-hydel generators of 100 kW and 56 kW capacity, respectively. The power supply was limited to the Imphal town area until 1950. At the end of the first five-year plan (1955–56), the electricity installation capacity of Manipur was only 165 kW, whereas electricity generated was merely 5.13 kWh, and per capita consumption stands at 0.62 kWh.[4] The state witnessed a steady growth of electricity from 1955 to 1956 and 1960 to 1961: the installed capacity increased from 165 kW to 731 kW, electricity generation from 5.13 to 14.91 kWh and per capita consumption increased from 0.62 to 1.36 kWh. In the same year, the per capita electricity consumption of all-India average was 30.0 kWh. The low energy consumption in the state was primarily due to inadequate installation and electricity was limited to the valley areas of the state – i.e. Imphal. This implies that electricity was still unknown in the hill areas of the state.

The growth of the power sector in Manipur is most visible following the elevation to full-fledged statehood in 1972. By 1975–76, the installed capacity stood at 9390 mW; the electricity generated was 149.50 kWh, and per capita consumption was 9 kWh, which is far below the all-India average of 124 kWh. This growth can be attributed to an increased budgetary allocation to the power sector. A sum of Rs. 2056.78 lakh (30.87 per cent of the total expenditure) was earmarked for the power sector alone during the fifth five-year plan period (1974–78). A similar trend in investment continued in all five-year plan periods and so contributed to the growth of the power sector in the state. In 2010–11, the installed capacity stood at 45,020 mW with 1,930.1 kWh electricity generated, and the per capita consumption stood up at 230. 93 kWh. Though there was a sharp increase in the power sector over the years in the state, compared to the all-India average, Manipur is far below.

Apart from a road infrastructure deficit, as discussed in the previous chapter, the state is facing a huge electricity deficit, both in terms of infrastructure and power supply position. Yet this deficit is manifested mostly in the hill areas of Manipur or, in other words, in tribal territories. By and large, Manipur represents a case of an *electricity deficit state*. The state-owned resources for electricity generation are minimal. Thus electricity generated from the state is not even sufficient to meet the demand of basic domestic use. The consumption rate of electricity is disproportionate to its generation rate. During 1985–86, the electricity generated in the state was merely 3.260 million kWh, whereas consumption stood at 54.014 million kWh. This trend continues even today. Although there was a steady increase in per capita electricity consumption in the state, the generation of electricity decreased from 1985 to 1986 onwards. Hence, Manipur heavily depends on the central electricity project share to meet the demand of its citizens.

The first mega-hydropower project in the state – i.e. Loktak Hydro Electric Project – was commissioned in 1984 by the central government. This project was developed and controlled by the National Hydroelectric Power Corporation (NHPC). By virtue of the project being located in the state, Manipur received a limited free share of power supply. In order to meet the growing demand of electricity by the valley dwellers, the GoM purchased power from central sector plants mainly located within the northeastern region: the Loktak Hydro Electric Plant, Kopili-Khangdong Hydro Electric Plant, Assam Gas Based Power Plant at Kathalguri and Agartala Gas Turbine Power Plant at Ramchandranagar, Eastern Regional Electricity Board, Ranganadi Hydro Electric Plant and Doyang Hydro Electric Plant.

The GoM in 2000–01 thus purchased from central sector plants to the tune of 3,556.25 kWh. This was further increased to 4,651.21 kWh in 2009–10. This constitutes about 90.89 per cent of the total electricity in the state (GoM, 2011). It implies that the state's own generation of electricity is less than 10 per cent. In 2011, it cost the state exchequer a sum of Rs. 187.92 crores on purchasing electricity. However, the revenue collected from the consumers was only Rs. 67.36 crores, with an outstanding amount of Rs. 311.08 crores. This created huge arrears accumulated over the years and the state owes a sum of Rs. 84.93 crores to central sector plants (ibid.). During the lean season,[5] even the central sector plants are not in a position to meet the demand of electricity made by various states from the region, as major electricity generation depends on hydel plants. Of all the northeastern states, Manipur is the worst affected state since it depends entirely from the central sector plant's share of electricity. The severity of this problem and shortage of electricity are reflected in the government report which stated, 'Sometimes, the availability of power from these plants are so poor that even the demand of vital installations like hospital, radio station, doordarshan kendra and other telecommunication stations could not be met' (GoM, 2015: 118). A shortage of electricity on the one hand and non-payment of electricity bills by consumers on the other hand placed Manipur in a distinct state. This is best encapsulated in the words of an ex-minister:

> Manipur generates small amount of electricity and cannot even meet the demand or give 24X7 electricity to 1/3rd of the Imphal city. We

> buy power mainly from NEEPCO and Assam. The state government spent more than Rs. 20 crores per month approximately on purchasing power. Even then we cannot provide 24 hours power supply and worst is in hill areas where they get approximately two hours of electricity in a day. Every month, the government incurred a loss of Rs.10 crore in power sector alone.[6]

This echoes the gravity of neglect to the hill areas by the state, and it can be gauged from the fact that the power supply is a priority in Imphal city or the valley, whereas the hill areas barely get two hours of electricity. It gives the impression that the hill areas receive only the spillover electricity from the valley. This reinforces the valley-centric development approach of the state and denial of agency to tribes wherein the growth of an alternative centre (hill areas) remains stagnant if not impossible. It is thus imperative to be introspective and rethink the edifices of state practice.

Shortage of electricity is indeed a great concern for development. The shortage of power is mostly attributed to non-payment of electricity bills by consumers. However, oftentimes, we failed to unearth who the consumers were and why they didn't pay their electricity bills? According to 2015–16 data, domestic consumption of electricity amounted to 298.85 million kWh – i.e. 62.9 per cent of the total consumption of the state (GoM, 2017). Logically, if the hill areas get approximately two hours of power in a day, then about 90 per cent of domestic consumers are valley dwellers. Predominantly, the valley is inhabited by the Meitei. Thus the demand and supply gap of electricity is effectively created by the dominant community in the valley. This can be gauged from the fact that in 2003–04, the Imphal East and Imphal West Districts alone consumed 67 per cent of the total electricity available in the state, whereas the five hill districts' consumption was merely 16.73 per cent. Besides the physical infrastructure gap between the hills and the valley, the distribution/supply of power follows the same pattern. This approach leverages injustice to hill people or the tribals in the state. Thus taking the state as a unit of analysis does not reveal the social reality of the power shortage and consumption by different ethnic communities. Nevertheless, in absence of ethnicity and a district-wide pattern of electricity consumption and power shortage, a quick overview of the power shortage is merited to see where Manipur stands as a whole. This is demonstrated in Table 5.1.

The demand for electricity by consumers increases over the years whereas generating capacity remains stagnant, thus resulting in a shortfall and creating a demand-supply gap. The state's own capacity to generate power remains at a minimum and so too the investment in the power sector. In 2005–06, the peak power demand by consumers was 117 mW, whereas it could supply only 103.8 mW, leaving a gap of 13.20 mW shortfall (Table 5.1). In the following year, the peak power demand was 134 mW and could meet only

Table 5.1 Electricity demand and supply gap

Year	*Peak power demand (mW)*	*Peak demand met (mW)*	*Shortfall (mW)*
2005–06	117	103.8	13.20
2006–07	134	96	38
2007–08	145	97	48
2008–09	157	100	57
2009–10	170	110	60
2010–11	175	110	65
2011–12	180	115	65

Source: Department of Electricity, GoM

Table 5.2 Cost of power in Manipur and India (in paisa/kwh)

State	*2007–08*	*2008–09*	*2009–10*	*2010–11*	*2011–12*	*2012–13 (R.E)*	*2013–14 (A.P)*
Manipur	585.53	783.81	782.4	798.97	976.55	915.61	855.31
India Average	404.42	459.58	471.09	506.29	569.84	592.75	593.13

R.E: Revised estimate, A.P: Annual Plan

Source: Planning Commission, GoI

96 mW. With the increase in power demand, the shortfall also increased. In 2011–12, the demand was to the tune of 180 mW, whereas it could supply only 115 mW, leaving a shortfall of 65 mW (Table 5.1). The consequences of an irregular power supply also echoed during my fieldwork when the concerned officer was unable to give me data because of load-shedding and because the office did not have a power backup.

Non-payment of electricity bills is associated with high cost. On the one hand, the government increases the price of electricity to recover the cost, and on the other hand, consumers' dues escalate, resulting in non-payment of bills. Each unit of electricity in Manipur cost 585.53 paisa in 2007–08, whereas the all-India average was 404.42 paisa/kwh. The cost escalated to 915.62 paisa in 2011–12. In contrast, the all-India average for the same year was 569.84 paisa/kwh (see Table 5.2). The cost of electricity per unit in Manipur is much higher than the national average. In a nutshell, the following attributes can be characterised as the status of electricity in Manipur: (1) acute shortage of power, (2) irregular power supply to hill districts, (3) high cost, (4) disproportionate power supply and consumption between the hills and the valley, (5) total dependent on central sector plants, (6) high T&D loss and (7) poor governance of electricity department, amongst others.

Rural electrification: hill-valley divide

Electrification in the hill or tribal areas started only after 1972 – i.e. post-statehood. In contrast, electricity supply in Imphal valley started as early as 1930, when the first mini-hydel plant was set up at Leimakhong. Hence there is a difference of 42 years between the hills and the valley in terms of electrification. Until 2018, many villages in the remote hill areas neither had roads nor electricity, as was the case with the Tingsong village. Roads and electricity in the hills have a close correlation. Wherever there is no road in a village, there is no power infrastructure either. The distribution line of electricity closely follows the path of the road to the villages. This is done to prevent people from electrocution on the one hand and to ensure that the felling of trees in the hilly terrain does not block the supply of electricity on the other hand.

Rural electrification is one of the indicators that reflects the status of accessibility and availability of basic infrastructure in villages. There are 2,557 villages in Manipur according to the 2011 census. Out of this, 2,212 are officially electrified, which accounts for 86.51 per cent of the villages. As compared to other northeastern states, Manipur has a high village electrification rate per the official record. However, it is associated with a recurrent phenomenon of load-shedding. In fact, electrified villages, particularly in the hill areas, hardly get two hours of power supply and then on alternate days. In the words of the director, 'Electricity is regularly irregular in the hills'.[7] This came from a government servant who echoed the gravity of the electricity supply situation in the hills. The temporality and suspension of the electricity supply in the hill districts is what defined the status of rural electrification in Manipur. In cases of breakdowns in electrical infrastructure, such as poles, wiring, voltage transformers and regulators, amongst others, it takes months for repairs and replacements to be made. In the perpetual absence of departmental staff in rural areas, the onus of repairs falls on the villagers who are not professionally trained in that field. Hence the probability of electrocution is very high, and, in fact, many such cases have been reported in rural areas. Whereas in valley districts, electricity supply is far more regular. In terms of rural electrification, valley districts achieved 100 per cent. The hill-valley divide on rural electrification is ably presented in Table 5.3.

The hill-valley divide continues to be a marker of development in Manipur, as shown in Table 5.3. A comparison between hill and valley districts reveals a wide disparity in rural electrification. Villages in all valley districts are electrified with a record of 100 per cent, whereas the average hill district rural electrification stands at 83.83 per cent as of 2014. However, the state average rural electrification stands at 86.51 per cent. This does not echo the reality of rural electrification, as all the valley districts have a record of 100 per cent electrification. Amongst the hill districts, Senapati, with the highest

Table 5.3 Rural electrification in Manipur (villages per the 2011 census) as of 31 March 2014

Name of district	*No. of rural Villages*	*Total nos. of rural villages electrified*	*Percentage of villages electrified*
Valley districts			
Imphal East	193	193	100
Imphal West	112	112	100
Bishnupur	49	49	100
Thoubal	106	106	100
Hill districts			
Senapati	683	621	90.92
Churachandpur	597	563	77.55
Ukhrul	213	183	85.92
Tamenglong	174	152	87.36
Chandel	430	333	77.44
Total	**2,557**	**2,212**	**86.51**

Source: Department of Electricity, GoM

number of villages, achieved 90.92 per cent rural electrification. This is followed by Tamenglong (87.38), Ukhrul (85.92), Churachandpur (77.55) and Chandel at the bottom with a 77.44 per cent rural electrification rate. It is interesting to note that the total number of four valley district villages (460 nos.) is less than in the Senapati District with 683 villages (Table 5.3). This partly explains the slow pace of rural electrification in the hills, and the element of subjugation by the state continue towards the tribals. Thomas pointed out from his lived experience that even though 83.83 per cent of rural villages are officially on the list of villages with electricity, in most cases, load-shedding for long durations is a normal everyday experience for the villagers. He further posited that electricity was, until recently, an urban phenomenon. The penetration of electricity up to 60 km from the district headquarters is very recent.[8] This resonates with my lived experience. During monsoons, the roads are not drivable, and electricity is so irregular that in some places, there are electric poles with no wires. People have to climb to the hilltops and mountains for cell service. To get to school, students have to walk for miles.

As experienced by this researcher, in the hill villages, electricity is supplied during odd hours. In rural areas, people hardly need electricity during the daytime since they are all engaged in their subsistence agriculture and allied activities. Unlike other societies where agriculture is heavily dependent on irrigation and bore wells, agriculture productivity in the hill areas does not depend on such factors. The consumption pattern of electricity in tribal society is mainly for domestic use. During the peak hours – i.e. the evening – there is hardly a supply of electricity in those villages which are officially electrified. The reasons often cited by the concerned department staff members include underdeveloped hydroelectric projects, low installation capacity, high transmission and distribution losses, non-payment of dues and overload in the transformer, amongst others. In contrast, the inhabitants of valley districts do not face such issues as their counterpart tribal districts. This echoes my position on infrastructural injustice, or in this case it may be called a transmission of injustice via irregular electricity supply to the hills.

The dynamics of a power supply in villages is such that there is no electricity when it is required. At times, the power supply is cut off for months with officials citing overload in the transformer or default in the distribution lines. A case in point is the technical problem concerned with transformers installed in villages. The concerned department rarely visits villages to rectify the technical problems, even after repeated requests and filing complaints. Thus villagers are forced to make repairs by themselves and buy transformers through collective contribution. There are also cases of electrocution taking place during the process of repairs carried out by villagers. Thonta, who is about 24 years of ages, was part of the volunteer youth squad in the Hiimai village to fix the disconnected electric wire between two poles when he was involved in an unfortunate accident. Prior information was passed to the nearest sub-power station, which is 20 km away from the village, that repairs would take place on that fateful day. While Mr. Thonta was on top of the pole connecting two disjointed electric wires, there was sudden power supply, and he was electrocuted and fell from a 40-feet (12 metre) electric pole. Fortunately, he survived the electrocution after being rushed to Imphal (105 km away from the Hiimai village) for treatment.[9] It is interesting to note that the work which is supposed to be done by the electricity department is executed by the concerned villagers. The processes involved with village electrification makes for interesting reading. It is the villagers who literally carry electric poles and erect them to connect to the nearest distribution lines/sub-power station. The following was reported by Mr. Daile (who is about 48 years of age):

> I was in class eight when we got the news that electricity will finally come to our village. We went to carry necessary equipment by foot (such as electric poles, wire, plates etc.) as given by the government without going to school. For nearly one month we were engaged on clearing dense forest for distribution line to pass through and digging pits for electric poles. It took more than a year to finally complete the process of creating electric infrastructure. However, to our utter disappointment, the power supply was given only on the day of inauguration and thereafter got disconnected for months.[10]

The mere provision of materials for rural electrification and being listed as an electrified village are gross violations of the very definition of electrified village, as defined by GoI. The recurrent phenomenon of load-shedding overshadows the physical existence of electrified villages. Corruption within the electricity department is deeply entrenched in the supply of power. As pointed out earlier, a section officer sold off the electric wires meant for the Tingsong village. There are also cases of other materials being sold on the black market by the department staff members. Bribery in the form of giving 'pocket money' to the staff members posted at the sub-power station for additional electricity supply is a common practice. Any village desiring a few hours of extra electricity supply during special occasions has to bribe the departmental personnel in its jurisdiction. Such is the situation and status of electricity in the hill villages in Manipur.

Manipur, like other states, also implements centrally sponsored schemes, such as Rajiv Gandhi Grameen Vidyutikaran (RGGVY), Restructured Accelerated Power Development and Reform Programme (R-APDRP) for rural electrification. Under RGGVY, there is a provision for free power supply to below poverty line (BPL) families. However, the GoM is not in a position to contribute to the state share of 10 per cent to fully implement the scheme. The severity of non-fulfilment can be gauged from the fact that the number of BPL households with electricity connection in the Ukhrul and Senapati Districts are merely 5 and 9 per cent, respectively.[11] Besides central sponsored schemes, Manipur is also the beneficiary state of the World Bank aided North Eastern Region (NER) Power System Improvement Project. This is implemented by the Power Grid Corporation of India. The project aims to improve power transmission and sub-transmission in six of the northeastern states. Out of the total budgetary support of Rs. 5,111 crore, Manipur is earmarked Rs. 442.22 crore (World Bank, 2015). However, it is interesting to note that the improvement and renovation of the transmission line passes through the hill districts, but the improvement and extension of distribution lines are mostly concentrated in the valley districts. Apart from the extension of the existing 33/11kV sub-station at Chandel, the other six distribution lines are in valley districts (ibid.). The benefits of international financial institutes, such as World Bank–aided projects, did not accrue to the tribal people in the state. Rather, these projects are appropriated by the dominant community since they have the political power and occupy the seats of governance. This is just one of such instances. The list continues. The systemic denial of agency and persistent injustice perpetuated by the state and dominant community towards tribals or hill districts in Manipur makes tribes more vulnerable. Hence they continue to assert their political rights to carve out their own path of development and administration.

Politics and dynamics of billing

Reliable and timely dispatch of electricity bills to consumers is key to recover the cost of electricity. Educating consumers to pay their electricity bills on time could be one way forward in addressing the persistent issue of non-payment. Unlike industrial states in India, Manipur falls into a category with no medium or large-scale industries; hence, industrial consumption of electricity is very low. In 2015–16, the industrial consumption of electricity was just 23.81 million kWh, whereas domestic consumption was as high as 298.85 million kWh (GoM, 2017). Domestic consumers include its citizens as well as various government department offices where electricity is in use for daily functioning. Less than 17 per cent of total electricity is consumed by five hill districts; hence, the biggest defaulters are those settled in the valley districts. It is true that there are many consumers from the hill areas who default in paying electricity bills/charges, but their share is significantly low when compared to their valley dweller counterparts.

The nonchalant attitude of consumers on the one hand and the inefficient and poor maintenance by the department of electricity on the other hand is the reality of electricity in Manipur. This phenomenon has a direct correlation with an irregular power supply and huge loss in revenue. Both the government and consumers are responsible for the failure of the electricity sector and even more so the system of operation and governance at the department of electricity under the GoM. The electricity department is responsible for installing the postpaid metre system and generating usage bills, and it has failed miserably in the state. In most of the tribal villages or in hill districts, there was no system in place for generating electricity bills until 2014.[12] In the absence of any technology to determine the usage of electricity, generating bills becomes problematic and questionable. Often the practice by the department of electricity is that it sends electricity bills to its consumers by calculating the average usage without taking into account the actual usage. One hardly finds a case in which electricity bills are sent on a monthly basis. The gravity of the inefficiency can be gauged from the fact that the electricity department, for instance, sends electricity bills to its consumers once a year or in some extreme cases after five years in the hill districts. There are also cases where the electricity department notified its consumers of ten years of usage in a single bill. In the words of Louniiru (an illiterate consumer, who is about 64 years of age),

> The electricity department notified us to pay a bill amounting to a sum of Rs. 74,000 as an arrear/due for the past ten years. But we wonder how did the department calculate our usage bills for ten years without installing metre in my house. In no way, we could pay this much amount. We never receive any such bill before.[13]

This situation requires serious introspection on such practices by the concerned department. Notifying an illiterate consumer whose annual family income is less than electricity bill is a gross violation of human rights. The family is not in a position to pay the billed amount since they come under the category of BPL. The two options in this case are either disconnect the electricity or waive the amount under the RGGVY scheme.[14] Ideally, it should have been the latter since BPL households are entitled to free electricity connection and usage. Yet Louniiru's family was notified to pay the bill, which implies blatant corruption within the department and failed governance.

The other extreme case is the nexus between government employees and electricity department staff members. It is interesting to note the modus operandi of this nexus. The strategy often employed by government servants is bribing the electricity department staff to get a *no-due certificate*. The GoM introduced a policy for its employees to mandatorily get no-due certificates from the electricity department before releasing their respective salary. This was done in order to recover the cost of electricity and to make it mandatory for its employees to pay electricity charges on time or else face a consequence of deduction in their salaries. And yet this policy is rendered ineffective due to various levels of systemic loopholes and unethical practices by government servants vis-à-vis the staff members in the electricity department. Often the easiest and most popular strategy is to bribe the concerned officers in the department to get an instant no-due certificate and submit the same to their respective departments to release their salaries. What is more interesting is the case of those employees who are posted in the rural hill villages. They hardly report to their workplaces. Instead, they employ an untrained teachers from the local area to teach on their behalf (proxy teachers) for minimum pay. Hence those proxy teachers take the responsibility of getting no-due certificates as well. During my fieldwork in a village, I had an interaction with a schoolteacher posted in government primary school. In her case, she didn't bribe the electricity department. By virtue of living in a remote village, she was able to obtain a letter from the village chairman/chief that stated that there was no electricity connection in her house. Hence when she gave the letter to the electricity department, a staff member issued her a no-due certificate.[15] This is another common strategy to avoid paying electricity bills, especially by those employees posted in rural villages. Others avoid paying electricity bills by bypassing the postpaid metre system or outsmarting technology. What consumers often do is take two electricity connections – the official connection to the postpaid metre box and the direct connection to household – and bypass the metre system. Hence the metre box remains idle and non-functional since it is not in use at all. Due to non-physical verification by the concerned department, such a practice is rampant in remote villages. Against this backdrop, the GoM initiated the process of corporatisation of the electricity department in 2013, or was it just the replacement of postpaid metres with prepaid metres?

Electricity reform or prepaid metreing?

To augment and revive the electricity department from the recurrent loss of revenue, the GoM initiated various policies. These include (1) mandatory clearance of electricity consumption dues before issuing any certificate by the deputy commissioners, (2) no-due certificate from government employees, (3) an incentive scheme for waiving 74 per cent of the outstanding surcharge amount for domestic consumers in the one-time clearance of their dues, (4) detection and disconnection of unauthorised consumers and (5) spot collection of dues, amongst others (GoM, 2014). Yet these strategies remain ineffective due to unabated malpractice and the nexus of consumers and electricity department staff members. Taking into consideration the gravity of persistent issues of electricity, the GoM passed the Electricity Act in 2003. This act empowered the setting up of two courts to deal exclusively with issues related to electricity in Manipur: the special court (electricity), Manipur east, and the special court (electricity), Manipur west. These two courts were entrusted to deal with the theft of electricity, tampering with metres and any other cases related to electricity in their respective jurisdictions.

The landmark initiative undertaken by the GoM was the corporatisation of the electricity department in 2014. Following the cabinet decision on 14 February 2013, the electricity department unbundled into two companies: Holding Company (HOLDCO) and Distribution Company (DISCOM). This was done through a notification of the government – vide Manipur State Electricity Reform Transfer Scheme, 2013. This notification came into force on 1 February 2014. The Manipur State Power Company Limited (MSPCL) was assigned as the HOLDCO with the responsibilities of discharging the functions of the state transmission and generation utilities and state load dispatch centre. Whereas the Manipur State Power Distribution Company Limited (MSPDCL) took the role of DISCOM with its main function being the distribution of licences. All the existing employees of the electricity department were assigned either to MSPCL or MSPDCL (GoM, 2014). However, the two aforementioned companies remain 100 per cent GoM undertakings under the command of the power minister. All the existing employees were merely transferred with new designations; otherwise, they performed the same responsibilities and duties. For instance, the director position was rechristened managing director, executive engineer changed to deputy general manager, section officer changed to deputy manager and so on.

The two companies introduced new initiatives to revamp the former electricity department. The initiatives include (1) provisioning of new electronic metres, (2) outsourcing of metre reading and collection of bills, (3) increasing underground cabling and ABC cable for low-tension connection in high-consumption areas, (4) provisioning of Distribution Transformer (DT), feeders and sub-station metres and (5) installing of prepaid energy metres in urban areas. The key feature of corporatisation of electricity is the introduction of the prepaid electricity metre system. In South Africa, the prepaid electric metre system was assembled as a device of counter-insurgency against the anti-apartheid rent boycotts and to curb the non-payment of service charges. In light of this, Schnitzler (2013) termed the prepaid metre a 'techno-political device'. In the context of Manipur, the prepaid metre was introduced to address power theft and non-payment of bills, to regulate power consumption by consumers, to increase the efficiency of the power supply and to enforce payment, amongst others. However, the element as a device for counter-insurgency is absent, even though Manipur has the highest number of insurgent groups in the country.

The company makes it mandatory in urban areas to install prepaid electric metres for every consumer or they will face the consequences of disconnection of electricity. Hence, installation of prepaid metres began in Imphal in a phased manner. In the first phase, 11,000 metres were installed followed by 1,000 metres in three phases in Imphal areas. Under this new initiative, every consumer has to recharge to use electricity and operate in a similar fashion to our prepaid mobile phone service. The supply of electricity automatically gets disconnected once the recharge amount is used up by the consumer. The consumers can regulate their own capacity of electricity usage according to their purchasing power. This echoes the neo-liberal agenda of cost recovery from consumers for the services provided by the company. According to the power department, GoM, the outcome of this initiative has resulted in the substantial reduction in load demand, improvement in quality of power, drastic increase in revenue generation and efficient power supply. The quantitative output of electricity reform is presented in Table 5.4.

From Table 5.4 one can infer that the introduction of prepaid energy metres in Manipur revamped the then debt-stricken electricity department. The load profile percentage has come down to 56 per cent, which is a reduction of 44 per cent in load demand. The revenue thus generated has

Table 5.4 Postpaid versus prepaid energy metres in Manipur

Items	*Pre-installation*	*Post-installation*	*Remarks/Impact*
Load profile percentage	100 per cent	56 per cent	44 per cent reduction in load demand
Revenue (6 months)	Rs.3.18 crore	Rs.6.07	About double-fold collection
Staff requirement	MR-16, JBC-19, total: 35	Ten staff members at five staff members per vending machine	70 per cent reduction in manpower requirement
No. of consumers	9,300	12,000	Due to the regulation of load beyond 5 kW by the prepayment metre
Billing efficiency	63 per cent	100 per cent	Cent per cent billing without metre reader
Collection efficiency	64 per cent	100 per cent	Collection in advance

Source: Power department, 2013–14

doubled – i.e. from Rs. 3.18 to Rs. 6.07 (six months accounting period). However, it is interesting to note that the number of consumers has increased from 9,300 to 12,000 (see Table 5.4). Does this mean that there were many households without electricity connection prior to the prepaid system in Imphal?[16] This posits a juxtaposing situation wherein the number of consumers has increased but load demand has decreased drastically – i.e. by 44 per cent. One possible explanation of this absurd phenomenon is that in a single household, there might be more than one prepaid metre box being installed. The most notable achievement of the prepaid energy metre according to the GoM is the 100 per cent billing efficiency and bill collection (Table 5.4).

At present, the electricity sector in Manipur is in a transition phase. The company has not completely revamped the old electricity department, nor has it totally embraced as an autonomous company free from government interferences in its governance system. Moreover, various initiatives undertaken so far are limited to urban inhabitants. In rural villages, there is neither improvement in the electricity infrastructure nor an increase in the frequency of electricity supply. The benefits of electricity reform did not accrue to rural Manipur, especially the hill villages. As a matter of fact, the rural population in the state accounts for more than 70 per cent of the total population. Hence, the imperative of improving rural electricity infrastructure along with regular power supply augments a minimal justice to hill people/tribals. In reality, what the company does is install postpaid metres in rural villages following electricity reform without actually improving the transmission system and the old electric poles and wiring. The company is streamlining to install single metreing at the transformer for a whole village wherever the postpaid metres are not installed. To this end, the question arises as to who will pay the electricity bill if the metre is installed at the transformer? This approach could create a conflict amongst the villagers and escalate the existing chronic conflict in the state.

The widespread non-payment of electricity charges by consumers and 'neoliberal imperative for cost recovery' (Schnitzler, 2013) prepayment technology has become the default mode of connecting electricity to urban Manipur. With prepaid metres, the affordability of electricity becomes a question and hence the low-income households and rural inhabitants are excluded from new technology. If prepaid metreing is a means for cost recovery, then bypassing the metre becomes the antithesis and challenges the reform initiative. For instance, to have their prepaid metres bypassed, consumers indulged in hiring skilled labour to connect electricity to their households. This service is also extended by the contract employees hired by the company to earn a side income. It must be mentioned that MSPDCL hires skilled labour on a contract basis for installing and reading prepaid metres. Often their salaries or remunerations are not paid for months. An anonymous contract employee who is posted in a district headquarters enunciated that they at times help consumers bypass prepaid metres to earn money for their sustenance since the company does not pay their salary for months.[17] This resonates with the old mode of operation by the electricity department and the unethical practice, or what may be called the assembling ethics and the politics, of metreing. This raises an interesting question: Is it a reform in itself or merely prepaid metreing? The major change is rechristening the electricity department to MSPCL and hiring skilled contract labour for installing and reading prepaid metres.

(Un)harnessing untapped hydro resources

The persistent key issue confronting electricity in Manipur is the shortage of power. This stems from underdeveloped hydropower and failed governance, coupled with varied ethnic conflicts, contestation and chronic breakdown in law and order situations. Against this background, the GoM initiated hydropower generation as a thrust area of development to bridge the power supply and demand gap and sell surplus power since the state is rich in hydro resources. 'Manipur has identified hydropower potential of about 2190 MW' (GoM, 2012: 1). Hence the government started developing hydro projects for power generation. Yet these projects are enveloped with mis-governance, coupled with a long gestation period without meeting its objective. One such project was the Khuga Multipurpose Dam in Churachandpur. This project was commissioned in 1983 with an objective of generating 4.5 mW of electricity and providing the irrigation of 15,000 ha of land. The dam was completed and inaugurated by Smt. Sonia Gandhi[18] in 2010 – i.e. after 27 years of commissioning. Strangely, however, the dam neither generates electricity nor provides irrigation facilities. In contrast, it has submerged large agricultural lands and villages and displaced hundreds of tribes residing in the vicinity of the dam site. During an interaction with locals, it was revealed that since the inauguration of the dam, they have not seen a single unit of electricity being generated. The dam serves only as a picnic spot, fishing site and occasional tourist setting. And yet it is heavily guarded by the Indian Reserved Battalion (IRB) for reasons best known to the government.[19]

The Mapithel Dam in Phungyar, the Ukhrul District, is a case marked by land alienation, displacement and heavy militarisation. The dam was commissioned in 1980 against the wishes of local communities living in and around the affected areas. Despite a long battle and agitations by the affected villages and civil societies, the GoM went ahead with the proposed dam under heavy deployment of army, paramilitary and state armed forces. As pointed out by the affected people, there have been lapses even in rehabilitation and resettlement. The dam started filling up in 2015, which led to the displacement of villages and submerging of forests agricultural and grazing lands. The Mapithel Dam Affected Villagers Organisation, the Citizens Concern for Dams and Development and the Centre for Research and Advocacy, Manipur, observed,

> Manipur witnesses' series of mega dams commissioned in 1980s and 1990s which are either failed or seriously underperforming. The Khuga Dam, the Singda Dam, the Khoupum and the Loktak Project have all failed to fulfill its objectives. Indeed, some of the dams like Khoupum dam failed to provide irrigation and power. The Singda dam failed to generate a single unit of its intended 750 KW of power. Similar is the case with Khuga Dam, which failed to generate single unit of power, despite its component to generate 4.5 MW of power. The Government of Manipur instead pursued construction of more hydroelectric power projects under the controversial Manipur Hydro Power Policy, 2012. Of late, International Financial Institutions like the Asian Development Bank, the World Bank and the Japanese Bank for International Cooperation etc. are financing energy and allied infrastructure projects, and thus facilitating development injustice.[20]

As Chakravarti (2015) noted, the Mapithel Dam is to provide irrigation for 17,500 ha of land, generate 7.5 mW of electricity and supply 10 million gl of water per day for the state capital, Imphal, and valley districts. This echoes the political economy of dam development. In this case, tribals are the victims and the benefits of such development have accrued to the valley population at the cost of tribal lives, livelihoods and resources. This reality amplifies other parts of the country's development model where development and economic growth of a nation is seen as a necessary tool for tribal displacement and destruction. In yet another hydropower project enveloped with controversies is the case of the Tipaimukh Dam on the Barak River. This dam was commissioned in 1984 as a project for flood control and to generate 1,500 mW of electricity. However, the project is in the midst of controversy due to international river and water policies, ecological issues, morphological structures, displacement of locals and bilateral issues with neighbouring countries, amongst others.

Clouded with varied controversies, shortages of power and underperformance of the existing hydropower projects in the state, the GoM passed the Manipur Hydro Power Policy in 2012. This policy paved the way for private developers to harness the massive untapped hydro resources in the state. The GoM, under this policy, has identified six hydro projects with a total capacity to generate 516 mW and shortlisted ten private companies for development. Beside this, the GoM, at present, is engaged in developing

1,701 mW of electricity from four mega-hydropower projects: (1) Loktak Downstream Hydroelectric Project (90 mW), (2) Tipaimukh Hydroelectric Project (1,500 mW), (3) Irang Hydroelectric Project (60 mW) and (4) Tuivai Hydel Project (51 mW) (GoM, 2014). The protest against these hydropower projects in Manipur echoes the conceptual metaphor of what Guha and Martinez-Alier called 'environmentalism of the poor' (Guha and Martinez-Alier, 1997). Mega-hydropower projects and dams in Manipur, as elsewhere in the country, pose a threat to tribal intrinsic relationships with the natural environment and its resources – namely land, forests and minerals.

> Traditionally, these resources were either individually or collectively owned. The tribes at least had usufructuary rights over these. But because of the measure adopted by the state, there has been a steady erosion of the control over and use of these resources by the tribes.
>
> (Xaxa, 2008: 64)

Notes

1 I interacted with members of the village council and the village headman at Senapati on 24 September 2014.
2 Part of this section appears in *Economic and Political Weekly* as a letter. Vol. LI No. 13 (2016).
3 Retrieved from https://indianexpress.com/article/north-east-india/manipur/leisang-indias-last-electrified-village-narendra-modi-5165019/ (accessed on 31 October 2018).
4 Data pertaining to electricity is taken from Manipur Electricity Department's annual reports and a statistical handbook unless otherwise mentioned.
5 In a lean season, the generation of electricity reduces substantially due to the recession of the water level in the rain-fed reservoirs.
6 Excerpt from the personal interview with the ex-minister at his official quarters located in Imphal on 13 September 2014.
7 Excerpt from the personal interview with the director of the Department of Tribal Affairs and Hills, GoM, at his office located in Imphal on 18 July 2014.
8 Excerpt from the personal interview with Thomas (it is a pseudonym), the leader of UPF at Lamka on 12 May 2014.
9 Excerpt from the personal interaction with the Hiimai village youth on 15 June 2015.
10 Excerpt from the personal interview with Daile, a farmer in the Hiimai village on 2 June 2014.
11 Data from the GoM (2013).
12 The GoM corporatised the electricity department and began the prepaid metre system in the valley and hill districts' headquarters.
13 Excerpt from the personal interaction with Mrs. Louniiru (it is a pseudonym) at Senapati on 15 April 2015.
14 The GoI implemented RGGVY in 2005, which aims to provide electricity connection to all unconnected houses and provide free electricity to BPL households.
15 Extracted from the personal interaction with Mrs. Zuveiru (it is a pseudonym) at Hiimaiki on 2 May 2014.

16 Data accounting during this period was limited to Imphal where prepaid metres were first introduced.
17 Excerpt from a conversation with a contract employee of MSPDCL (who didn't want to be named due to possible repercussions on his job) on 15 July 2018.
18 Sonia Gandhi is the 48th Indian National Congress Party president.
19 Excerpt from a personal interview with Mr. John (it is a pseudonym and named changed on the request of the participant) at Lamka on 18 May 2014.
20 Retrieved from http://landislife.org/news/2015/2/20/baldvaz5zaw38u2vgf47maxhx-9cqpk (accessed 28 October 2015).

References

Chakravarti, S. 2015. *Dignity for the Displaced*. Retrieved from www.livemint.com/Opinion/DaD1SKQPZm3HD7GUDXDl3J/Dignity-for-the-displaced.html (accessed on 28 October 2015).

Government of India. 2004. *Ministry of Power Vide Letter No. 42/1/2001-D(RE) Dated 5th February 2004*. Retrieved from www.ddugjy.gov.in/portal/definition_electrified_village.jsp (accessed on 31 October 2018).

Government of Manipur. 2011. *Annual Administrative Report 2010–11*. Imphal: Department of Power.

Government of Manipur. 2012. *Manipur Hydro Power Policy 2012*. Secretariat: Power Department, p. 1. Retrieved from http://manireda.com/wp-content/uploads/2016/02/Hydro-Power-Policy.pdf (accessed on 7 November 2018).

Government of Manipur. 2013. *Annual Report*. Imphal: Department of Electricity.

Government of Manipur. 2014. *Annual Administrative Report 2013–14*. Imphal: Electricity Department.

Government of Manipur. 2014. *Annual Administrative Report*. Imphal: Department of Electricity.

Government of Manipur. 2015. *Economic Survey 2014–15*. Imphal: Directorate of Economics and Statistics.

Government of Manipur. 2017. *Statistical Handbook of Manipur 2017*. Imphal: Directorate of Economics and Statistics.

Guha, R. and Martinez-Alier, J. 1997. *Varieties of Environmentalism: Essays North and South*. London: Earthscan Publication.

Lenin, L. I. 1920. *Eight All-Russia Congress of Soviets Part II: Report on the Work of the Council of People's Commissars, December 22, 1920*. Retrieved from www.marxists.org/archive/lenin/works/1920/8thcong/ch02.htm (accessed on 3 October 2017).

Neog, A. K. 2009. 'Electrification in North-East India: An Economic Evaluation'. *Northern Region. Journal of North-East India Council for Social Science Research NEICSSR, Shillong*, 33 (2).

Richmond, J. and Patwardhhan, A. 2018. 'Universal Electricity Access: Can Cooperatives Strengthen Electric Connections?' *Economic and Political Weekly*, LIII (23): 12–15.

Schnitzler, von A. 2013. 'Travelling Technologies: Infrastructure, Ethical Regimes, and the Materiality of Politics in South Africa'. *Cultural Anthropology*, 28 (4): 670–693.

UNDP. 2007. *Human Development Report, 2007*. New York: UNDP.

World Bank. 2015. *Initial Environment Assessment Report for Manipur/IEAR/Tranche-1/2015. Power Grid Corporation of India Ltd.* Retrieved from www-wds.worldbank.org/external/default/WDSContentServer/WDSP/IB/2015/07/29/090224b083033bb1/1_0/Rendered/PDF/Initial0enviro0p0Tranche0100Manipur.pdf (accessed on November 2015).

Xaxa, V. 2008. *State, Society, and Tribes: Issues in Post-Colonial India*. New Delhi: Pearson.

6

SOCIAL AND POLITICAL PROCESSES OF INFRASTRUCTURE DEVELOPMENT

Infrastructure in the hill districts

This book accepts the limitations and boundaries set forth by its objective. One of these limitations is the inter-tribal infrastructure disparity. There are disparities in terms of accessibility, location, socio-economic status and populations within and amongst tribes in Manipur. However, it is beyond the framework of the present book to examine these dimensions. Moreover, there are more than 33 officially recognised tribes if one takes into account the sub-tribes. However, the hill-valley infrastructure divide, the marker of development and injustice, has been discussed in detail. Hence, in this section, I limit my analyses to variations and patterns in five hill districts that are predominantly inhabited by STs. Tribes in Manipur, as discussed in Chapter 3, can be broadly subsumed under two distinct categories: the Naga and the Zo (Kuki-Mizo-Zomi). Before delving into infrastructure disparity, I shall briefly highlight the socio-economic status of all the hill districts. This is presented in Table 6.1.

Tribal districts in Manipur stand out distinctly in terms of literacy rate. The literacy rate is above 70 per cent in the five tribal districts, unlike their counterpart tribal districts in other parts of the country. Amongst tribal districts, Churachandpur, with a literacy rate of 82.8 per cent, is above the national average of 74 per cent and the second-highest literate district in Manipur – i.e. next to the Imphal West District (86.1 per cent). Literacy rate is the only indicator where a hill district stands at par with those of the valley districts, and there is not much variation amongst the hill districts. In terms of sex ratio, besides the Chandel District with a sex ratio of 933, the other four hill districts are placed above the national average of 933 (see Table 6.1). Senapati is the least urban populated district with just 1.56 per cent of the total population. According to the 2011 census, there is no urban area, except Kangpokpi, which is listed as a census town. In contrast, Ukhrul's urban population is 14.78 per cent; this is followed by Tamenglong

Table 6.1 Socio-economic status of the hill districts

Name of the hill District	*Sex Ratio*	*Literacy rate*	*% of Urban population*	*Percentage of household availing/having assets*			
				Banking Services	*Landline Telephone connection*	*Mobile phone*	*Car/Jeep/Van*
Senapati	937	74.1	1.56	18.88	1.51	32.5	2.65
Ukhrul	943	81.4	14.78	16.13	1.15	31.4	3.09
Churachandpur	975	82.8	6.70	39.99	1.63	44.21	3.62
Tamenglong	943	70.1	13.77	10.50	0.70	22.01	2.02
Chandel	933	71.1	11.68	19.32	2.30	38.51	3.12

Source: Census 2011

with 13.77, Chandel with 11.68 and Churachandpur with 6.70 per cent, respectively. The average urban population of the hill districts stands at only 9.69 per cent. This partly explains the poverty of infrastructure in the hill districts.

Financial inclusion in terms of accessibility and availability of banking services is another crucial dimension of socio-economic development. The lack of credit/loan facilities for tribal populations reveals the extent of the financial exclusion. With a perpetual absence of rural cooperative bank or credit services, often, rural populations depend on money lenders (who charge exorbitant interest rates) to meet even emergency needs, such as paying hospital bills and children's schooling/college fees. Rural cooperative bank branches rarely operate in the hill districts and block headquarters from leaving villages. Of late, a few nationalised banks besides the State Bank of India have started operating at the district headquarters. Yet more than 70 per cent of the total households in the hill districts do not have access to banking services. Amongst the hill districts, with 39.9 per cent of households accessing banking services, Churachandpur stands at the top. This is followed by Chandel (19.32), Senapati (18.88), Ukhrul (16.13) and Tamenglong, the lowest with just 10.5 per cent (see Table 6.1). This data reveals an interesting trend – i.e. for those districts predominately inhabited by Naga tribes (Senapati, Chandel, Temenglong and Ukhrul), household access to banking services is consistently low. In contrast, the Churachandpur District, where Zos reside, has much higher household access to banking services. Availing banking services, such as credit/loan facilities (housing, personal, agriculture, entrepreneurship, etc.), depends on government approved/recognised/legal documents. For instance, any individual wanting to obtain a housing loan need to furnish land patta (proof of landownership) documents and guarantors. However, amongst Naga tribes, such documents are not available since their landownership pattern is determined by their traditional and customary laws. Hence they automatically become ineligible to obtain credit from banks.

Telephone connectivity, especially landline connection, is extremely low in all the hill districts. The average household with landline telephone connectivity is as low as 1.4 per cent. To illustrate, the Tamenglong District has merely 0.7 per cent of households with landline telephone connection. In a similar trend, households with assets such as a car/jeep/van are very low, with an average of only 2.9 per cent whereas more than 33 per cent of the total households have mobile phones. Yet there are different issues plaguing the use of mobile phones in the hill areas. One amongst them is the phenomenon of irregular electricity, as discussed in Chapter 5. Telecommunication exclusion of tribes in digital India is a serious concern. This stems from non-availability of communication infrastructure in the hill districts.

Within the hill districts, there are variations in terms of infrastructural availability and distribution leading to disparity. However, these variations do not differ significantly. The composite infrastructure index/score, as presented in Table 2.3, points in this direction. It unravelled major economic and social infrastructure (transport, energy, water supply, telecommunication, health, education and banking) availability. With a composite infrastructure score of 114, the Senapati District is the highest ranked amongst the hill districts in the state. This is followed by Ukhrul (83.80), Tamenglong (73.69), Churachandpur (73.13) and Chandel as the lowest ranked in the state with a score of 70.49 (see Table 2.3).

The Chandel District is consistently behind the other hill districts in all dimensions/indicators of infrastructure. The poverty of infrastructure in Chandel can be gauged and attributed to its demographic composition and geographical location. Chandel is an assemblage of diverse ethnic communities. It is predominantly inhabited by STs with some non-tribals being mostly merchants who are settled in the vicinity of Moreh, the only border trade centre in Manipur. Both Kuki and Naga claim the Chandel District as their ancestral land, resulting in conflict of varied kinds. It is interesting to note that tribes such as Aimol, Chote and Kom, due to their minuscule population size and contestations, oscillate between Kuki and Naga ethnic groups. Because of this oscillatory status, they are known as an intermediary tribe.

Geographically, Chandel shares a large part of the international boundary on the east with Myanmar. It is the gateway to the Southeast Asia where AH-1 on the Indian territory ends at the Chandel District and connects to Myanmar. The district is also a transit point for many insurgent groups operating in Manipur that smuggle arms and ammunition, as well as conduct other illicit trade, such as cocaine and heroin distribution. Major insurgent groups, be they Meitei, Naga, Kuki or Zomi, operate in this district. The higher the number of insurgent groups, the more siphoning of any development fund. The Chandel District is thus experiencing the phenomenon of high manipulation of development fund/projects. Moreover, it has only two constituencies representing at the state assembly. And their representatives rarely get any ministerial or cabinet berth in any government in Imphal. These are some of the factors that have been detrimental for infrastructure development in the Chandel District.

The dynamics of inter-tribe relations in the hill districts has bearing on infrastructure development and access to such benefits. 'There is no doubt that tribal societies have relatively more egalitarian in comparison to non-tribal societies, but they are not altogether free of inequality' (Xaxa, 2008: 73). Besides inequality, there is an inherent domination by larger tribes over smaller tribes with low populations. Amongst the three major ethnic groups in the hills, Naga, Kuki and Zomi, there is always a dominant tribe within these larger ethnic communities. Tangkhul dominance amongst the Nagas, Paite amongst the Zomis and Thadou Kuki amongst the Kukis. This is true even in the case of insurgents and tribal civil society leadership. However, the intensity of domination and dynamics varies in time and space. This can be gauged from the fact, for instance, that in the Ukhrul District, Tangkhuls are the majority and often the deciding factor in all key decision-making processes. But this is not the case in the Chandel or Senapati Districts since their populations are relatively smaller. Hence development projects are invariably influenced by the dominant tribe in each of the hill districts. This deepens and leverages the contestation amongst different tribes, leading to differential access to infrastructure facilities. In the process, those tribes that are numerically small are either sidelined or assimilated into larger tribes, as in the case of intermediary tribes that oscillate between different larger ethnic groups. It is pertinent to note Dzuvichu's (2010) theorisation in which he posited that 'access to space, both physical and metaphorical, as well as ideational and symbolic, are all about question of power, culture, location, and identity. Access is conceived, managed controlled, and contested in space' (: 2). Infrastructural disparity and accessibility amongst tribes in the hill districts varies and depends on the location of the dominant tribes.

It is true that tribal social reality and social structure do not allow easy infrastructure development due to varied contestations and domination. But on top of this, there is a pervasive structure – i.e. the politics of the dominant community and the state – that disallows the growth and rise of tribal territories, which may be called alternative centres. State-level politics in Manipur is characterised by a deep divide between tribes and non-tribes or between the plains people and the hills people. State-level politics is dominated by the non-tribes, who are numerically dominant and socially and economically powerful. Not only do they tend to dominate tribes but also the politics they follow tends to thwart and scuttle the functioning of traditional institutions and ADC by blocking grants and creating other impediments (Xaxa, 2008). Against this backdrop, I shall unearth the social and political processes and some key factors and hurdles associated with the poverty and the crumbling infrastructure in the hill districts.

Key stakeholders of infrastructure creation/development

I have classified key stakeholders into four broad categories: (1) international stakeholders, (2) national stakeholders, (3) state's stakeholders, and (4) key ethnic stakeholders. Amongst these, it is the state's stakeholder's modus operandi which has the most detrimental implication on infrastructure development in Manipur. The international stakeholders, such as World Bank and ADB, and national stakeholders, such as GoI, are the major funders for infrastructure development, whereas the GoM is the core state stakeholder responsible for executing and laying infrastructure. The following section analyses each of these stakeholders' roles and their linkages with one another.

International stakeholders

International stakeholders investing in Manipur's infrastructure development include the World Bank and the ADB. The World Bank provides funding to improve power transmission and sub-transmission in Manipur under its NER System Improvement Project, whereas the ADB is funding road infrastructure. It has listed six roads under its projects with an estimated cost of Rs. 1800 crore. They are

(1) NH-2 from Impha-Moreh (110 km);
(2) Imphal-Wangjing-Heirok-Khudengthabi (85 km) and greater Imphal ring road (34 km);
(3) Imphal-Kangchup, Tamenglong-Tousem and Haflong;
(4) NH-37 from Imphal-Jiribam (197 km);
(5) Imphal-Ukhrul (160 km); and
(6) Imphal-Moirang-Wangoo-Churachandpur-Behiang (120 km).[1]

These are a few of projects executed in recent times. International financial institutions thus play a critical role in providing resources to poor states like Manipur for developing physical infrastructure. However, the usual practice of manipulation and diversion of such projects for the interest of the dominant community always overshadows the process of proper planning and implementation. As noted in Chapter 5, the World Bank project for the improvement of transmission of power in Manipur is valley centric, as is the case of the ADB road infrastructure project. The alignment of these roads projects often bypasses the rural economy and people.

National stakeholders

The GoI and its ministry, such as MDoNER and agencies NEC and BRO, are the national stakeholders for infrastructure development in Manipur. The construction and maintenance of NHs are under the jurisdiction of the central government headed by the NHAI. The GoI is the single-largest stakeholder for infrastructure development not only in Manipur but also the country as a whole. The GoM, due to poor resources and small revenue share, heavily depends on the central government for any development projects/initiatives. All eight NHs and PMGSY roads in the state are fully funded by the GoI. Besides, MDoNER also supports funding for physical infrastructure development through the provision from the NLCPR, and NEC fully supports building inter-state roads, border roads and transport terminals. The BRO is the key partner in building highways in Manipur through its Border Road Task Force (BRTF). The central government, state government and BRO are intricately linked to each other. However, the actual construction of road infrastructure is carried out by BRO and state PWD.

State stakeholders

The state-level politics is manipulated by the state stakeholders. The forerunners of these includes (1) the GoM, (2) minister and MLAs, (3) contractors, (4) insurgent groups, (5) bureaucrats, (6) social elites, (7) civil societies and (8) key ethnic communities. These are the main players that shape infrastructure development in the state. The politics and dynamics of infrastructure build-outs revolves around these stakeholders. The state stakeholders operate in relation to two key factors: they are closely related to power dynamics within the state, and they are associated with the key ethnic stakeholders. It is the state stakeholders that actually implement and monitor all the development activities. Hence they are directly responsible for poverty and the crumbling physical and economic infrastructure. It is interesting to note the modus operandi and cordial nexus within this stakeholder. Before unfolding this unholy nexus, examination of each stakeholder's role and how each one operates in Manipur is merited.

The GoM

The GoM is the key authority in enacting laws related to transport infrastructure, electricity and the other 59 items on the state list of the Constitution of India. It is the responsibility of the government to look after the welfare of its citizens, fraternity, justice and empowerment, amongst others. In contrast, in Manipur, the citizens bear the brunt of frequent law and order issues, recurrent highway blockades, bandhs or economic blockades and quick formation of joint action committees over any issue plaguing their interests. The main source of power and domination stem from political representation and legitimise government actions. In the 60-member state legislative assembly, only 20 seats are reserved for tribes, while the remaining 40 seats are in the hands of the majority Meitei ethnic group. The political domination by the dominant community is one of the many factors leading to the disempowerment of tribes.

The cohesive and unilateral political stand of the dominant ethnic community's people's representative (though affiliated with different political parties) is evident in matters of Manipur's territorial integrity and the safeguarding of the interests of the dominant community. The Meitei legislators stand united in voicing their opposition to the extension of the Indo-Naga ceasefire without territorial limits, opposition to the extension of the Sixth Schedule to the hills of Manipur, support for uniform land laws or the extension of MLR&LR into the hill districts, support for ILP law and so on. This finds expression in various acts and resolutions passed in the legislative assembly.

In contrast, tribal MLAs/ministers due to internal power struggles are often influenced by the dominant representative. Hence the constitutional power conferred upon them in Article 371 (C) of the Constitution of India is toyed around with and often thwarted by the dominant ethnic community. Thomas (it is a pseudonym), a social activist, posited,

> Hill Areas Committee (HAC)[2] cannot assert their rights even though it has a constitutional power and the chairman of the committee enjoys the status of a deputy CM. Rather it has always been manipulated by the ruling party in the state. This has continued for the past three decades.[3]

Tiankhan made a similar observation that HAC seems to very good for tribes in Manipur but only in theory. In practice, the HAC is merely a puppet in the hands of the council of ministers in the state. Moreover, the committee was supposed to be very powerful could not function effectively, as it did not have any financial power (as cited in Guite, 1999). The protective measure for tribes in Manipur offers some power over non-tribes, particularly in relation to their land, by imposing restrictions on the power of non-tribes. However, they were given this right without any corresponding power to enforce it (Xaxa, 2008). According to Leo (Naga human rights activist),

> The rivalry among tribal MLAs and Ministers led to underdevelopment of infrastructure in the hills. Once they are elected, they become the puppet of the dominant Meiteis and act against the interest of the larger tribal society in the state.[4]

Lorho offered a different perspective from his lived experience as a former legislator and minister. According to him, tribals in Manipur know very well that they are the minority in the assembly. If they did not assert their rights, nothing would work out. It is not a question of majority versus minority but the assertion of rights that prevails. He reiterated that tribal MLAs and ministers are just busy begging rather than voicing their rights in the assembly.[5]

Urbanisation in Manipur unlike other parts of the country is not the by-product of industrialisation. With virtually no medium- or large-scale industries in the state, the process of infrastructure development became the sole responsibility of the government. This was aimed at creating infrastructure rather than as part of the organic process. This is even more so in the hill districts where infrastructure was created in the vicinity of the district headquarters to meet the basic needs of government offices. When the government put the interests of the dominant community at the forefront, this resulted in the crumbling of the infrastructure in hills. This is one of the major structural constraints for poverty of infrastructure in the tribal areas of Manipur.

Ministers/MLAs

In a parliamentary government, it is the people's representative who forms the government. Hence, they take decisions pertaining to when, where and for whom infrastructure will be built in the state of Manipur. Amongst MLAs, those in the ruling party have an edge over others, more so the cabinet council members, political elites and heads of government departments, who are assigned ministerial berth. They are part of the policy and decision-making body of the government. No doubt in the Manipur government there are tribal ministers within the council of ministers. However, when one critically analyses their portfolios and the departments assigned to them by the CM, often they are not given any significant or crucial departments. This can be gauged from the fact that, for instance, during the Ibobi-led congress party (2002–2017), all the important portfolios, such as PWD, revenue, finance, home, law and legislative affairs, were in the hands of Meitei legislators. Tribal ministers were assigned portfolios, such as tribal development, information and public relations, tourism, statistics and veterinary and animal husbandry, amongst others. Similarly, in the N. Biren-led coalition government (2017–), the portfolios of printing and stationary, agriculture, veterinary and animal husbandry, social welfare, tribal and hill affairs and youth affairs and sports are with tribal legislators, whereas crucial portfolios, such as PWD, power, rural development, finance, home and revenue are with dominant ethnic community. Ministers have significant power to influence any major decision making in the state. The internal imbalance of power within the council of ministers/cabinets can jeopardise major decisions pertaining to infrastructure creation in the hills. Hence the role of ministers and which ethnic community he/she represents is an important marker in Manipur.

It is interesting to examine the background of elected representatives or MLAs in Manipur. They can be broadly located in three categories: (1) those who come from contractor backgrounds, (2) those having close and direct links with insurgent groups and (3) those from the elite section of the society, usually with direct linkage and access to political elites and seats of governance. Their linkage to other stakeholders in the state, as unfolded by G. K.

Pillai (former home secretary, GoI), reveals the gravity of connivance and the clandestine nature of the nexus embedded in the system of operation. In the words of G. K. Pillai (2012),

> If you have the DGP of police, his very close relative is heading one underground group. You have the Chief Minister; CM brother-in-law will be in the underground group. There is a minister; his nephew or cousin is an important functionary in Meitei underground groups. It is that close, there is no difference between the government and underground because I still believe that they all are there to finally protect Manipur's territorial integrity.[6]

This echoes the background of those MLAs/ministers who have a close or direct linkage with insurgent groups in Manipur. Gaikhangam (former deputy CM), on the other hand, ably demonstrated those MLAs from contractor backgrounds during the by-election campaign in 2015. He said,

> The by-election has been necessitated because the two MLAs who were elected for five years terms could not walk the path of a people's representative. This is a tragedy resulting out of electing men who grew up as contractors and who are novices in politics.[7]

This category of ministers/MLAs have a direct connection with contractors in the state and invariably influence the decisions pertaining to awarding contract works. At the other end are those MLAs/ministers from elite backgrounds who own and control a large amount of land who are economically powerful and politically influential in society.

Contractors

The role of contractors is paramount in the construction of infrastructure. The dimension of temporality, quality and elasticity of any infrastructure, such as road construction, repair/maintenance and public buildings, amongst others, depend on the contractors. They execute the work orders after winning the tender. In Manipur, there are two types of contractors/firms who are registered with government departments (PWD, electricity department, etc.): the class-I contractor/firms (popularly called special contractor in local terminology) and general contractors/firms. The modus operandi of contract/tender bidding in Manipur evokes an interesting reality. Often contractors/firms that win tenders and secure work orders are either closely associated with the concerned minister or they have a close linkage with insurgent groups, or at the very least, they have a recommendation letter from the insurgent group. The nexus between contractor-minister-insurgent group is an open secret in a state like Manipur. This resonates with Michal Taussig's

(1999) concept of the 'public secret': those things that are generally known but not openly spoken about. In many cases, the process of bidding tender is just to fulfil the formalities, as the contractor is already pre-selected. Contractors/firms with limited assets (capital, manpower, tools, plants, etc.) have a higher chance of winning contract work if they have close associations with ministers or insurgent groups over qualified contractors/firms. The gravity of the nexus and nepotism in awarding contract work can be gauged from the fact that some work orders are either purchased or assigned to close associates of ministers even before the tendering process. It is worth quoting in verbatim the contractor's narratives.

> I recently purchased a work order of Rs. 1 crore by paying Rs. 5 lakh to the concerned minister. The minister assured me of the contract work and also agreed to pay me 50% of the total bill in advance, so that the process of bidding for the tender would be a mere formality. But in order to begin working, I have to take a recommendation letter from the insurgent group operating in the project area, to whom I paid 5 per cent of the total budget. Thus, much before the work begins, I have already spent Rs.10 lakh. It is also mandatory that the GoM take 11.75 per cent of the project's total budget. When the project started, the Public Works Department official again took 10 per cent. So in total, 31.75 per cent of the total budget is gone and am left with only Rs. 68.25 lakh. When the project begins, I have to pay the contractor dealing assistance (CDA) since he is the most important person as he maintains each and every file of the contractor. Since the billing is done at Imphal and the PWD is in Imphal, I have to again pay insurgent groups operating in the valley and normally we have a round table negotiation with these groups in a closed- door meeting. Again, to sanction bills, the cashier has to be given certain amount or else he creates lots of problem. During every visit by PWD staff for work inspection, I have to pay them to approve the work. Since all the raw materials are transported from outside the state, every load of goods has to pay taxes to both police departments at checkpoints as well as to insurgent groups. I am left with barely 50 per cent of the total budget so ultimately, the work quality gets compromised.[8]

The narrative points to a layer of corruption and the deep nexus of various agencies in the state. This vicious cycle perpetuated by the multi-stakeholders gets legitimatised in the realm of operation. Whoever disturbs this nexus is excluded or sidelined from the process. The rent-seeking behaviour, nepotism, favouritism and nexus, amongst others, are not new to Manipur, as elsewhere in the country. However, the uniqueness stemming from the state is the existence of multi-contractors and contractors within contractors or sub-contractors.[9] As pointed out, a well-established contractor (mostly valley inhabitants) who has a direct access to ministers and a good network with insurgent leaders often gets contract work. A valley-based contractor/firm often wins contract work, including contracts to be implemented in the hill district. Since the principal contractor is not from the hills and is unfamiliar with the local politics and dynamics of tribal insurgent groups, he/she leases out the contract to local sub-contractors. This greatly affects the work quality and, hence, the temporality of infrastructure is a recurring phenomenon.

Insurgents/militants

What distinguished Manipur from the rest of the northeastern states is the number of insurgent groups operating in the state in addition to highly polarised ethnicity. In fact, Manipur has the highest number of insurgent groups in India with more than 30 active groups. The major source of revenue for any insurgent group in the state is collecting illegal taxes and from government servants, departments, contractors, donation from ministers/MLAs and any development projects, be it NH construction, airport construction, electrification work or railway project, amongst others. The ramification of such subversion and diversion of development funds echoes the poor infrastructure and suspension of work. As Oliver pointed out, 'No contractor/firm can escape from the tax imposed by insurgent groups operating in the area'.[10] This was enunciated when a high-ranking leader of an insurgent group admitted to deducting a percentage of the total cost of a project being implemented in the group's geographical area of operation.[11] All the government officials with whom the present researcher interviewed during fieldwork pointed to insurgent groups for the poor quality of work due to blatant imposition of illegal taxes and kidnapping of contractors and labourers. For instance, a PWD engineer posited, 'Insurgency in Manipur affect the progress and quality of road construction and repairing'.[12] Disparately, the chief engineer of MSRRD attributed the slow pace of rural road construction to law and order problems plaguing Manipur state.[13] However, in a critical analysis of other stakeholders – i.e. ministers, bureaucrats and contractors – siphoning off development funds, it was found that their roles were no less detrimental than those of insurgent groups. Concomitantly, they all are part of or responsible for the poverty of infrastructure. Yet taking advantage of frequent law and order problems and insurgency, the government and other stakeholders conveniently blame insurgents for poor infrastructure. Insurgency, no doubt, is a serious threat to law and order and a challenge to the nation-state. Likewise, the militarisation in the form of counter-insurgency operations and enforcement of draconian law (AFSPA) hampers the development process in the state. Hence the imperative to explore beyond insurgency for laying basic infrastructure.

Bureaucrats

The cycle of the nexus is incomplete without bureaucrats. They are part of the policy and key agents of the government who oversee the implementation of development projects and the mediators between citizens and the government. As Sharma and Gupta noted, the direct contact for the majority of people with the state is with the local-level bureaucrats, such as block development officers, schoolteachers and staff members at civil hospitals, amongst others (Sharma and Gupta, 2006). Echoing the Weberian perspective, bureaucrats are indispensable to the functioning of the state and more so in a chronic conflict-ridden state like Manipur. However, in contrast to what Weber characterised as the rigid division of labour being one feature of bureaucracy in the western world, in Manipur, one can observe the rigid division of corruption. Bureaucrats, irrespective of their seniority and hierarchy within the structure of governance, make a conscious effort to establish links with elected members (ministers and MLAs). Often, IAS cadres posted in the northeast and other conflict areas are perceived as being assigned to punishment postings. Likewise, those middle-level bureaucrats posted in the hill districts of Manipur are also seen as being assigned to punishment postings. Hence they make a conscious effort to network with ministers to transfer them to valley districts. They work and function in close proximity with ministers and MLAs. Local-level bureaucrats often act as the agents of the elected representatives for their constituencies. Due to their direct access to the power centre – i.e. ministers and MLAs at Imphal – their irregularity at the place of posting and corruption at the grassroots get legitimised and protected.

Elites

In every society, be it caste or non-caste, the emergence of social elites is inevitable. Amongst the tribal societies in Manipur, be it Poumai or Tangkhul, Kuki or Paite, social differentiation has begun to emerge. Yet this differentiation is not based on the pervasive features of the caste system. Xaxa (2008) posited,

> Such social differentiation is rooted in forces outside of tribal societies, such as introduction of private property in land, growth of trade and the emergence of market, emigration of non-tribes in search of land and employment, spread of modern education, opening up of new occupations, state-sponsored programmes, and similar activities. Accordingly, social differentiation has moved along different lines.
> (:119–120)

Social differentiation amongst tribes is based on occupation, income, ownership of property, age, gender, clan and lineage, amongst others. One way to conceptualise elites amongst tribes could be in regard to social differentiation based on socio-economic and political privileges and power relations. At the top of this differentiation are minority sections of tribals who took advantage of the forces unleashed by market- and state-sponsored programmes. Hence they became very influential politically, socially and economically. They may be called elites amongst tribes. They occupy the highest social strata and are influential in any decision making in their societies. Ovung (2012) observed amongst the Naga society that 'the whole problem of distribution of power, prestige, and privileges has been operated through different elite group such as social, religious, political, business, intellectual, professional, and bureaucratic elites' (:1). Elites amongst tribes include clan leaders, chiefs and headmen, businessmen, government servants, contractors and politicians, amongst others. Often, political parties identify elites in a society as a points of contact to leverage their political agendas. In return, they get petty contract work and government schemes and some go on to become personal assistants to ministers and MLAs. Their role in local area development for basic infrastructure is crucial since they have direct access to powerhouses and seats of governance. In the words of Thang (it is a pseudonym),

> The role of these elites in the process of development is very crucial. During election, they support the potential candidates who are likely to win the election. Once their candidates are elected they become equally powerful since they now have a direct access to Minister/MLAs. They move around in government offices with the blank letterheads of Minister and access everywhere. All officers can't do anything since they have Minister letterhead and government servants are to do what is written in the letterhead brought by elites to their offices. Superior officer cannot take any action since they are well connected to the Minister. These elites are the most dangerous group which one simply cannot mess with them.[14]

He called these elites the *native intelligent* due to their knowledge of various government schemes and contracts (both existing and forthcoming) in various government departments. In addition, they are well connected with local-level politics and the dynamics of different villages, which they pass on to ministers and MLAs to further their political careers. Bribing and negotiating with insurgent groups, as well as influencing voters during elections, are the tactics carried out by these elites.

Civil society

Civil societies are formed and organised on the basis of ethnicity. The number of civil societies is also in proportion to, or even surpasses, the number of ethnic communities. Each tribe in the state has its own civil society with the tribe's name prefix; for instance, amongst the Poumai Naga tribe, they are called Poumai Naga Union and Poumai students are organised as Poumai Naga Tsiidoumai Me. Likewise, Poumai Naga tribe women have their own body called Poumai Naotoumai Me. Amongst the Naga tribes in Manipur, the UNC is the apex body. Likewise, Kuki Inpi and Zomi Councils are the apex civil society for Kuki and nine frontal tribes. Amongst the Meiteis, there are three frontal civil societies: (1) the All Manipur United Clubs' Organisation (AMUCO), (2) the UCM and (3) the Committee on Civil Societies (CCSK).

Invariably, these apex civil societies' organisation's stand opposed to each other's political articulations and deepen their contestations, often igniting ethnic tensions, anxieties and insecurities. There are many instances of contestations which are antipathetic to each other. To illustrate, the UNC political assertion for an AA of Nagas in Manipur is opposed by UCM, AMUCO and CCSK. Similarly, UNC, the Kuki Inpi and Zomi Councils stand opposed to uniform land laws and the implementation of ILP, as demanded by UCM, AMUCO and CCSK (Meitei-based civil societies). Competing interests amongst these apex civil societies based on ethnic lines often cause major unrest in the state. They resort to varied modes of protests, bandhs, economic blockades, rallies, political mobilisation and so on. They are the biggest pressure groups in Manipur and at the forefront of political articulation of their respective ethnic communities.

Key ethnic stakeholders

There is a thin line between civil societies and ethnic communities in Manipur in terms of its objectives and political goals. It is the ethnic communities which give rise to the formation of civil societies in the state of Manipur. Ethnicity is part of the state-level politics that shape infrastructure and development discourse. The dominant ethnic community invariably influences the planning and location of infrastructural sites. Major ethnic stakeholders include (1) Meitei: Meitei and Meitei Pangan; (2) Naga: Poumai, Mao, Tangkhul, Rongmei, Anal, Maram and Thangal, amongst others; and (3) Zo: Kuki, Mizo, Gangte, Paite, Simte, Hmar, Vaiphei, Zou, Shuhte, Ralte and so on. Meiteis are the key players amongst varied ethnic communities. They dominate development, along with public discourse. This stemmed from an imbalance of the power structure, coupled with the advantage of numerically large, economically and politically powerful seats of governance. The roots of social exclusion and denial of agency, especially to tribes, can be located within this framework. This part of the discontentment and shared antagonism of tribes towards the dominant ethnic community and the state. The varied political assertions, anxieties and insecurities apparent in the faces of the ethnic minority or hill people in the state of Manipur are accentuated in the denial of justice, poverty and crumbling infrastructure and valley-centric development, amongst others. It is interesting to note that correlation between ethnicity and infrastructure. Wherever the dominant ethnic community reside, infrastructures are far more developed as compared to the places inhabited by ethnic minorities – i.e. hill districts. The relationship of dominant ethnic stakeholders with state stakeholders in infrastructure development is cordial in nature. In short, the relationship of major state stakeholders can be diagrammatically represented in Figure 6.1.

The connivance and clandestine nature of the nexus amongst these stakeholders – namely, ministers-insurgents-contractors-bureaucrats-elites (see Figure 6.1) – is deeply embedded in the structure while operationalising infrastructure development projects. In the order of hierarchy and power, ministers occupy the top layer. They are directly connected to all the other stakeholders and responsible for awarding contract work. Contractors, irrespective of their credibility, can purchase contract work if they have a good network and internal connection with the ministers and insurgent groups. There are cases wherein contractors come with a recommendation letter from the insurgent groups to pressurise the state authority to award certain contract work to them. In return, insurgent groups get a certain percentage of the total project cost when contractors get the contract work. Local elites work closely with minsters/MLAs, and often they act as gatekeepers for contractors to get access to the ministers and even insurgent groups. Commenting on the nefarious cycle of connivance between various stakeholders, Haokip (2012) observed,

> The nexus between the politicians and the militants is sometimes conscious and voluntary, while at some other times forced and imposed for the sake of safety and security of the former. Sometimes the

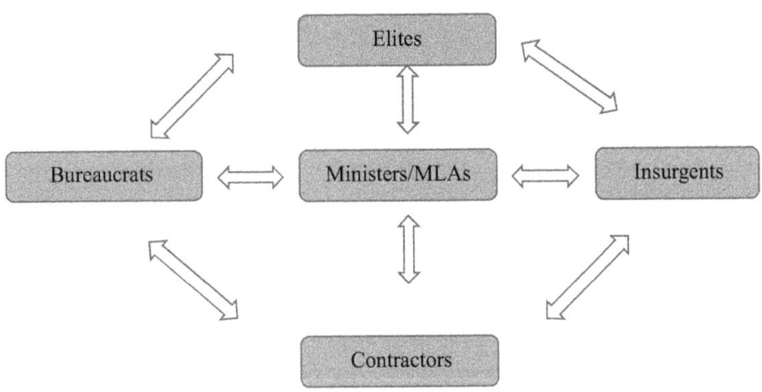

Figure 6.1 Vicious cycle of state stakeholder relationships

Source: Author

> bureaucracy has to serve the interest of the militants by extending government benefits either to them or to the people identified by them. (:226)

Political condition and political negotiation

Political instability is one of the many impediments of infrastructure development. It is closely related to insurgency, law and order problems, ethnic conflicts, political assertions, etc. The frequent blockades, bandhs, protests and law and order issues, amongst others, delay the completion of infrastructure projects, and in some case, they are suspended indefinitely without due dates. The cordial relationship between civil societies and insurgent groups is best encapsulated during economic blockades or bandhs. For instance, when Naga civil society called for economic blockades on all NHs passing through Manipur state, the Naga insurgent group extend its support. Likewise, when Kuki- or Zomi- or Meitee-based civil societies called for bandhs or blockades, their respective insurgent groups extended their due support. Often, the justification or rationale for endorsing such a radical approach by civil societies is that the state only responds to or listen when it directly affects them and calls for negotiation. Besides the political implication of such blockades, these activities come with a heavy price for the state exchequer and the public. The price of all essential commodities skyrocket during blockades. The political economic impact of a blockade or bandh involves the steep rise in the underground economy or black market. Hence it is the common citizen who bears the brunt of a blockade, both in terms of losing a day's wage and paying heavy prices for commodities. This escalates when blockades and counter-blockades continue for more than a month, as these cases are not new in Manipur.

The unequal power relations between various ethnic communities, more so the polarisation of hill-valley divides as manifested in socio-politico-economic spheres, deepened the already stale relationship between the state and tribes vis-à-vis tribes and non-tribes. Demographic domination enveloped with power politics led to the process of ethnic domination by the majority over the ethnic minority. Shimray (2004) postulated that the politics of ethnic power hegemony tends to induce assimilation. The ramification of the pan-Manipuri identity or the totalising project as envisaged and moved by the dominant community was not received well and vehemently opposed by tribes in the state. Hence, to counter the totalising project, tribes have been articulating their own political paths, as discussed in Chapter 3, led by three tribal stalwart organisations – i.e. UNC, KNO and UPF, respectively. The state prioritising the dominant ethnic community's interests and patronising the tribes has created considerable hostility between the tribes and the state on the one hand and between tribals and non-tribals on the other hand. A series of unproductive negotiations between the state and tribal civil society organisations have become the hallmark in Manipur whenever the latter groups resort to a radical form of protest. Hence a good amount of government energy has also been spent on political negotiations of varied kinds. This has bearing on infrastructure development. The parallel forms of civil administration, one by the GoM and the other by insurgent groups, have placed common citizens in a perpetual state of insecurity and anxiety. As Haokip (2012) noted,

> It is an undeniable truth that the government's authority and legitimacy has been eroded to such an extent that the militants have acquired the courage to literally run parallel governments in Manipur as elsewhere in other states of North-East India.
>
> (:226)

Corruption: context and sector

Value-loaded concepts, such as corruption and good or bad governance, have become buzzwords in development discourse. The terminology has been used indiscriminately by politicians and pedestrians. However, it is plausible in reference to unfair means of practice, bribing, extortion, diversion and subversion of funds, nepotism, nefarious and unholy nexus in the context of Manipur. Corruption as Harvey and Knox contextualised in public works 'is a disruptive or shattering force, and one that, in social terms, work against a sense of healthy integrity' (Harvey and Knox, 2015). Echoing this perspective, every layer of government, from the traffic police to the top bureaucrats and elected members, is involved in one form or another of corruption. Corruption is deeply imbedded in the system of governance and its administration. A traffic officer on duty take bribes from daily wage labourers, such as rickshaw pullers and vegetable vendors, operating on the side of the road and allows them to do their daily business. Ministers sell contract work to contractors prior to the tender process. Insurgents or militants and government department officials deduct an agreed upon percentage from development project funds. These are only a few instances of corruption.

Corruption in the form of injustice to the ethnic minority disparately stems from budgetary outlays prepared by different government departments. In the context of physical infrastructure development, the PWD, MSRRD and the electricity department are the main players. For instance, the PWD prepares a separate annual budget for the hill and valley districts. The annual PWD budget for the year 2011–12 was Rs. 68,587.96 lakh, out of which a sum of Rs. 27,540.25 lakh (40 per cent) was earmarked for the hills, whereas Rs. 41,047.71 lakh (60 per cent) was designated for the valley districts. Similarly, a sum of Rs. 21,564.81 lakh (35 per cent) was earmarked for the hill districts and Rs. 39,561.36 lakh (65 per cent) for the valley districts during 2013–14 (GoM, 2014). Taking into consideration the total geographical areas, road density, total unsurfaced roads and persistent impassable roads in the hills, the total budgetary allocation should ideally be greater for the hills than the valley. But this has not been the case since historical times to the present. The valley-centric budgetary allocation or, in other words, the budgetary injustice meted out to the hills can further be gauged from the fact that, for instance, the joint secretary of the Department of Tribal Affairs and Hills, GoM, pointed out that '60 per cent of the funds meant for tribals in hill districts are spent in Imphal i.e. the state capital'.[15] Strangely, funds meant for tribal development are spent in non-tribal areas – i.e. in the valley. This points to the case of fund diversion and subversion, and hence, the hills remain further deprived due to non-percolation of development.

Horam (2000) pointed out that merely 27 per cent of the state total annual budget outlay goes to tribal areas. Supposedly, keeping in mind the density of the population, 73 per cent of the annual state budget outlay is spent entirely on the valley people who live in and around 10 sq mi. This is another form of corruption within the structure of governance and what I call injustice embedded in infrastructure planning and development. The valley-centric budgetary allocation can be attributed to the composition of employees of various departments. In PWD, the chief engineer to the clerks are dominated by the Meitei-ethnic community; there are hardly any tribal employees at the managerial level. During my fieldwork and thereafter, I found some cases where the PWD and other offices located in the hill districts are operated from the officer's residence at Imphal.[16]

Corruption: systemic loopholes

The corruption that takes place in the infrastructure sector or in any other sector is mainly due to systemic loopholes and unethical practices. Corruption is so deeply rooted that any honest endeavour ends up being excluded and sidelined in the process. Unravelling when and where corruption starts and ends is methodologically challenging since the vicious cycle of corruption flows continuously uninterrupted. Nevertheless, one can take any aspect as a starting point. However, one will soon realise how deep the structure of corruption is and how stakeholders get intricately linked into that structure. To illustrate, in many villages, exercise of adult franchise on the day of voting is just a mere formality, as the votes are already bought prior to election. As pointed out earlier, whoever has an economic advantage and the backing of insurgent groups normally wins the election regardless of the opponent's political credibility.

To win over the insurgent groups and get their support is, again, a complicated process and involves good networking. Amongst the insurgent groups, there is a dimension of hierarchy and geo-specific area of operation. For instance, if any candidate from the Senapati and Ukhrul Districts wants to contest those constituencies and tries to build a network with insurgent groups, it will be futile to link up with Meitei-based insurgent groups since Naga-based ethnic insurgents are very active in these constituencies, and they literally control their respective zones of operation. Likewise, it will be pointless for candidates from the Churachandpur District to attempt to build a network and get the support of Naga- or Meitei-based insurgent groups, as Kuki and Zomi ethnic-based insurgents operate actively, and they are often the deciding factors. Fulfilling the demands of insurgent groups and getting their support involves a lot of cash transactions on the part of the intending candidates. Often, the most productive form of election campaigning is cash in hand to insurgent groups. As opined by Thomas (it is a pseudonym), who is about 54 years of age and an ordinary voter from a remote village, 'I accepted some cash from the candidate since that would be the last time I will ever see him again after election and that's the only benefit I can get from him'.[17] Voters developed this perception because time and again, elected representatives make so many promises but rarely fulfil any of them after being elected. It is, again, extremely difficult for ordinary citizens to meet their ministers or MLAs to voice their concerns since their offices and residences are located in Imphal, and they hardly pay visits to the villages once elected.

It is interesting to note the voting behaviour on the day of election in villages. Either all the members of a village decide to cast their votes for a particular candidate or they are forced to vote for certain candidates by militants stationed at the respective booths. If a particular insurgent group decides to support candidate 'A', then they will deploy cadets to various polling booths to coerce and manipulate voters. There have been cases of kidnapping voters (ring leader of opposition party), booth capturing, proxy voting and threatening pooling officials, amongst others, by militants to favour their candidate or those candidates who have the so-called *blessing of the insurgent group*. The cycle of the nefarious nexus does not stop on the day of voting. The more intricate system of operation and nexus begins after a candidate has been elected and becomes a minister, for example. There is pressure from insurgents who supported him/her, as well as the desire to recover money which he/she spent during the election period. In order to repay the money borrowed from businessmen, contractors, social elites, etc., along with interest, he/she becomes involved in illicit transactions. This is often done by siphoning off development projects and MLA local areas development funds, taking bribes for awarding government schemes and contracts and accepting backdoor appointments of services. Hence the elected representative does not find time to work for the welfare of his/her constituency's needs. The nexus between politicians and insurgents as discussed earlier is obvious, and many cash transaction from the former to the latter have been reported. For instance, former CM Mr. Rishang was reported to have paid a sum of Rs. 3 million to the undivided NSCN and supplied uniforms to NSCN-IM. Mr. Phungzathang (former health minister) from the Churachandpur District provided two vehicles and a sum of Rs. 2.6 lakhs to ZRA. In 2005, Ibobi Singh (former CM) was accused of paying Rs. 10 million to PLA and Rs. 5 million to KYKL. The accusations were denied by both sides. However, KYKL admitted to having received financial help from politicians (Routray, 2007 as cited in Singh, 2011).

Dynamics and processes of contracting work

Manipulation of paperwork in awarding contracts is not new in Manipur or elsewhere in the country. The blatant manipulation and nexus of different stakeholders in building infrastructure projects continues unabated. Hence the output of such a system of operation is seen in pitiable highways and dusty and bumpy roads. The clandestine nature of awarding a contract at the tendering process and at the stage of implementation is a serious concern. This process is perpetuated by different stakeholders and legitimised by the state. The phenomenon of sub-contracting, or contractor within contractor, continues with different permutations and combinations. Often, it is the tribal contractors who constitute the sub-contractors since they don't have the negotiation power and stipulated assets to win the official tender. One of my respondents pointed out, 'Contractors from hills are just like bus conductor, who are busy collecting bus fare and negotiating with different passenger, but the real driver sits and direct from the front'.[18] The modus operandi of awarding contracts, as narrated by G. K. Pillai (former home secretary, GoI), makes for interesting reading and notes the gravity of the situation in Manipur:

> A contractor comes to the minister and the minister says its 10 crore work. You pay me 2 crore. So, he pays him two crore. Once the 2 crore is paid then the minister writes, please sanction this road work from here to here at the cost of ten crore. Send it to the PWD secretary of Manipur. Who open the files, sends it to the finance, who clears it because that's the Minister's order. And the money is given and write 50 per cent advance and 5 crore may be released. So, by evening the contractor who has paid 2 crore already got 5 crore. Then the work is sent to concerned person in the field and that's the time when PWD engineer comes to know that such road work has been sanctioned. Then, he starts preparing an estimate and the contractor also gives him some money, so he makes an estimate and then two weeks later, he will certify saying that 50 per cent of the road work has been completed and gives utilisation certificate. The concerned contractor come back to Imphal and take next 5 crore. This happen and who's monitoring this? Is CAG monitoring any of this? Thousand and thousands of crore worth of mis-utilisation and nobody bothers. I remember Mr. X,[19] came to me and they wanted

> a work for about 12 crore, saying that from this areas to this area it covers so many tribal villages which have not connectivity etc. And I was so satisfied, I said actually let's sanction this work and sent it to NEC. And promptly I got a reply from NEC in two weeks saying Sir, but this road was already sanctioned and it was completed in 1992 with Rs. 4 crore budget being sanctioned. Then nothing on the ground happen. And there I can tell you the contractor who built that 1992 road was actually the PWD Minister of Manipur subsequently who came with the work. I meant that's the system. It's going to take time. . . . It's a tough battle, but it has to be done and only when the local community get involved in such project.[20]

This narrative points to the deeply embedded nexus of different stakeholders in building infrastructure and how the very system, which otherwise is there to strengthen the community, becomes a part of the clandestine nature of the operation. Singh estimated that more than 45–50 per cent of a development project or public work is being siphoned off by state and non-state actors involved in rent-seeking behaviour (Singh, 2011). Thumra (2000) opined that too often in Manipur, there is an unholy trinity that consists of politicians-bureaucrats-businessmen/contractors. Despite many developmental schemes, the benefits are not percolating to the masses because of the corruption that is prevalent at all levels. Apart from the unholy trinity, as observed by Thumra, there is also the nexus between other stakeholders who are equally responsible for the poverty and the crumbling infrastructure. A nexus of one kind or another has become the hallmark of infrastructure development in Manipur.

Internal needs and demands: change in agenda

Various contestations, ethnic conflict, historical processes of political negotiations and corruption have led to a change in the internal needs and demands of the locals. As corruption becomes legitimised and the flow of money from illegitimate sources into the hands of elites increases, society also changes. The monetary economy has taken over the subsistence agrarian economy. What was once people's want has now become their need. Money plays multiple roles as an agent of transformation in landownership. Power and status attached to land was affected by money factors (Shimray, 2009).

The waves of the monetary economy, along with market forces and corruption, have altered the perception of locals on the very notion of development. This change is best encapsulated on the conception of development between the rich and the poor. It is an undeniable fact that in any society, the poor are numerically large. Development for the rich means an increase in private income, material accumulation and high living standards, amongst others. Development is thus conceived as a materialistic term, and it can be argued that development is not taking place. For the elites, the indigenous system of governance, tradition, customary laws, etc., is seen as the hurdle for development. In contrast, development for the poor means collectivity where community comes first, and decisions are made collectively for/on what is best for their society. Yet their voices are superseded by the rich and sidelined from decision making. The primacy change in the development agenda is now based on social differentiation and stratification rather than collective growth where every individual has a say in village development.

The state is well aware of the hill-valley divide in all spheres of development and the widening gap between the rich and the poor. Yet the state and its agents are consciously looking for the elites in a society to penetrate their agenda and maintain status quo. A case in point is awarding contract and government schemes by ministers and MLAs in their constituencies. Invariably, it is the influential and the rich who get such work orders and schemes since they are considered the ring leaders in their respective villages and constituencies. The poor are wrestling and trapped between the state notion of development on the one hand and the elites' conception of development and their agenda on the other hand. The state developmental processes have brought about changes in both village morphological structure and the social system. The morphological changes can be seen in the construction of unfinished village approach roads, non-functional electrification and water supply. Also improved communications and market forces are changing the village ecological setting and economic system considerably (Shimray, 2009).

Notes

1 Construction World. 2013. *Six Road Projects in Manipur to Be Funded by ADB*. Retrieved from www.constructionworld.in/news.aspx?nid=ntNnHBJFd4cEwpihYQXsdA== (accessed on 2 November 2015).
2 The HAC consists of all elected representatives from the hill districts.
3 Excerpt from the personal interview with Thomas (it is a pseudonym), social activist and leader of ZRO at Lamka on 12 May 2014.
4 Excerpt from the personal interview with Paul Leo (Naga Human Rights Activist) at Karong on 19 August 2014.
5 Excerpt from the personal interview with Soso Lorho (former deputy CM, GoM) at Imphal on 20 August 2014. He passed away on 19 April 2018.
6 Pillai, G. K. 2012. *Manipur: The Way Out*. Internal Security Lecture Series. Institute for Defence Studies and Analyses (IDSA). New Delhi. Retrieved from www.youtube.com/watch?v=KCt87g_AFX4&frags=pl%2Cwn (accessed on 14 October 2015).
7 Staff reporter. 2015. Verbal duel between BJP, Cong hots up between pro-Manipur and anti-Manipur, says Dy CM. The Sangai Express. 7 November 2015. Retrieved from www.thesangaiexpress.com/page/items/59198/verbal-duel-between-bjp-cong-hots-up-between-pro-manipur-and-anti-manipur-says-dy-cm (accessed on 7 November 2015).
8 Excerpt from the personal interview with Mr. Oliver (pseudonym requested) who is a first-class contractor registered with the PWD, GoM, in Senapati on 28 August 2014.

9 This phenomenon is a common practice especially work implemented in the hill districts.
10 Excerpt from the personal interview with Mr. Oliver (it is pseudonym) who is a first-class contractor registered with the PWD, GoM, in Senapati on 28 August 2014.
11 Excerpt from the personal interview with the defence secretary of an insurgent group operating in the Churachandpur District on 13 May 2014. The name of the insurgent group is not mentioned here due to security reasons, and the interviewee requested a pseudonym. Hence, I used anonymous.
12 Excerpt from the personal interview with the additional chief engineer, PWD, in Imphal on 6 August 2014. The person remains anonymous as requested.
13 Excerpt from the personal interview with the chief engineer, MSRRD, in Imphal on 12 August 2014. The person remains anonymous due to the sensitivity of the issue as requested.
14 Excerpt from the personal interview with Thang (it is a pseudonym) IAS (senior officer at the Department of Tribal Affairs and Hills, GoM, at the time of interview) in Imphal on 18 July 2014.
15 Excerpt from the personal interview with the joint secretary of the Department of Tribal Affairs and Hills, GoM, at his office located in Imphal on 18 July 2014.
16 During my fieldwork, I asked for district-level data pertaining to roads from the office of the executive engineer, PWD, located in the Senapati District headquarters. Strangely, however, his office was always locked whenever I visited. On further probing, I was told by his staff that the executive engineer is hardly in his office in Senapati. Rather, all official work is carried out at his residence in Imphal for security reason.
17 Excerpt from the personal interview with Thomas (it is pseudonym) in the Tingsong village on 18 September 2014.
18 Excerpt from the personal interview with Daniel Pou (social worker) in Senapati on 23 September 2014.
19 The name of Mr. X is not mentioned here due to ethical reasons.
20 Pillai, G. K. 2012. *Manipur: The Way Out*. Internal Security Lecture Series. Institute for Defence Studies and Analyses (IDSA). New Delhi. Retrieved from www.youtube.com/watch?v=KCt87g_AFX4&frags=pl%2Cwn (accessed on 14 October 2015).

References

Dzuvichu, L. 2010. *Opening Up the Hills: The Politics of Access Along the Northeast Frontier of British India 1866 to 1942*. A Ph.D Dissertation submitted to Centre for Historical Studies. New Delhi: Jawaharlal Nehru University.

Government of Manipur. 2014. *Demand No. 8 Public Works Department*. Imphal: Government of Manipur.

Guite, C. H. 1999. *Politico-Economic Development of the Tribals of Manipur*. New Delhi: Anmol Publication.

Haokip, T. G. 2012. 'On Ethnicity and Development Imperative: A Case Study of North-East India'. *Asian Ethnicity*, 13 (3): 217–228. https://doi.org/10.1080/14631369.2012.630571.

Harvey, P. and Knox, H. 2015. *Roads: An Anthropology of Infrastructure and Expertise*. Ithaca: Cornell University Press.

Horam, M. (ed.). 2000. *The Rising Manipur: Including other North Eastern States*. New Delhi: Manas Publication.

Ovung, A. 2012. *Social Stratification in Naga Society*. New Delhi: Mittal Publication.

Pillai, G. K. 2012. *Manipur: The Way Out*. Internal Security Lecture Series. Institute for Defence Studies and Analyses (IDSA). New Delhi. Retrieved from www.youtube.com/watch?v=KCt87g_AFX4&frags=pl%2Cwn (accessed on 14 October 2015).

Routray, P. B. 2007. 'Manipur: The Nexus Again'. *South Asia Intelligence Review*, 6 (4), October 15. Retrieved from www.satp.org/satporgtp/sair/Archives/6_14.htm#assessment2 (accessed on 18 November 2015).

Sharma, A. and Gupta, A. (eds.). 2006. *The Anthropology of the State*. London: Blackwell Publishing Ltd.

Shimray, U. A. 2004. 'Socio-Political Unrest in the Region Called North-East India'. *Economic and Political Weekly*, 39 (42): 4637–4643.

Shimray, U. A. 2009. 'Land Use System in Manipur Hills: A Case Study of the Tangkhul Naga'. In F. Walter and S. Barbora (eds.), *Land, People and Politics: Contest Over Tribal Land in Northeastern India*. Guwahati: North Eastern Social Research Centre.

Singh, G. K. 2011. *Security and Development: The Political Economy of Insurgency in Manipur*. New Delhi: Akansha Publishing House.

Taussig, M. T. 1999. *Defacement: Public Secret and the Labour of the Negative*. Stanford: Stanford University Press.

Thumra, J. H. 2000. 'Development in the North-East: Constraints and Prospects'. In M. Horam (ed.), *The Rising Manipur: Including Other North-Eastern States*. New Delhi: Manas Publication.

Xaxa, V. 2008. *State, Society, and Tribes: Issues on Post-Colonial India*. New Delhi: Pearson.

7

CONCLUSION

Beyond unholy trinity

Laying physical infrastructure, or, for that matter, any infrastructure creation/construction, requires large amounts of capital and time. It is often marked with long gestation periods and mired with multiple issues: land acquisition, compensation, rehabilitation and resettlement, cost inflation/escalation, non-availability of materials, suspension, poor governance and corruption, amongst others. This is even more so in a chronic conflict-ridden state like Manipur, which is marked by varied ethnic contestations, deep hostility between communities living in the hills and the valley, frequent breakdowns in law and order situations and existence of a parallel underground government formed by some of the major insurgent groups in the state of governance between insurgents and GoM. Manipur is one of the most expensive states in India for any construction work.

> As per the CPWD rate, if the cost of construction is Rs. 100 in Delhi then the same work will cost Rs. 200 (double the amount) in Manipur, Rs. 160 in Nagaland, Rs. 150 in Arunachal Pradesh, and Rs. 127 in Assam.[1]

The high cost of construction is mainly due to exorbitant logistic costs and rampant illicit taxes imposed by both state and non-state actors. All construction materials for any infrastructure projects are imported from other states, which adds to the already high transportation costs.

The high cost of construction, on the one hand, and the layers of corruption inherent in the system of governance coupled with a nexus of dubious stakeholders between the state and private entities, on the other, are the hallmarks of Manipur's infrastructure development. The system of governance and the underlying social dynamics and political processes in creating infrastructure, such as roads and electricity, are conceptualised in Figure 7.1. The conceptual map points to the linkages and relationships amongst different stakeholders and the factors leading to poverty and the crumbling infrastructure in the hills, as well as the disempowerment of the tribes. The poor state of infrastructure and the hill-valley divide go beyond what Thumra (2000) and

Horam (2000) called the infamous 'unholy trinity' (the nexus of politicians-bureaucrats-contractors) to include insurgents, elites and influential people, as well as civil society. The whiff of corruption and dubious the nexus swirls around infrastructure projects. The connivance and clandestine nature of the nexus between ministers-elites-bureaucrats-contractors-insurgents-civil societies is deeply embedded in the structure while operationalising governance and development programmes. Hence the outcome of infrastructure projects is well reflected in the form of dilapidated rural roads and highways, collapsing bridges, schools without proper infrastructure and electrified villages without electricity, amongst others. Whoever disturbs this nexus is either terminated or excluded or sidelined from the process. This is demonstrated in the modus operandi of the assignment of contract work and its vicious cycle of corruption that has been unravelled in this study.

Figure 7.1 illustrates the social and political processes of building infrastructure and demonstrates how each stakeholder is related and the issues that link them to one another. One can take any dimension/element as a starting point. For example, a key stakeholder is directly related to an international, national, state or ethnic stakeholder. The state stakeholder is related to and closely linked with power dynamics, corruption and dynamics of contracting. Corruption in return is linked to systemic loopholes in various institutions, political negation, political condition and major state stakeholders. Political negotiation is again directly related to historical processes of varied ethnic communities and the infrastructure sector, which further links internal needs and demands to the question of land and varied contestations to demography.

The existing quality of roads and electricity in each district echoes the output of government (dis)investment. It also reflects how social dynamics play a crucial role in shaping infrastructure. It is interesting to note the correlation of ethnicity and infrastructure in a chronic conflict state such as Manipur. The hill-valley infrastructure divide corresponds to the ethnic polarisation between the two categories. Both primary and secondary data consistently point to a widening infrastructure gap between the hills and the valley. It is fair to conclude that there is no poverty of infrastructure or infrastructural deficit in the valley districts as compared to the hills districts. In other words, in all of the hill districts where tribes reside, infrastructure is either poorly developed or suffers from quality and quantity. This is evident from road density, total surfaced roads, location of public infrastructure and institutions, per capita consumption of electricity, village electrification rates and frequency of electricity supply, amongst others.

It is undeniable that within hill districts, there is variation in infrastructure. This is best encapsulated in the hill districts predominately inhabited by either Naga or Zo (Kuki-Zomi-Mizo) ethnic communities. Disparately, infrastructure in the Zo ethnic dominated district is placed ahead of Naga dominated districts both in quality and quantity. This raises an interesting

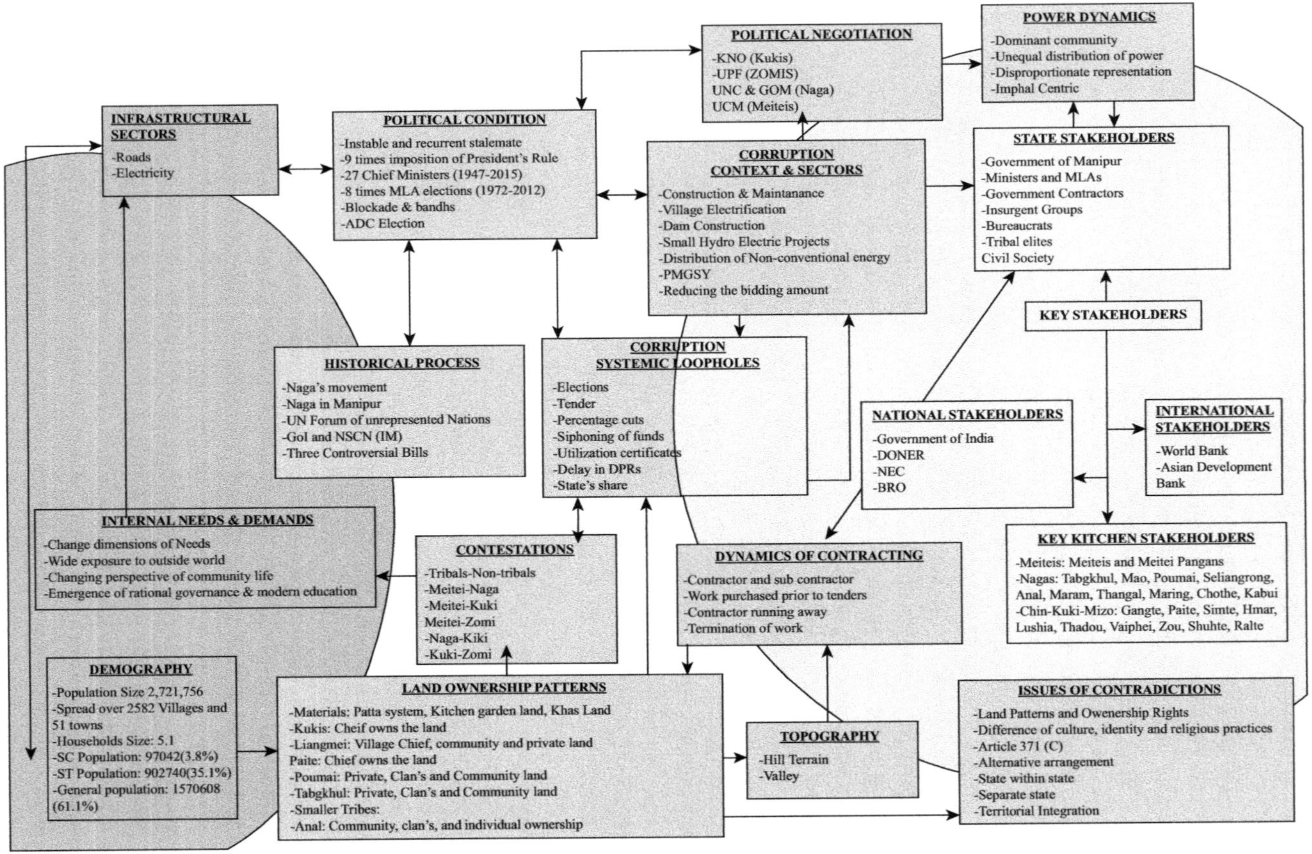

Figure 7.1 Social and political processes of infrastructure building

question: why are Naga-dominated areas lagging behind their counterpart Zo's territory in Manipur in terms of infrastructure? The hill-valley infrastructure divide has been largely due to structural inequality and injustice perpetuated by the state. However, this is not the case amongst tribes and hill districts. The differences amongst Naga and Zo ethnic communities stem from their historical roots, which can largely be attributed to their political orientations. Nagas have been preoccupied with their larger political vision for an integrated homeland with all Naga-inhabited areas merged with Nagaland, an endeavour that echoes Anderson's (1991) notion of a nation as an 'imagined political community'. Hence their political goals overshadow the dismal state of physical infrastructural needs. Naga civil society, which otherwise is at the forefront of Naga political issues, rarely organises protests or blockades to raise their voices regarding the poverty of infrastructure. This gives the impression that Nagas only need political rights. In contrast, Zos prioritise the question of development, along with their political goals. Hence, this explains why infrastructure in Zo territories is relatively better than in Naga territories within the hill districts.[2]

Emerging pattern of commonalities and point of difference

The overarching framework of infrastructure development has been from the statist perspective. The state solely decides why, when, where, how and whom infrastructure is for. Yet infrastructures that are delivered by the state are never quite the infrastructures that were promised, either in their material quality or in their planned routing. Vested interests are commonly assumed to derail the process: politicians, insurgents /militants, bureaucrats and contractor take a cut; contracts and subcontracts are circulated through friends and families; and funds and materials are siphoned off by those who hold positions of responsibility (Harvey and Knox, 2015). The material transformation, such as laying of roads and electricity, are solely decided by the state; hence, it often differs from the local community imaginaries of such infrastructure. Infrastructure that aims to ensure progress, growth, and development also generates deep uncertainties, which are manifest in the absolute and shared conviction that public works are always steeped in corruption and a nefarious nexus (ibid.). Private investment on physical infrastructure development is invisible in Manipur. The reason underlying this is there are no returns on such development projects in the state. No doubt, there are contractors/firms from outside the state engaged in road construction and maintenance of NHs. However, this has more to do with contract work than investment. It is interesting to note the temporality and suspended dimension of human agency while embarking on building infrastructure. Contractors/firms, especially those from outside the state of Manipur, at times terminate contracts or abandon them in the pre-execution phase or midway. This occurs mainly due to high monetary demand by non-state actors. Contractors are thus ensnared between state and non-state actors. In a nutshell, this results in the suspension of projects either for a short period or indefinitely.

The intersection of human and non-human often forms a nebulous space of uncertainty and ambiguity coupled with a dubious nexus embedded in injustice. Roads/highways in Manipur as public spaces and networks of connectivity constitute important markers of political life. They have been routinely engaged as sites of protest, contestations, and negotiations to engage with the state and effectively deployed by varied ethnic communities. The political highway, as discussed in Chapter 4, is best encapsulated from the lens of protests, political assertions, emblems of exclusion, politics of access and means of conflict resolution. Electricity, on the other hand, results in the transmission of injustice across the hills through load-shedding, temporal infrastructure, irregular power supply, shortage of human resources/staffs in sub-stations and total absent in rural/hill villages, amongst others. Harvey and Knox's (2015) ethnography on Peruvian roads has shown us how a focus on material transformation opens up a world of tensions, negotiations and contestations that extend our understanding of political life (: 203). Drawing from this perspective, Manipur's infrastructure build-out elicits an additional dimension of ethnicity besides an unfolding contemporaneous state development practice. Different permutations and combinations of the nexus are what distinguish Manipur's political economy of infrastructure development.

Roy-Burman (2000) observed that unlike other states in the country or even in the northeast, the NH dominates the entire transport system in Manipur. This means that the transport system in Manipur is basically oriented to the external market or for security consideration rather than to meet the requirements of internal mobilisation, or, in other words, it bypasses the local economy and people. Kamei (2000) posited, 'The philosophy of road making should not only be to link up with the administrative and marketing centres but to reach out to every village in the state'. This is also applicable to the philosophy of electrification, which should not be confined to an urban agglomeration. Rural roads and rural electrification are poorly developed and, worse so, they seldom draw the attention of either the state or contractors despite the provision of maintenance, as in the case of PMGSY for five years. The contractors go scot-free since they are protected by politicians and local elites. Rural roads during monsoon season are not motorable, even with the implementation of PMGSY, thereby defeating the objective of building an all-weather rural road. The same is witnessed in the case of rural electricity, where an irregular power supply is the hallmark despite RGGVY being in force. Either one finds no power infrastructure or the absence of a power supply for months in remote rural villages.

The most deplorable roads with no maintenance or budgetary provisions are state highways, major and minor district roads and rural roads. It is interesting to note that the state pays scant attention to roads that connect various tribal districts. The IT Road connecting the Senapati and Tamenglong Districts, the Ukhrul-Senapati Road (recently elevated to NH status) and the Tengnoupal-Ukhrul Road are a few such roads. Strangely, none of these roads pass through valley districts. Concomitantly, NHs that pass through hill districts are poorly maintained. In contrast, those stretches of highways in valley districts are regularly maintained and have been extended to four lanes. Roads connecting tribal districts with neighbouring states Mizoram and Nagaland are poorly developed and can be used only in the dry season. The case in point is Guite Road or NH-102B. This road otherwise connects the Churachandpur District with the state of Mizoram. Likewise, the portion of NH-202 is supposed to connect the Ukhrul District with the State of Nagaland. In contrast, the state, as well as the dominant community, gives every effort to develop the road connecting Imphal with Jiribam.[3] This road is a direct extension of dominant power since NH-2 is often disrupted by different ethnic communities. Concomitantly, Jiribam is the only railway station in Manipur and the development of 110 km of the Jiribam-Imphal railway line is in progress. This raises some interesting questions: why does the state pay scant attention to roads connecting tribal districts? Are good roads amongst tribes a threat to Manipur's territorial integrity and Meitei hegemony? What is the political economy of such neglect? What is the politics of access? Do ethnicity, cultural ties and autonomy movement play a role?

Churachandpur is the homeland of the Zo ethnic community. The district shares a boundary with Mizoram state. They have a close cultural affinity, ethnic ties and shared history with Mizos. Likewise, Tangkhul Naga predominantly inhabits the Ukhrul District and shares larger political goals with other Nagas tribes over the Meiteis. Roads connecting inter-tribal districts with neighbouring states Mizoram and Nagaland are economically and political not viable for the state, as well as for the dominant community. These roads bypassed the Meitei-dominated districts (valley areas), and hence the benefits of such physical connectivity accrued only to the tribes. The state and the dominant community consciously and deliberately delay the process of construction and repairs of these roads either by the subversion or and non-release of funds, suspension of projects indefinitely or wrong alignments, to cite a few examples. Leveraging inter-tribe road connectivity especially across tribal states poses as a direct threat to the Meiteis' hegemony and their totalising project vis-à-vis the government resolution on Manipur's territorial integrity. This may lead to an alteration in the existing power equation and the status quo of Meiteis might be in question. The rise and growth of alternative centres – i.e. tribal districts – is seen as an antithesis and counter to the Meitei totalising project or pan-Manipuri identity. Deepening of economic and social infrastructure development directly correlates with the growth of small towns, tribal towns and urbanisation. Hence the deliberate and conscious attempt by the dominant community to deny such growth. The perceived sense of insecurity is demonstrated by the Meiteis from their movement and demand for ST status. This is best encapsulated in the words of the vice-president of the STDCM:

> When Meitei become ST, all kinds of loss of the future of the youths and loss in service career will be protected, . . . there is no question of loss of religion or down-gradation of Dharma in the community rather there lies uncountable benefits.[4]

A critical analysis of the demands and various protest strategies shows how hard Meiteis try to appropriate tribal land in Manipur. As per the Constitutional provision, tribal land in Manipur, as elsewhere in scheduled areas, cannot be sold nor transferred to non-tribals. The equation of land between tribes and non-tribes is in the ratio of 10:1. The ramification of recognising Meiteis as ST would open up a floodgate of land grapping in hill districts, as they have both political power and economic resources. The possibility of denuding the 31 per cent reservation of jobs in the government sector for the present ST cannot be ruled out, and Manipur would get the tag of a tribal state. The price paid by tribes living in the shadow of the Meiteis' hegemony includes the denuding of tribal rights, destabilising tribal ethnic identity, poverty and the crumbling infrastructure and denial of agency, amongst others. In a nutshell, it is marked by injustice.

Discrepancy in building infrastructure

The empirical data, as pointed out in previous chapters, reveals five broad discrepancies in building infrastructure. The first discrepancy is the non-participation of locals. From planning to execution, infrastructure projects in the state suffer from non-participation/non-involvement of locals.[5] To illustrate, tribes were not at all a part of the process of planning and building the Mapithel Dam. Rather, they were against such development, which accrued the benefits to other populations at the cost of their land and resources. Yet the government implemented the construction of the dam by deploying large armed forces to suppress the resistance from tribes. This echoes what Xaxa (2018) has termed 'coercive development'. The second dimension of discrepancy relates to the siphoning of infrastructure funds. The very act of infrastructure creation involves a large capital investment in the form of budgetary allocation. Yet these funds are often distributed to various stakeholders in the form of percentage cuts and create an ambiguous space of corruption and unethical practices. The worst affected out of this rampant practice of corruption and the nefarious nexus are the hill districts. Apart from state budgetary discrimination towards the hills, contractors from the hills pay more than their counterpart Meitei contractors to insurgent groups and bureaucrats. All the bills related to any contract works are passed and released from Imphal; hence, in every bill, the contractor ends up paying a certain percentage to insurgent groups and departmental staff members. So by the time investments reach implementation, more than 50 per cent of the total project cost has already gone into a popular concept of 'unseen expenditure'.[6]

The third paradigm of discrepancy relates to the local governance system/traditional institution. The local governance system/traditional institution, though recognised by the state, is neither part of the infrastructure planning and implementation process nor involved in identifying the locations where the infrastructure will be the most beneficial. Hitherto, the framework of infrastructure development has been conceived from the statist perspective, thus widening the gap between state and society/tribes (Ziipao, 2018: 487). Besides, there is an element of geopolitics which plays a pertinent role in mega-infrastructure development projects. Manipur is strategically crucial for India's foreign policy due to its land proximity with Southeast Asia, as well as from the security point of view. Manipur is projected as the gateway for building trade relations with Southeast Asian countries under India's AEP. The current infrastructure development, such as building AH-1 and mega-hydropower generation projects, are in tune with the vision and mission of the AEP and not so much in addressing the local needs and aspirations. Bypassing local customary laws and traditions in the process of implementing these projects is an emerging trend.

The fourth and recurrent phenomenon of discrepancy is Imphal-centric investment and development. Imphal has historically been the seat of governance and power. All major government offices, departmental headquarters and institutions are located in Imphal. It is the centre of all hubs ranging from medical facilities to corruption and law and order issues. The fifth dimension of discrepancy pertains to global processes. All investments from international stakeholders, such as World Bank and ADB, are mostly rooted in the valley, which benefits only certain sections of the society and leaves out the tribes. The global process of investment/subsidies, by the time it reaches the hills, gets altered and diverted in such a manner that one does not know where such investments end up. The discrepancy between policy and processes in the creation of infrastructure has the dimension of ethnicity and identity.

The state fleeing from tribes

Historically, the state has always put the interests of the dominant community at the forefront, and this continues to be the case in contemporaneous development practices. Infrastructure development encapsulates and amplifies this reality. I, therefore, posit that the state is fleeing from its citizens (the converse of Scott's argument in his seminal book *The Art of Not Being Governed: An Anarchist History of Upland Southeast Asia*). Scott ably placed the historical context of Southeast Asia and made an argument of Zomia, the term coined by Williem van Schendel that refers to a distinctive zone of geographies inhabited by highlanders or hill peoples who are aloof from the lowlanders. Conceptually, hill people or tribals in Manipur fit into the category of Zomia. More so, the geographical location of tribal societies in Manipur invariably fits into Scott's argument about Southeast Asia; the tribes Naga and Zo, in his terms, would form a non-state space – an 'illegible space' from the perspective of the states in the lowland. For Scott, Zomia is a 'shatter zone' or a 'zone of refuge' where people escape the lowland-state coercion, taxation, conscription into military services and epidemic diseases. In short, people flee from the state. Echoing this perspective, it elicits the situation of 'then' in the context of tribes in Manipur. However, the situation of 'now' with time and space differs significantly; it is the state[7] which is actually fleeing from tribes. This can be gauged from the fact, for instance, that politicians, once elected hardly, visit their constituencies. Besides the occasional visit to the district headquarters and selected villages as a chief's guest to grace the events of important celebrations or the laying of a foundation stone for an infrastructure project, they are otherwise confined in their respective bungalows located at the powerhouse and seat of governance – i.e. Imphal.

The ability of common people to meet their ministers and MLAs and voice their concerns becomes even more difficult with poor road connectivity and other infrastructure and the sheer fact that they have to travel long distance to Imphal. With much difficulty, some manage to travel to Imphal, but often they are not entertained since they did not make an appointment. They are either advised to come back at another time or wait for a few days, which invariably means an extra expense. It is to be noted that ministers and MLAs mostly cater to elites and social leaders from their respective constituencies. These are the ring leaders of their communities and have the potential to influence or woo voters in next assembly election. As discussed, these elites and social leaders are paid off by the ministers/MLAs to penetrate their vested interest rather than addressing the core issue, such as basic infrastructure plaguing most of the villages. This nexus is conscious and deliberately carried out; hence, these leaders choose to remain silent over non-performance by politicians. The collusion and concealment of public voices over public works by politicians and their associates silences the public discourse concerning basic infrastructure issues.

It is interesting to note that, in the case of Zomia, Scott observed that the period following the Second World War, the power of the state to 'deploy distance-demolishing technologies – railroads, all-weather roads, telephone, telegraph, airport, helicopters, and now information technology – so changed the strategic balance of power between self-governing peoples and nation-state' (Scott, 2009: xii). Strangely enough, however, in the case of tribal areas in Manipur, the state does not maintain nor repair inter- and intra-village roads or districts roads (link road to NHs), making it more difficult for tribals to reach the state. In May 2018, the GoM initiated a policy of 'go to village', wherein it envisages a doorstep service delivery and the state coming to its people, which otherwise remains a mundane space (hill territories). Yet as usual, it was only on the day of inauguration of the policy that elected members, along with bureaucrats, visited villages. Thereafter, it fell back to the same system of governance. It is imperative to note that the go-to the village policy is inadequate if it is a mere visit by ministers, MLAs and bureaucrats to a village for a day. These visits, rather than fulfilling the doorstep service delivery as promised by the government, would disempower locals/villagers and create further hierarchy. Various photos circulated in social media and newspapers on the maiden launch of the initiative speak volumes regarding this hierarchy. People's representatives and bureaucrats were accorded with grand welcome by the host villages. However, it is not clear whether this welcome really depicts the true feelings of villagers or is an impressment from street bureaucrats and the intermediaries. The hierarchy and the binary between the core very important persons (VIPs) and the voiceless (villagers) echoes from such a reception.[8]

The existing gap between the state and tribes thus contributes to poverty and the crumbling infrastructure in the hills. Despite this gap and the state remaining a mute spectator, many tribal communities have remarkably taken recourse in a 'do it yourself' framework and deployed their collective labour to the repair and construction of various infrastructure rather than wait for the state to intervene. This is encapsulated in the case of the people's road construction, electrification of the Tingsong village and the Manipur Tribal Movement for Road Construction Committee (MTMCC),[9] which repaired the portion of NH-102B connecting the Churachandpur District with Mizoram state. This echoes the sense of cultivating public assets and claiming ownership, which otherwise remains an untouched domain. These initiatives, even though they are at the nascent stage, are welcomed endeavours. However, mobilising resources for large-scale maintenance of roads and other infrastructure is beyond the reach of tribes since they have little economic and political capital.

The politics of ethnicity and socio-political unrest stemming from the unequal power relationship posited by Shimray can further be extended from my data, as discussed in this book (Shimray, 2001, 2004). Not only the unequal power relationship between tribes and non-tribes but also the question of land and identity, inter-tribe feuds, identity oscillations and ethno-cultural assertions are intricately linked to shaping the infrastructure development process and socio-political unrest in the state. Xaxa (2018) pointed out that development and identity are not antithetical. Drawing from the lived reality of tribes from central India, Xaxa argued that tribal resistance is not against development but development of a kind that is antithetical to their very existence as a people. However, with the tribes in the northeast, the question of development has been directly linked to the assertion of political rights: Bodoland for Bodos, Nagas for greater Nagalim, Kukis for Zalengam and so on. There are autonomous councils in place for tribals under the Sixth Schedule of the Indian Constitution. For instance, in Manipur, there are six ADCs for tribals. Yet with no legislative or financial power, often their functions are thwarted and hence the concept of local-level democratic institutions does not guarantee political rights. The imperative of development, along with political rights, may be a way forward to empower tribes in the state and address the socio-politico-ethnic unrest.

Echoing Bhatia's (2010) argument that peaceful co-existence in Manipur is possible only if rights are fulfilled and historical injustice corrected, the present data points out that the development imbroglio policy followed by GoM needs to reorient towards infrastructure development based on justice framework. The challenge on the part of the state is to provide space for synchronising tribal lived experiences, their traditional institutions, value systems, along with modern values of equality, justice, freedom, fraternity, mutual respect, emancipatory and non-discriminatory, while formulating and executing infrastructure development. For too long, the state has been catering to the dominant community, which has tended to induce assimilation through the politics of ethnic power and hegemony over the ethnic minorities (Shimray, 2004). Horam's observation on the dominance of a particular ethnic group has always aroused ill feelings on the part of others. In every respect, the various ethnic groups contest keenly, whether it is over jobs, politics, etc., which often aroused mutual jealousy and hostility, and this widened the gap in their relationship, which is even more relevant in contemporary Manipur's political economy of development (Shimray, 2004: 3676). Development policy conceptualised and based on the premise of population size and dominant culture has further escalated the ethnic tension and development disparity between the society living at the margin of the state, history, economy and identity crisis with those of the dominant ethnic community. Bodhi's (2013) observation on the widening politico-historical gap between the Indian state and the Adivasi finds it place in the context of Manipur's social reality.

> The manifest situation, unfortunately, is the widening politico historical gap that already existed between the Indian State and the Adivasi peoples. The end result of this problematic, characterized by a brutal imposition of the state framework on Adivasi realities, being the disconnect, deprivation and further estrangement of Adivasis from Indian State couples with a wringing subjective distortion of Adivasi lived-reality. This is related in many ways to their subjective alienation and felt-loss of command over what they conceived to be their naturally endowed resources and their culturally embedded life worlds.
>
> (: 7)

In light of the three controversial bills passed in Manipur's legislative assembly, as pointed out in Chapter 3, the contestation between tribals and non-tribals have escalated and hence further widened the hill-valley divide. The contrasting interpretations and issues enveloped in the bills are interesting to note. The state, vis-à-vis the dominant community, see these bills as an act of (1) protecting the people of Manipur, (2) regulating tenants from outside the state/migrants, (3) checking the influx of non-Manipuri and (4) regulating the sale and transaction of land. The state placed these bills as money bills and bypassed the mandatory consent of the HAC constituted under Article 371 (C) of the Indian Constitution. Tribes, on the other hand, assert that these bills are a direct infringement of their rights over their ancestral lands, forests, resources, customary laws and traditions, as well as their very identities. As orchestrated in the bills, the dominant community's assertions supersede the tribal worldview. The very act of drafting the bills and passing them in the assembly and more so the interpretations are predominantly resonating with what the dominant community advocated for. The element of ethnicity, as discussed, is part of the process of enacting bills and hegemonic dominance of the majority over the minority. Echoing the perspective of legal realism and sociology of law, these bills find express the dominant community's location, ethnicity, class, caste, gender, etc., while interpreting and legalising them. The dynamics of the articulation of tribes and non-tribes are problematic since articulation in itself is an act of domination. There is an articulation, assertion and resistance from tribes, and yet there is continuous domination that is deeply rooted within the structure of operations, resulting in structural inequality. This finds expression in socio-politico-economic spheres, as well as numerically. In a nutshell, the politics of dominance, denial of rights, historical injustice and contemporaneous development practice of injustice, amongst others, are the hallmarks of Manipur's social reality in the development sector.

Politics of infrastructure

The book examined the politics of infrastructure development in Manipur. Infrastructure has always been an act of power, which has at different times been leveraged to smooth relationships, (dis)connect people, enable trade, create spaces of contestation or dilute boundaries between varied ethnic groups.[10] These are key to unravelling a larger political discourse. The focus of the study was on roads and electricity. Although there are other areas of critical infrastructure, such as airways, waterways, railways and telecommunication which are equally important, these are either at the nascent stage or yet to be developed in Manipur. And, therefore, they have had minimal impact on the political and economic power play in the state. The infrastructure of roads and electricity has been the most politicised in the border state and the most visible upon breakdown, thus presenting a rich subject of study. As discussed in previous chapters, infrastructure plays a major role in power politics and co-constructs the notion of modernity and development while at the same time breeding injustice and disempowering certain communities. For instance, the reasons for politicisation of electricity are availability, accessibility and affordability for household consumption; some degree of employment; recruitment of experts; corporatisation of electricity; reclamation of land; rehabilitation and resettlement of displaced inhabitants; power generation; and environmental issues, amongst others.

The key issue in the politics of infrastructure is the power dynamics in that has its historical roots. The main players in the politics are the major ethnic communities of Meitei, Naga and Zo. These communities are marked by a dissymmetrical land relationship. Every community has its own ancestral claim over its land system. While some are antithetical to each other, as is the case with Nagas and Kukis, which witnessed the bloodiest ethnic conflict over the claim and assertion of ancestral land and territory, other ethnic communities simply make historical claims over land through legal institutions and constructed histories. Physical infrastructure invariably builds upon land, and it is thus a political activity. The power relationship determines how infrastructure is planned and executed.

A dissymmetrical land relationship is embedded in the history of communities in Manipur. It is in this relationship that conflict of history emanates. Communities have engaged in the production and claim of history, reconstructing history and constructing new history. The contestation of history results in tension and conflict between various communities. It is in this conflict that one can observe how history acts as a powerful tool in the negotiation of power. Contestation of history over land, resources and forest, on the one hand and the manipulation, fusion and fission of ethnicity on the other have led to the amplification of what is called a community asymmetric relationship. This phenomenon cuts across communities in Manipur, be it Poumai, Mao, Kuki, Kom, Paite, Hmar or others. The central issue in shaping this relationship is tied to history. It could be historical events, manufactured history, invented history or even creation of new history. Hence the conflict of history is imminent amongst varied ethnic communities. When one places such a context in the development framework, these histories in reality have turned against themselves in terms of development. For instance, the moment Poumais assert something, Maos will contest, similarly Kukis and Paites contest with each other and above all there is a contestation between tribal and non-tribals or hill and valley people. Taking the location of development projects as a point of reference, these contestations are most encapsulated in the case of AH-1/NH-2, World Bank aided power system improvement project, ADB project on road development, Indira Gandhi National Tribal University, Regional Campus Manipur, the National Sports University and so on. The communities which are excluded from these projects have questioned the very idea and location of such projects.

Thus embarking upon physical/critical infrastructure deepened the material agency and relationship, fostering close relationships with ethnicity and co-constructing modernity coupled with injustice and prejudices.

In Manipur, there is no fairness in the distribution of infrastructure across varied social groups. The hill-valley divide or tribals and non-tribals binary in terms of infrastructure facilities stemmed from complex historical processes and systematic discrimination meted out to tribes. Suan (2011) unravelled that 'the hill-valley divide germinates from the historical baggage. This has an indelible bearing on all developmental or non-developmental trajectories of the state encompassing socio-economic, cultural, and political spheres' (:274). His observation that the state of Manipur/Meiteis totalising project has failed to incorporate the hill people into its fold is pertinent to the debate of justice and injustice. When the dominant community appropriates infrastructure and other development projects, it amounts to injustice to tribals in Manipur. Based on the principle of justice as fairness, this distribution becomes unfair, and hence it amplifies injustice.

Fundamental to the life of physical infrastructure is its intrinsic connection to land. Infrastructure is built on land. Land and identity amongst tribes are intrinsically related to each other. Mega-infrastructures invariably fragment land, village community and identity. The fragmentation of the holistic construction of identity in the processes of infrastructure build-on amounts to injustice and creates varied kinds of conflict within the community vis-à-vis community and state. Infrastructure, as much as it connects and builds networks, also destroys community structure and identity. When land is turned into a commodity and the state and dominant community appropriate such land for infrastructure development, the original inhabitants loss control over their land, leading to injustice. More so, when the benefits from such infrastructure development is not accrued to tribes, which is often the case, then it perpetuates injustice or what I called infrastructure of injustice. With such development, a new governance system comes into play and tribes are forever dispossessed of their land.

Towards an alternative development discourse/ epistemology

The existing development discourse in Northeast India has been popularly examined and analysed from the perspective of underdevelopment, isolation, periphery and security, as well as and from the lens of neglect theory by the central government (Ahmed and Biswas, 2004; Bhattacharya, 2011; Sharma, 2011; Sharma, 2012). What has often been ignored or paid scant attention is within the specific political context and state-level politics that breed injustice. Bhattacharya's (2011) volume titles *Development Disparities in Northeast India* makes a case for political economy as an approach to unfolding development. She drew her argument from indicators such as law and order, health, education, consumer market, investment, per capita income and poverty, amongst others, to compare the northeastern states with others. While arguing for development disparities, she consciously or otherwise deliberately ignored the dimensions of structural inequality, dynamics of power relation, ethnic polarisation within respective states and the region as a whole. As a matter of fact, infrastructural development in places like Guwahati, Kamrup, Imphal, Shillong, Dibrugarh, etc., are in no way underdeveloped or isolated. Such an approach tends to invisibilise the voices and the lived experiences of people without political power while attempting to objectively engage development disparities. Perceiving development from the existing theory without contextualising the social reality, her argument for privatisation and integration becomes problematic. This is more so in a state like Manipur where the dominant community makes a conscious effort to destabilise the tribal reality: their customs, culture, land, traditions and local governance, as well as the denial of the rise and growth of alternative centres. It is an undeniable fact that failure in governance, insurgency and corruption, as posited by Bhattacharya, are some of the factors leading to the widening development gap. But unravelling structural inequality and the dynamics of power relations within the region and state, as well as amongst ethnic communities, can enrich development discourse in Northeast India. The concept of 'hostile geography' and 'unfortunate history' in the region needs to be revisited from the people's perspective and historical events (ibid.: vii).

In the northeast and Manipur in particular, ignoring the multi-facets of marginality and injustice perpetuated by the state and the dominant community amounts to the denial of ethnic minorities' existence. For instance, Sharma (2011) problematised the issues of insurgents and development in Manipur based on the premises of the dominant community's reality. Such a framework disallowed the voices from the margin and alternative centres and the internal dynamics that shape the development that attributes to disparities. It rather points towards totalising projects and placed Manipur as a whole in the status of periphery from the nation-state framework. In contrast, my data consistently pointed out the hill-valley infrastructure development divide and the dichotomy between tribes and non-tribes. Hanjabam Sharma's thesis on understanding underdevelopment in Manipur is yet another case of a totalising project from the lens of neglect theory. He argued, 'Manipur has for long had a peripheral status, not only in spatial terms, but also on the development index right from the colonial times to its merger with the Indian union' (Sharma, 2012: 71). This argument failed to capture and unpack the internal dynamics and unequal power relations between tribes and non-tribes. Conceptualising Manipur's underdevelopment from the lens of the core periphery within the federal structure undermined the existence of ethnic minorities and the power play of state-level politics.

The waves of internal colonisation unleashed by the dominant community in colluding with the state is orchestrated by an array of laws and policies that have been put into place. One of the many such laws is the MLR&LR Act and several amendments henceforth made to extend the act to the whole of Manipur. Often, the dominant community subsume tribes within their discourses and deny agency for an alternative narratives, categories, and epistemologies emerging from within tribes. In this overarching process, there is no place for investing in infrastructure except in cases where infrastructure extended the state's power and the interests of the dominant community. The vested interest is in land and maintaining the status quo over their hegemony. This echoes the British colonialism and the colonial mindset towards hills people in the northeast; they did not have a genuine interest in developing infrastructure in the hills. This is best accentuated to the concept of 'internal colonialism', as propounded in the work of Leo Marquard (1957). Tribes, on the other hand, attempted to decolonise through various articulations, resistance and autonomy movements. Yet their attempts, even today, have not fructified into any amicable political alternative nor intensified infrastructure development. Rather, this has deepened the space of contestation between tribes and the state vis-à-vis the dominant community.

In this new politico-economic regime of the neo-liberal era, the push for mega-infrastructure development as the basis for driving economic growth is often presented in the language and framework of modernity. This approach to development has penetrated tribal habitats and begun to fundamentally alter their reality to such an extent that tribes are beginning to experience a new wave of colonisation or what may be called *developmental colonialism.*[11] This form of colonialism is taking place in light of the state's current 'development paradigm', which is framed in such a way that tribe/Adivasi displacement and destruction are seen as necessary for national economic growth. This stems from a dominant (mis)conception that tribes/Adivasis are mere objects for necessary alteration rather than thinking, reflecting subjects with historical rights over their land, culture and territory (Bodhi, 2016). This approach to development further perpetuates injustice rather than leveraging basic infrastructures of tribal habitats.

Scapegoat syndrome

The responsibility for the development imbroglio in the conflict-ridden border state of Manipur lies with multiple agencies. Yet each of the stakeholders finds an excuse for the lack of development, and the general tendency amongst them is to blame the others – what may be called a *scapegoat syndrome.* My data revealed that political economy indicators, such as population, economic growth, per capita income, poverty and economic size, are not enough to comprehensively capture and unravel the political-economic reality in a region where tribes form an important section of the population. The issues of geopolitics, government policy, lived experiences of tribes, power dynamics, land and identity are of equal relevance. This study emphasised these additional indicators as key to the substantive understanding of the political economy in Manipur, opening an important new area for further research. The political life of infrastructure, non-human agency enveloped in a shadow of ethnic contestation and insurgency steeped in corruption and the nexus reveal contemporaneous development practices. It opens up new avenues to unfold the spaces of injustice, as well as sites for protest and negotiation.

Notes

1 Excerpt from the personal interview with the advisor of transport and communication, North Eastern, Shillong at Nongrimbah on 14 June 2014.
2 This observation is purely based on the subjective experience of the present researcher.
3 Until December 2016, Jiribam was part of the Imphal East District and dominated by the Meitei ethnic community.
4 Vice-president (STCDM). ST status for Meiteis/Meetei. The Sangai Express, 20 December 2014. Retried from www.thesangaiexpress.com/scheduled-tribe-status-for-meiteimeetei/ (accessed on 8 March 2016).
5 For details, seeZiipao, R. R. 2018. 'Look/Act East Policy, Roads and Market Infrastructure in North-East India'. *Strategic Analysis*, 42 (5): 476–489.
6 Contractors, or, for that matter, the government, often refer to percentage cuts given to different stakeholders from projects as unseen expenditure.
7 'State' in this sense is not in the conceptual and theoretical formulation of Marx nor that of Max Weber. State in the mind of the popular or ordinary citizens is that of ministers, MLAs, bureaucrats and various institutions controlled and administered by them.
8 For details, see Ziipao, R.R. 2018. Go to Hills to Go to Village. *Imphal Free Press*, May 23, 2018. Retrieved from www.ifp.co.in/page/items/49272/go-to-hills-to-go-to-village/ (accessed on 18 November 2018).
9 This committee was formed by the Joint Action Committee Against Anti-Tribal Bills passed in Manipur. Its goal is to ensure an uninterrupted supply of essential items into tribal territories through the repair and construction of important roads and highways passing through the territories while fostering cultural and emotional integration amongst tribal people. Phase one of their plan involves the repair of a 14 km stretch of the 127-km long Guite Road, which is a part of NH-102B, which connects Lamka (Churachandpur) with Mizoram state (MTMCC 2016).
10 For details, see Ziipao (2018).
11 Developmental colonialism here refers to State vis-à-vis corporates imposed form of development into tribal territories where the benefits did not accrue to tribals. Rather it serves the interest of the State and the corporate sectors wherein tribes are further push to periphery and marginality and perpetuate injustice .

References

Ahmed, R. and Biswas, P. 2004. *Political Economy of Underdevelopment of North-East India*. New Delhi: Akansha Publishing House.

Anderson, B. 1991. *Imagined Communities: Reflections on the Origin and Spread of Nationalism* (Revised Edition). London: Verso.
Bhatia, B. 2010. 'Justice Denied to Tribals in the Hill Districts of Manipur'. *Economic and Political Weekly*, XLV (31): 38–46.
Bhattacharya, R. 2011. *Development Disparities in Northeast India*. New Delhi: Foundation Book.
Bodhi, S. R. 2013. 'Of Savagery Disruption, Historical Injustice and Political Distortation: Reflections on Chottanagpur, Adivasi, State and Empowerment'. *Journal of Tribal Intellectual Collective*, 1 (2): 1–24.
Bodhi, S. R. (ed.). 2016. *Social Work in India*. Kolkata: Adivaani.
Harvey, P. and Knox, H. 2015. *Roads: An Anthropology of Infrastructure and Expertise*. Ithaca: Cornell University Press.
Horam, M. (ed.). 2000. *The Rising Manipur: Including Other North Eastern States*. New Delhi: Manas Publication.
Kamei, G. 2000. 'Problems of Development of the Tribal Areas of Manipur'. In M. Horam (ed.), *The Rising Manipur*. New Delhi: Manas Publication.
Marquard, L. 1957. *South Africa's Colonial Policy*. Johannesburg: Institute of Race Relations.
Roy-Burman, B. K. 2000. *Social Factors of Development in Manipur in Horam: The Rising Manipur Including Other North Eastern States*. New Delhi: Manas Publication.
Scott, C. J. 2009. *The Art of Not Being Governed: An Anarchist History of Upland Southeast Asia*. New Haven: Yale University Press.
Sharma, H. I. 2012. 'Understanding Underdevelopment in Manipur: A Critical Survey'. *Economic and Political Weekly*, XLVII (46): 71–77.
Sharma, S. H. 2011. 'Conflict and Development in India's North-Eastern State of Manipur'. *The Indian Journal of Social Work*, 72 (1): 5–22.
Shimray, U. A. 2001. 'Ethnicity and Socio-Political Assertion'. *Economic and Political Weekly*, 39 (28): 3674–3677.
Shimray, U. A. 2004. 'Socio-Political Unrest in the Region Called North-East India'. *Economic and Political Weekly*, 39 (42): 4637–4643.
Suan, H. K. K. 2011. 'Hill-Valley Divide as a Site of Conflict: Emerging Dialogic Space in Manipur'. In S. Baruah (ed.), *Beyond Counter-Insurgency: Breaking the Impasse in Northeast India*. New Delhi: Oxford University Press, pp. 263–289.
Thumra, J. H. 2000. 'Development in the North-East: Constraints and Prospects'. In M. Horam (ed.), *The Rising Manipur: Including Other North-Eastern States*. New Delhi: Manas Publication.
Xaxa, V. 2018. 'Coercive Development'. *Economic and Political Weekly*, 53 (45). Retrieved from www.epw.in/journal/2018/45/alternative-standpoint/coercive-'development'.html (accessed on 18 November 2018).
Ziipao, R. R. 2018. 'Look/Act East Policy, Roads and Market Infrastructure in North-East India'. *Strategic Analysis*, 42 (5): 476–489.

INDEX

Note: page numbers in *italic* indicate a figure and page numbers in **bold** indicate a table.

www.ingramcontent.com/pod-product-compliance
Ingram Content Group UK Ltd.
Pitfield, Milton Keynes, MK11 3LW, UK
UKHW020004200926
475702UK00015B/2470
* 9 7 8 0 3 6 7 4 9 3 5 8 5 *